Leo Kofler's Philosophy of Praxis: Western Marxism and Socialist Humanism

Historical Materialism Book Series

The Historical Materialism Book Series is a major publishing initiative of the radical left. The capitalist crisis of the twenty-first century has been met by a resurgence of interest in critical Marxist theory. At the same time, the publishing institutions committed to Marxism have contracted markedly since the high point of the 1970s. The Historical Materialism Book Series is dedicated to addressing this situation by making available important works of Marxist theory. The aim of the series is to publish important theoretical contributions as the basis for vigorous intellectual debate and exchange on the left.

The peer-reviewed series publishes original monographs, translated texts, and reprints of classics across the bounds of academic disciplinary agendas and across the divisions of the left. The series is particularly concerned to encourage the internationalization of Marxist debate and aims to translate significant studies from beyond the English-speaking world.

For a full list of titles in the Historical Materialism Book Series available in paperback from Haymarket Books, visit: www.haymarketbooks.org/series_collections/1-historical-materialism.

Leo Kofler's Philosophy of Praxis: Western Marxism and Socialist Humanism

*With Six Essays by Leo Kofler
Published in English for the First Time*

Christoph Jünke

Translated by
Nathaniel Thomas

Haymarket Books
Chicago, IL

First published in 2021 by Brill Academic Publishers, The Netherlands
© 2021 Koninklijke Brill NV, Leiden, The Netherlands

Published in paperback in 2022 by
Haymarket Books
P.O. Box 180165
Chicago, IL 60618
773-583-7884
www.haymarketbooks.org

ISBN: 978-1-64259-787-5

Distributed to the trade in the US through Consortium Book Sales and Distribution (www.cbsd.com) and internationally through Ingram Publisher Services International (www.ingramcontent.com).

This book was published with the generous support of Lannan Foundation and Wallace Action Fund.

Special discounts are available for bulk purchases by organizations and institutions. Please call 773-583-7884 or email info@haymarketbooks.org for more information.

Cover art and design by David Mabb. Cover art is a detail of *Construct 21, Kathleen Kersey for Morris & Co. Arbutus / Kasimir Malevich, Fabric Ornament No. 10*, paint and wallpaper on canvas (2005).

Printed in the United States.

10 9 8 7 6 5 4 3 2 1

Library of Congress Cataloging-in-Publication data is available.

Contents

Preface to the English Edition VII
List of Illustrations X

1 A Border Crosser of the Twentieth Century 1

2 From Classical Socialism to the Critique of Neoliberal Globalisation: Leo Kofler's Marxism as Theory Intended for Practice 17

3 Kofler's Critique of Stalinism 52

4 Socialist Humanism, Human Nature and Marxist Anthropology 78

5 The Debate over a Marxist Aesthetics: Going beyond Adorno and Lukács with Kofler and Lefebvre 107

6 Pseudo-Nature and Pseudo-Critique: Krahl, Kofler, and the Critique of the Frankfurt School Intended for Practice 125

Timetable of the Life and Work of Leo Kofler 141
Illustrations 145

Appendix: Six Essays by Leo Kofler

On Freedom [1951] 149
Liberalism and Democracy [1959/1972] 158
The Progressive Elite [1959] 181
The Concept of Society in Historical Materialism [1956] 192
The Three Main Stages of Dialectical Social Philosophy [1966] 210
The Anthropology of Consciousness in the Materialism of Karl Marx [1983] 227

Bibliography 240
Index 247

Preface to the English Edition

Dialectical thinking, Ernst Bloch wrote shortly before his death in in 1977,

> is more than assuring oneself of what has come to be without it. For it always knows itself as an aspect of what it understands. For dialectical materialism in particular, there can therefore be no one-sided derivation of consciousness from economic being in such a way that this determines everything else as the ultimate *causa sui*. To a greater degree, the essence of human conditions amounts to the conditions of acting people endowed with consciousness who pursue their purposes. Marxism is thus the attempt, far removed from a purely contemplative relationship of thought to being, to achieve a historical self-knowledge of the productive subject-object of society. This is particularly true of the thought of Leo Kofler, which, like Lukács's *History and Class Consciousness*, is dedicated to the revival of a Marxist dialectic.[1]

If Ernst Bloch ranked him with the early Georg Lukács, Wolfgang Fritz Haug called him a 'Marxist solitary' and Oskar Negt an 'unmutilated, living Marxist'.[2] For Ernest Mandel, too, his way of presenting the dialectical method in historical materialism was 'the only correct one', and moreover one that 'enabled the education not of epigones, apologists or "red professors", but of independent (revolutionary) thinkers'.[3] Yet the left socialist dialectician Leo Kofler (1907–95) remained an all too often forgotten pioneer of Western Marxism and the New Left of the twentieth century.

This is primarily, but not completely, due to structural reasons. Kofler, as a left-wing crosser of borders, naturally had a hard time in the dichotomies of the Cold War (as comes up again and again in this work). While the German bourgeoisie ignored Marxists and socialists on principle and as part of a long tradition, the Social Democrats had a hard time with this critic of social-democratic integration into the emerging social (welfare) state. If for the East German Communists he was an anti-Stalinist hostile to the state, West German Communists regarded him as an unreliable character. For the Marxists he was too anarchist; for the anarchists too Marxist. After all, he did not make it easy for his New Left audience before and after '1968': his programmatic

---

1 Jakomeit et al. 2011, p. 143.
2 Jakomeit et al. 2011, p. 190.
3 Jakomeit et al. 2011, p. 75.

talk of a socialist humanism and human nature, his development of a Marxist anthropology, but also his criticism of modernist aesthetic concepts and the hegemonic critical theory of Adorno and others – all this was instrumental in making him the *persona non grata* of leftist intelligentsia, even if he was at the same time flesh of their flesh, spirit of their spirit, as I have attempted to make clear with myriad examples of his affinities with New Left intellectual greats throughout this book, such as Theodor W. Adorno, Georg Lukács, Henri Lefebvre, Herbert Marcuse, Isaac Deutscher, E.P. Thompson, Raymond Williams, Ernest Mandel, Perry Anderson, Terry Eagleton, Hans-Jürgen Krahl, Peter Brückner, and so on. Yet Kofler ended up on the margins of German society and its opposition movements – never completely gone, but never really there either. However, this does not do justice to his historical and theoretical significance. In the 1950s and 1960s it was Kofler who introduced hundreds and thousands of party and trade union activists, apprentices and students, workers and employees to Marxist theory. As a pioneer of a renewal of Marxist theory after fascism and war, he was one of the vanguard thinkers of both 'Western Marxism' and radical socialist humanism, and as such tackled problems of the emancipation movement of the twentieth century that were as profound as they were lasting, in an original and often still relevant way.

While I already described Kofler's life and work in detail in my comprehensive biography published in 2007, this book is primarily concerned with an introductory overview of his theoretical and political thinking. Accordingly, the following chapters present and discuss Kofler's philosophy of practice and, in my opinion, its enduring relevance.

The first chapter offers an overview of the close connection between his biography and his theoretical work, while the second chapter offers a tour through the theoretical underpinnings of his oeuvre. It discusses the cornerstones of his understanding of Marxist philosophy, introduces the historian of bourgeois society and its history of ideas as well as the critic of neo-capitalism and its late bourgeois ideology, before finally examining Kofler's critique of the organised labour movement and his theory of a progressive humanist elite as the programmatic core of a New Left, and attempts to place his work in a historical context. Various aspects of these central themes of his are explored in greater depth in the following chapters. Chapter 3 traces the continuities, changes, and ruptures in his theoretically adept criticism of Stalinism from the 1940s to the 1980s. Chapter 4 takes up this analysis again, and shows its connections to Kofler's humanistic understanding of Marxism, and his inventive historico-theoretical attempt to establish an anthropological epistemology as a science of the unchanging preconditions of human changeability. In these two chapters, the specific contours of a socialist humanism, of which

Kofler must be considered the pioneer, become clear, while the following two chapters look more closely at Kofler as a 'Western Marxist'. In the fifth chapter, Kofler's critique of aesthetic avant-gardism is assessed in terms of his theory of the progressive elite and his critique of Frankfurt's 'Marxo-nihilism' using the notorious Adorno-Lukács debate as an example, while in Chapter 6 his critique of critical theory is placed in the larger context of other critiques and the inherent contradictions of Western Marxism.

In contrast to the German edition, I have omitted two further chapters here, because they focus too much on discussions within the German-speaking world. Instead, six of Kofler's essays have been translated into English for the first time and included to illustrate some of the essential lines of his thinking. The first three deal with Kofler's political theory, the last three with his original understanding of Marxism. The fact that these essays and the overview of his work can now be published in the English-speaking world fills me with particular joy for two reasons. First, Kofler's work (he wrote over 30 books and pamphlets) has so far been almost completely ignored in the English-speaking world (still the most important language in international discussion of Marxism). Second, I personally owe a great deal to this English-speaking Marxism, as one can easily see on the following pages. Accordingly, I have to thank my colleagues from Historical Materialism, the Brill publishing house and the translator for their meritorious work; I associate with this publication the hope that it will find interested and adept readers.

Christoph Jünke, July 2020

Illustrations

1. Leo Kofler (m.) in the early 1940s performing work duties in a Swiss refugee camp   145
2. Leo Kofler with his wife Ursula in their new hometown, Cologne, 1950s   145
3. Leo Kofler working at his desk in the late 1960s   146
4. Leo Kofler teaching at the Cologne Academy of Art, 1971   146

CHAPTER 1

A Border Crosser of the Twentieth Century

Marxism had just been solemnly buried at the end of the twentieth century when the exorcised spirit announced its return at the beginning of the new century, as a new left once again demanded: 'Marx on campus!' What such a battle cry means, however, was and is not obvious, if one thinks of the manifold and not always compatible currents and traditions of Marx interpretation. We can find an original approach to this discussion in a little article in a provincial student paper. In June 1986 the *Bochumer Studenten-Zeitung* (*BSZ*) remembered the social philosopher Karl Marx and that this figure had made an idea of the 'beautiful human' his own, an 'erotic image of man' that also had something to do with university scholarship. Man, Marx formulated in the 1840s in figurative and popularising language, must be enabled to fish in the morning, to criticise at noon, and to make music in the evening – that means to take an active role in reproducing his life, to recover himself physically, and by means of art and philosophy, to actively cultivate himself. In the *BSZ* article, the author therefore argued for an erotic university, in which education is not only an act of discipline-specific training, but also an aspect of the human striving for happiness. The goal of the 'beautiful human' had to stand at the centre of university education, and the responsibility of individual scholars for the consequences of their work lay in not only not forgetting this guiding principle, but also, as much as possible, implementing it now.

Today, 40 years later, such an article would, even amongst many leftists, more likely cause a shake of the head than at the time – and yet this would say more about the head-shaker than about the article and its author. This was no idealistic, effervescing student activist, but rather an almost eighty-year-old sociology professor at Ruhr University Bochum: the renowned social theorist and philosopher Leo Kofler – an academic outsider who in his lectures sometimes enjoyed breaking out into song, animated his university pupils to found a tradition-creating uni-wide dance club and also in his old age did not think it beneath himself to publish in small student papers.[1] Kofler had an outstanding effect on the intellectual life of the Ruhr University for two decades, from 1972 to 1991, first as a visiting lecturer, than as an honorary professor in the faculty of social sciences. His weekly lecture on Wednesday mornings at 10:00

---

1 Kofler 1987.

not only reached students in the humanities and social sciences, but also natural scientists, physicians and lawyers – and many a non-student from outside the campus. Semester after semester his lectures almost completely filled a medium-sized auditorium in Building C, and in the 'Red 1970s' even regularly filled it close to bursting (at a time when the universities were not hopelessly overfilled).[2]

The Ruhr University Bochum professor Kofler, deemed a maverick, was an institution, what we would today call a location factor. But more than that, he was – as I would like to show in the following chapter, by the nature of this short chapter, in very broad strokes – a special kind of border crosser. For his wanderings across the regional, cultural, political, and theoretical borders of his time distinguish Kofler's life and his theoretical work – and this was, I think, no coincidence.

Border Crossing One: from Judaism to the Workers' Movement

Leo Kofler was born the eldest of two children on 26 April 1907 in Chocimierz in eastern Galicia, a tiny hamlet in the extreme northeast of the former Austro-Hungarian Hapsburg monarchy. Eastern Galicia, in today's Western Ukraine, belonged not only to Europe's poorest border regions, it was also the home of that Eastern European Judaism later destroyed by fascism and war, of which the Kofler family was an integral part. The mother, Minna, as well as the father, Markus, as far as we know, came from Jewish property-owning families, which allowed the children an admittedly modest but still relatively carefree childhood in undoubtedly traditional but liberal family surroundings. Jewish orthodoxy was still orthodoxy with a capital 'O' on the father's side of the family, in contrast to the mother's, but Markus Kofler had already largely detached himself from it.

It was the First World War that provided the occasion for the still young Leo Kofler to become a threefold border crosser. As a child of Eastern European Judaism, the eight-year-old had to leave his home due to war; his family, fearing the anti-Semitism of the Tsarist army, resettled in Vienna. He thereby exchanged, regionally, the Austro-Hungarian borderlands for the metropole of the Hapsburg dual monarchy – one of the capital cities of European modernism at the beginning of the twentieth century – and, culturally and socially, the Eastern European milieu marked by poverty and backwardness for the milieu

---

2   See Jakomeit et al. (ed.) 2011, pp. 169–70, 174–5.

of Central European Jewish assimilationism. The First World War and the subsequent global revolutionary wave (which, in addition to the disintegration of the Ottoman Empire led to the collapse of the three great European monarchies, Russia, Germany and Austria-Hungary) thereby marks this third, historical rupture of epochs, which would eventually lastingly alter the young Kofler.

In the 'Red Vienna' of the 1920s, Kofler intermingled the cultural legacy of Judaism with the modern workers' movement in its classical and radical expression. He graduated from primary and commercial school at a time when new paths were being forged in social and education policy, just as they were in the social housing policy that would become legendary in Social Democrat-governed Vienna. While the Austrian provinces remained stuck in peasant and bourgeois conservatism, three-fourths of the city dwellers voted for a social democracy that consciously referred to its Marxist foundations and understood socialism as a comprehensive anti-capitalist reform of life. His father, Markus, an old supporter of Ferdinand Lassalle, also read the *Arbeiter-Zeitung* out loud to his family on Sundays, while the passions of young Leo still pertained more to sport and art. He had no particular goals and lived for the moment. However, in 1927, as Leo Kofler took on a position as a clerk, he came upon the clerical trade union and was discovered by Manfred Ackermann, one of the most significant trade union activists of that time, for educational work on trade union policy.

The path that Kofler took here was a not-at-all untypical path for a 'non-Jewish Jew'. As the structurally excluded and discriminated against, Jews were at that time generally outsiders, social pariahs. Judaism was itself divided in multiple ways, between religious separation, cultural assimilation and oppositional inclinations. The strong assimilationist tendencies as well as the inclinations to defiance found their forerunners in a Jewish enlightenment tradition that bore a markedly progressive and rationalist character. This mixture of assimilation and Jewish enlightenment tradition in turn brought forth a certain kind of intellectual type whom Isaac Deutscher would later call the 'non-Jewish Jew': those people of Jewish origin who, through their own tradition of enlightenment, outgrew their Jewish religion (because they experienced it as archaic and constricting) and attempted, one way or another, to energetically integrate themselves into the emergent bourgeois society. In manifold areas these 'non-Jewish Jews' not uncommonly became outstanding thinkers and 'they represent the sum and substance of much that is greatest in modern thought' – not only, but also not least, when they connected themselves with the then powerfully rising radical workers' movement.[3] Intellectuals like Baruch Spinoza and

---

3 Deutscher 2017, p. 26.

Heinrich Heine, Karl Marx and Sigmund Freud, Rosa Luxemburg and Leon Trotsky (many more could be named) embodied, according to Deutscher:

> ... the most profound upheavals that have taken place in philosophy, sociology, economics, and politics in the last three centuries ... They had in themselves something of the quintessence of Jewish life and of the Jewish intellect. They were *a priori* exceptional in that as Jews they dwelt on the borderlines of various civilizations, religions, and national cultures. They were born and brought up on the borderlines of various epochs. Their mind matured where the most diverse cultural influences crossed and fertilized each other. They lived on the margins or in the nooks and crannies of their respective nations. Each of them was in society and yet not in it, of it and yet not of it. It was this that enabled them to rise in thought above their societies, above their nations, above their times and generations, and to strike out mentally into wide new horizons and far into the future.[4]

Biographically and intellectually formed in situations of historical rupture and under social conditions that allowed no reconciliation with nationally or religiously limited ideas, these non-Jewish Jews were generally driven to a universalist approach with certain philosophical principles. The world was consistently regarded by them as ruled by inner boundaries and laws – even within dreams and slips of the tongue, as with Freud; society was not something static for them, but rather something deeply dynamic – not least because it was possible to see society in constant flux at the borders of nationalities, religions and cultures, and more clearly appreciate its contradictions. None of them, according to Deutscher, believed in either absolute good or absolute evil, all had been able to observe communities that were bound to different moral benchmarks and ethical values. Thus, for all of them, knowledge and morality were things that were fundamentally practical, contradictory, and relative – a fundamental insight out of which they created a deeply optimistic belief in the ultimate solidarity of people.

Literally almost all of these descriptions and attributes that Isaac Deutscher assigns to the non-Jewish Jew also apply to Kofler, born into Eastern European Judaism and socialised in Central European Judaism. He, too, would develop, as conditioned by his family, into a renegade who was nonetheless in the Jewish tradition. He would also be a border crosser in the sense of regions, political

---

4 Ibid.

practice as well as social theory. He was a child of cultural and political peripheries and would, as much as he also exerted himself, never entirely arrive in the society in which he later lived. He would soon think beyond society, nation and the present to a rationalist irreconcilability that is only typical of a few. Kofler's later thought also holds true to the fundamental philosophical concerns of the non-Jewish Jew: he would think dialectically through and through, connecting in a special way the search for sociological determinacy with the emphasis on interventionist and deeply practical thinking. Later, dabbling as a Marxist anthropologist, he would also decline to believe in an either-or, in the either good or bad person. He too will never lose sight of the operative principle of hope, the optimistic belief in human solidarity. His legacy would be the same as those other great non-Jewish Jews – 'the message of universal human emancipation' (Deutscher).

This was made possible by the border crossing from Judaism to the workers' movement. In the red 1920s the young Kofler also said farewell emotionally to his Eastern European roots and became an enthusiastic Viennese social democrat. It was the 'Red Vienna' of the interwar period, with its somewhat different workers' movement, that had a lasting influence on him. Here in the framework of 'socialism in one city' and a political education system that resonated far beyond Austria, he experienced a party between reformism and bolshevism, a reformist workers' party with revolutionary expectations of its ultimate goal, as the Social Democratic Workers' Party of Austria (SDAP) would later be characterised.[5] He politicised himself here at the end of the 1920s and became an enthusiastic and enthusiasm-provoking social-democratic educational speaker – half rationalist, half educator of the masses on the red cause.

Border Crossing Two: from Social Democrat to Left Socialist

The great world economic crisis of 1929 and the following years led not only to the next epochal rupture, the rise of fascism, but also the radicalisation of Red Vienna's social-democratic youth. In the face of reformist achievements and the fascist danger, the youth and the left wanted more and revolted against the fatalistically wait-and-see social-democratic reformism of their party leadership grouped around Otto Bauer. The young social-democratic educational speakers from Vienna became the vanguard of politicisation, the carriers of a new left opposition. They found their ideologues on the left wing of Austrian

---

5 Kulemann 1979, p. 155.

social democracy, with Max Adler, the contemporary philosopher of European left socialism, who explicitly wanted to educate the youth to revolt against capitalism and, in his educational theory, urged that young people should become unsuitable for integration in the dominant system.[6] Leo Kofler was one of these politicised educational speakers. For many years, he became a staunch supporter and pupil of Max Adler, attending his lectures at the university, and was actively involved in the 'Marxist workgroup' headed by Adler, while at the same time travelling 'on the road' through the countryside or in the Lobau, the Danube floodplains east of Vienna, camping, making merry and politicising with the like-minded. In the last battles of this first republic, Kofler argued with Ernst Fischer and many others for a left opposition whose crossover with the Communist movement in the 1930s would be fluid.

The seemingly inexorable demise of the Austrian Social Democratic Workers' Party (SDAP) nonetheless took its course. After its last rebellion, the spontaneous and bloodily crushed February Uprising of 1934, it was banned, democracy was smashed, and an Austrian semi-fascist corporate state (*Ständestaat*) erected. The workers' movement and Austromarxism were relegated to illegality, and Kofler dedicated himself, besides occasional wage labour, entirely to autodidactic study.

Border Crossing Three: from Practice to Theory

This second border crossing of Leo Kofler – from Social Democrat to left socialist – segued once again in the years after 1933–4, after the political collapse of social-democratic Austromarxism and its left opposition, to a turning point in Kofler's life and thought, and also to a third border crossing. After the Anschluss of Austria to the fascist German Reich, the just 30-year-old Jew and Marxist fled in 1938 to Switzerland. Here in Basel, in the enforced global political isolation of the Swiss work camp and its political as well as psychological strain, he once again took up the academic studies he had begun in Vienna, and moved in intellectual and Communist circles. Called up from mid-1940 for the physically taxing work of the emigrants' work service, he worked during the week in road construction and peat digging, while in the evenings he devoted himself to intellectual accountability in the form of work on a book manuscript.

These deprivation-filled, ascetic conditions would not only leave a lasting influence on Kofler's character. They also formed the contemporary historical

---

6 See Adler 1926.

context for his process of theoretical maturation, since he wrote his first book as a social philosophical reflection on the broken relation of Marxist theory and practice and as the groundwork for a new understanding of Marxism.[7] Socialist and Marxist theory and practice required renewal, according to Kofler in this theoretically and politically groundbreaking work. Above all, the mechanism and determinism of previous Marxism must be overcome, the vulgar materialist Marxism as embodied in Social Democracy by Karl Kautsky as well as that embodied in Communism by Joseph Stalin. It was necessary to recapture the active element, the so-called subjective factor, that is, the role of consciousness in social being, for the theory and practice of a renewed Marxist socialism.[8] The previously so potent mechanical division of superstructure and base is rejected as inadequate and impracticable in social and historical practice.

Kofler's renewal of Marxist theory and practice relies above all on the philosophical tradition of Georg Wilhelm Friedrich Hegel and his subject-object dialectic, and on the young Marx and his radical humanism. The unique part in Kofler's approach lies as well in an original intellectual border crossing between his old teacher Max Adler and his new theoretical reference, Georg Lukács. From Lukács he adopts the central emphasis on dialectical thinking, while remaining true to Adler's central methodical emphasis on consciousness and his sociological thinking. Thus he becomes an, in many respects, not untypical yet original representative of the then-nascent 'Western Marxism' that with its tendency towards disengagement from political contexts would itself become a good deal academicised.

Kofler is one of those 'Western Marxists' who remained most true to the proletarian milieu and its organisational forms. Politically and practically he moved from then on between the left socialism of Adler and the reform Communism of Lukács.[9] This more practical and political side is reflected in his second work, his monumental study *Zur Geschichte der bürgerlichen Gesellschaft* ["On the History of Bourgeois Society"], published in the not-yet German Democratic Republic (GDR) in 1948, which brushes against the grain of the history of early bourgeois humanism and clarifies its internal and external contradictions.[10] In the antifascist context, Kofler updated the old teaching of the socialist workers' movement, which is that the workers' movement became

---

7   Kofler 1987a, p. 55.
8   See Chapter 2.
9   Reform Communism 'propagates de-Stalinisation not as an anti-bureaucratic revolution from the bottom up but as an anti-bureaucratic reform mainly from above' in societies ruled by Marxist-Leninist parties (see Chapter 3, Section 3).
10 See Chapter 3.

the historical heir of the early bourgeois radical democrats, and emphasised at the same time that socialism, having arrived at a crisis, could only renew itself if it did not play off social freedom against political freedom, but rather united both stages of world-historical freedom into a third, higher stage. For the social philosopher and theorist was crucially concerned about the freedom of an all-rounded individual in all its aspects, as well as collective development of a human species-personhood. This target idea of a 'beautiful human' did not, from this point on, let him go. It traversed all of his further work and became the reason for his next, his fourth border crossing, which once again is to be taken literally.

Border Crossing Four: from West to East

When Kofler had moved to the left in the 1930s and the beginning of the 1940s and connected his Western Marxism with hopes for a reformed Communism, he shared the hopes of many contemporaries that the foreseeable end of fascism and war would lead to an international expansion of the process of socialist revolution and to lasting de-Stalinisation in Soviet Russian socialism as well as the international Communist movement. He did not want to return to Austria. Not because a return to the homeland of the perpetrators scared him – although he already knew that his father, mother and large parts of his family had been murdered in the Holocaust. More likely, it was because there were no longer any prospects for avowed Marxists in academic and educational policy, as Austrian academia was firmly in conservative hands after the war – barely anyone there wanted to hear anything about a renewed Austromarxism of any kind whatsoever. Europe, on the other hand, was in open movement and Kofler was made aware that, in the East of the German motherland of Marxist socialism, a socialist teaching staff unburdened by involvement with the Nazis was sought. He therefore reacted with enthusiasm and great hopes to the ensuing offer at the beginning of 1947 to become a lecturer to the East German university in Halle an der Saale in the not-yet GDR. 'I thought: here you finally have socialism! My dream seemed to be fulfilled'.[11]

His first work, *Die Wissenschaft der Gesellschaft* ['The Science of Society'], was accredited as his doctoral dissertation and, with his *Zur Geschichte der bürgerlichen Gesellschaft*, the autodidact could subsequently qualify [*habilitieren*] as a professor of the philosophy of history. The ruling Socialist Unity

---

11 Kofler 1987a, p. 55. See also Chapter 3.

Party (SED) in East Germany, which he became a member of shortly after his arrival in Halle, had built up a parallel comprehensive educational system outside the university which was reminiscent in many aspects of the Austro-marxist educational tradition, and in which the university professor Kofler naturally was active at the same time. As an explicitly political intellectual, he actively intervened from that point onwards, and, wanting to contribute energetically and assertively, naturally took the liberty of levelling criticisms at tendencies that he held to be counterproductive. Accordingly, he sharply criticised the emerging bureaucratisation and Stalinisation tendencies of the new SED rule, and had already fallen out of favour by the end of 1949. After the SED's chief theorist Fred Oelssner publicly tagged him as a 'Trotskyite' and 'carrier of anti-Soviet contraband', Kofler understood the seriousness of the situation, as demonstrated by his withdrawal from the SED, and was placed on leave at the end of January 1950. For quite some time he nevertheless hoped to be able to return to office and dignity, but, in actual fact, his behaviour meant that open season was declared on him. In the autumn 1950, as it became clear that not only would there be no return to office and dignity, but that he was also being threatened with arrest, Kofler fled as one of the first dissidents from the GDR.

Border Crossing Five: from East to West

As an influential intellectual, Kofler had also attempted in Halle to bring together socialist theory and practice again and, with his Western Marxism, to foster the construction of Eastern socialism. That he failed in doing this, that he was first barred from his profession and finally threatened with arrest, that he was compelled to flee to the capitalist West of Germany which he had rejected, became what he later called the actual tragedy of his life. Once more the border crosser had come up against the wall of historical and social reality. Thus arrived the fifth border crossing: Kofler went to West Germany with his new wife Ursula and settled down permanently in Cologne.

How should he now employ his newly-won freedom? It was intimated to him: the denunciation of Marxism and socialism. He had already been unable to deny his history and identity in the hope-laden German East; how could he do so in the capitalist West? He countered attempts at co-optation with 'You must not forget that I am a Marxist'. Instead, he wanted to prove himself on Western soil as a Marxist. Yet the price was high. Just recently a publicly respected, materially more-than-well-provided-for professor, now an unknown travelling lecturer on the topic of Marxism, on the verge of poverty, moving in permanent material uncertainty, in the restorationist climate of the West German Adenauer state, of all places.

In the years 1951 and 1952, Kofler came to terms with his own experiences and composed several anti-Stalinist writings, which held fast to Marxist theory and his socialist convictions, and continued hoping for a future de-Stalinisation in the East. Nevertheless, he subjected Stalinism in theory and practice to a sharp critique. Stalinist Marxism was for Kofler explicitly a form of un-Marxist Marxism, a structurally undialectical theory and practice that was as mechanical as it was anti-humanist and anti-emancipatory, which Kofler identified as the ruling ideology of a new type of bureaucratic caste.[12] On the other hand, he did not want his criticism to turn him into an anti-communist renegade or a cold warrior. Such an attitude in West Germany at the beginning of the 1950s, however, made one once again into a dissident. In the Cold War West German frontline state, the Christian conservative Konrad Adenauer governed, and Communists were stamped as enemies of the state and persecuted in many ways. Since all roads ostensibly led to Moscow, Kofler, the committed Marxist, paid for his commitment with wide-ranging social exclusion. From then on, only on the left edge of the social-democratic movement and the trade unions could he be active as an educational speaker and wandering preacher. After the bloodletting of Nazi fascism, the need for new thinkers was great. Kofler brought the necessary qualities: undogmatic and original, sitting between all the theoretical camps, he was not only a distinctive personality but also a highly gifted speaker and educator. Yet one could not live off of this. Thus, his wife had to provide for the family's upkeep, and although she had been an academically-trained teacher in East Germany, she was not allowed to work in her actual profession for a long time.

Kofler's critical faculties did not abate in the West of Germany either. After he had made a certain name for himself as a Marxist critic of Stalin, he was increasingly active as a critic of social-democratic 'ethical socialism'. He levelled sustained criticism of the West German SPD before Bad Godesberg, clarifying the philosophical errors and confusions of the influential ethical socialists around Willi Eichler. These had made the socialist goal dissipate into the ethically noncommittal, thus paving the way for a political bureaucracy that was no longer able to address people affected by oppression and alienation in an emancipatory way. These ethical socialists, however, were not only those who attempted most consistently to theorise the new practice within social democracy, but also those who occupied important leadership positions in the

---

12 See Chapter 3.

party and trade unions. Kofler therefore made enemies, influential enemies. Conflicts were not a long time in coming.

On the other hand, he had close contacts with the left wing of the trade unions around Viktor Agartz and with left intellectuals such as Wolfgang Abendroth. And so, as a wandering preacher of social philosophy, Kofler became one of the minds of the forgotten 1956 revolt.[13] He attempted for the last time to openly cross the border between theory and practice, intervened practically, and propagandised the New Left as the third way between Social Democracy and Communism. All in vain. The banning of the West German Communist Party in 1956 and the treason trial against the left socialist social democrat Viktor Agartz led to a comprehensive criminalisation and ghettoisation of the left milieu in the Federal Republic of Germany, while in East Germany, the Harich trial and the campaign against Ernst Bloch symbolised the end of Communist liberalisation policy.

Intermittent attempts to procure a permanent position for Kofler within the trade unions or at the universities failed, partly through conservative resistance, partly due to his unwillingness to let himself be taken prisoner by such institutions and their bureaucratic logic. One had 'to already be a particularly strong personality, if one wanted to be capable of getting to leading positions without one's backbone being broken by the bureaucracy', he wrote in 1960 about late bourgeois bureaucracy, thereby also formulating his own anxiety.[14]

In the middle of this first generation of a New Left, he nevertheless grappled with the changes of the new, social state capitalism and, in doing so, developed his theory of a progressive elite, who sought an intellectual as well as political way out of the world-historical blockade of the intensifying Cold War.[15] The international left, according to Kofler, was caught in the bloc logic of this Cold War, re-Stalinising itself in the Communist current and bourgeoisifying itself in the social-democratic one. A new break from this logic of encompassing bureaucratisation therefore required a new socialist humanist left, which mostly moved on the dissident edges (in the niches, wrinkles and peripheries of society) or even entirely outside of social democracy and party Communism. The ongoing failure of an opposition within the social-democratic movement in the run-up to the SPD party congress in Bad Godesberg in 1959, however, finally brought this historical cycle of political opposition to an end. This failure of the first generation of the New Left was considerably undergirded by the new

---

13   See Jünke 2014, Chapter 6.
14   Kofler 1960, p. 335.
15   See Chapter 3.

social state – euphemistically termed the welfare state – being put into place at the time: the carrot and stick were also here.

Border Crossing Six: from the First to the Second Generation of the New Left

The crisis at that time of the first generation of the New Left was not only a German one, just as the New Left was not only a German phenomenon. Yet this development demonstrated a specific German sustainability. The generation gap that could be identified all over the international left, the alienation between '56ers' and '68ers', took particularly far-reaching forms here. The left socialist 56ers were largely ignored or ridiculed by the later, anti-authoritarian 68ers. Kofler, the somewhat different visionary of a New Left, was at first forgotten and displaced by the young SDS comrades, only to be partially rediscovered after the revolt of '68.

His political and intellectual path had already been separated for a long time from that Frankfurt variant of 'Western Marxism' that did not want to rely on an allegedly hopelessly integrated workforce.[16] Kofler, equally a homeless leftist like the Frankfurt School, remained more loyal to the reform Communist tradition and, furthermore, understood himself, despite all criticism, as an organic part of the workers' movement, and as a revolutionary humanist. The ongoing class antagonism found expression in the consciousness of ordinary workers, according to Kofler, and could also, when appropriately and consistently engaged with, be politicised. Critical consciousness is also contained in the reified consciousness and thus also the possibility of humanistic enlightenment. Although he considered himself to be a part of this New Left, he was nevertheless rarely perceived by his contemporaries as such. His writings had no reception, and he rejected getting personally involved from then on. He still feared, as an Austrian citizen, that a case of open political involvement would possibly result in expulsion from his newly chosen home. Only much later would he admit: 'If I am honest, this was to my advantage, since I prefer to concentrate more on theory'.[17]

Kofler was rightly upset at the time about being ignored by the young generation. Yet when debates did occasionally arise, he countered misunderstanding and resentment with a vehemence that had to hinder any meeting. As a result,

---

16   See Chapters 5 and 6.
17   Kofler 1987a, p. 69.

he barely received any more invitations to collaborate with groups or periodicals, was increasingly simply ignored, and renewed his contacts with Austria and Switzerland – if he wrote, it was for the press and publishers there. He was only freed from this personal isolation after the events of 1968. It was students who had full-throatedly demanded his appointment at the beginning of the 'Red 1970s' to the young Ruhr University Bochum, even if the young radicals could only make limited use of his theories. They were unable to appreciate the radicalism of an author discredited as a traditionalist, one who capped his socialist humanism in his manifesto *Perspektiven des revolutionären Humanismus* [Perspectives of Revolutionary Humanism], published in 1968, with the words of Gustav Landauer:

> The object of the democratic and socialist revolution can only be to abolish the proletariat once and for all. There should not be any proletarian, anyone doing without, any more. There should be people, with free mobility of spirit and life of the heart.[18]

His exceedingly original attempt, laid down here, at a theoretical mediation between Herbert Marcuse and Georg Lukács, between Marxist traditionalism and anti-authoritarian revolt, was widely unheeded.[19] His ambitious attempt at an alternative social philosophy to the Frankfurt School had no chance with the generation of young intellectuals. Adorno became and remained the hegemon of discourse. Kofler, on the other hand, was condemned to marginality.

Border Crossing Seven: from the New Left to the Epochal Break

Kofler continued, finally, to still be between all camps as he found a new domain at the Bochum Ruhr University in the 'Red 1970s'. He was considered old-fashioned, and his Lukács-trained aesthetics dogmatic. In other ways as well, he swam against the left current: he attacked Frankfurt critical theory ever more sharply; he also stood rather at a distance from psychoanalysis. Kofler's revolutionary humanism was even less compatible with the other fashionable intellectual current of that time: the French structuralism of a Louis Althusser, who reinvented Marxism as a theoretical anti-humanism. Kofler remained a loner, a misfit, and failed to come across as forming a school of thought.

---

18   Kofler 2007, p. 14.
19   Kofler 2007, pp. 93–4.

He experienced the demise of the New Left with a certain bitterness. Especially in the context of approaching postmodernism and the ideological triumphs of international neoliberalism, which he sensibly registered in the transition to the 1980s and sharply criticised, he despaired about the German left that had become an alternative subculture. Early on, he recognised the fresh wind coming out of the East, and struck out for the last time for new shores, becoming a propagandist for Gorbachev, in whom he thought he recognised a renaissance of classical socialism. As the Gorbachev project failed in 1989–90, Kofler's embitterment took on cynical features.

The great epochal break also left Kofler at a loss. Yet he behaved stoically and stubbornly. Although he was still a dues-paying member of the Austrian Social Democratic Party, he sympathised in 1990–1 with the new Party of Democratic Socialism (PDS), 'the one true opposition party', and he came to its defence against conservative and social-democratic attacks. 'I've been keen to underline that the PDS under Gysi's leadership can be formally, but not politically and intellectually, categorised as a "successor party" of the SED, just as the present SPD, which has long turned away from Marxism, cannot be understood as the successor party of the old, consistently Marxist SPD before Hitler'. He challenged what was, in his opinion, the inevitable '"ravenous" bloating of the FRG at the cost of other countries'.[20] In the old tradition of the socialist workers' movement, he conceded to the Germans the right to national self-determination and reunification: he wanted, however, to see this bound to a just as old and honourable tradition of a social and humanist goal. National thought does not obligate in any way a chauvinist nationalism and anti-leftist hubris; rather it obligates social and societal reforms, it obligates a humanist culture that remains to be achieved – according to Kofler in 1987 in front of an overwhelmingly conservative audience.[21]

Besides occasional lecture tours to, amongst other places, the still-existing GDR in 1990, he also continued to give his lecture every Wednesday at the Ruhr University Bochum, until multiple strokes befell him in 1991, from which he could no longer recover. On 29 July 1995, Leo Kofler died in his chosen home of Cologne, and for a last time countless contemporaries, some more prominent, some less so, bestowed the last honours on him in the large bourgeois and the small left and socialist newspapers and periodicals.[22]

---

20   Kofler 1992, pp. 66–7.
21   Kofler 1987b.
22   See Illian 1997.

A Border Crosser in the Age of Postmodernism

The figure of the border crosser today, in the age of postmodernism, enjoys enormous popularity and fascination. The marginal and the minority are not uncommonly celebrated as values in themselves, the niches and edges of social systems are viewed as places of refuge, and individualism is elevated. The collective and solidarity, the idea of a totality, of a collective practice and of a societal goal have, on the contrary, gone out of focus, have become just as suspicious as talk about humanity, about the subject, about consciousness.

In Leo Kofler's life and work, we encounter this figure of the border crosser, without him having participated in weaving an ideological veil of self-elevation over it. His life was a repeatedly broken life, in which the vicissitudes of the twentieth century were mirrored in not untypical, yet idiosyncratic ways. Kofler's work – today for the most part only available in secondhand shops – on the other hand, demonstrates a notable continuity. Its precious content has barely been excavated. The unifying and constant in this work is certainly the emphasis of the humanist goal; Kofler's specific devotion to the project of a universal human emancipation.[23] In his lifetime, he held fast to the old project of a comprehensive development of the human being as a species-being likewise capable of and damned to emancipation. He never tired of propagandising the 'whole person' and the idea of an 'erotic essence' of this person. This brought him, during his lifetime, into conflict with bourgeois capitalist society, whose lack of ideals he repeatedly and trenchantly characterised. Holding fast to the humanist goal, however, also brought him into conflict with many left currents that frequently made a virtue out of necessity and acted with reckless disregard for the many types of harm that resulted.

Kofler knew only too well that life in the twentieth century was a repeatedly damaged one. It was thoroughly clear to him in his case that holding fast to the humanist goal had to go hand in hand with specific biographical damages. He knew that the figure of the loner cannot and must not be an ideal that is actively strived after – and so he wrote once as a dedication in a copy of *Die Wissenschaft der Gesellschaft*: 'To go on the right path *together* a little ways is worth more than the pride of going on the path that one goes alone'. Despite that he became – one might say inevitably – a loner, a lone traveller and a border crosser in the sense of regions (East Galicia, Vienna, Switzerland, GDR, FRG), in the sense of political practice (SAPD, SED, SPD, New Left), in academic discip-

---

23   See Chapter 4.

lines (sociology, history, philosophical anthropology, aesthetics) and Marxist social theorists (Max Adler, Georg Lukács, Herbert Marcuse).

In Kofler we have the figure of the border crosser before us, the border crosser did not come into being out of abstract principle, out of personal passion, or on account of a consciously chosen life plan. Kofler became a border crosser and loner, because he held fast to his arduously acquired target idea of the 'beautiful human', especially under adverse conditions. This also seems to me to have been less the product of a personal quirkiness and far more the logical consequence of social and historical conditions, in which anyone who does not relinquish the ideas of a radical humanism is condemned to be, as it were, a border crosser.

CHAPTER 2

From Classical Socialism to the Critique of Neoliberal Globalisation: Leo Kofler's Marxism as Theory Intended for Practice

> So here we have arrived once more at the *philosophy of practice*, which is the path of historical materialism. It is the immanent philosophy of things about which people philosophise. The realistic process leads first from life to thought, not from thought to life. It leads from work, from the labor of cognition, to understanding as an abstract theory, not from theory to cognition.
> ANTONIO LABRIOLA, 1897

∴

> Criticism is no passion of the head, it is the head of passion.
> KARL MARX, 1844

∴

For half a century, the social philosopher and theorist Leo Kofler dedicated himself to the renewal of Marxist theory and its application to such diverse areas as the methodology of Marxism, the theory and history of bourgeois society, the sociology and critique of social state neo-capitalism, anthropology, and aesthetics. Yet as impressively diverse in reach and depth as his work is, it was to the same degree largely ignored, even in his lifetime, by the majority of German leftists (let alone the establishment). Was that down to the fact, as Klaus Vack surmised almost 40 years ago, that Kofler cannot be reclaimed for any left group or current? His path was 'too independent and idiosyncratic', according to Vack, 'and yet no adequate history of the socialist left ... could appear, without mentioning Kofler's work and his often rather latent influence'.[1] Oskar Negt supplemented this political classification a decade later from the intel-

---

1 Vack 2011, p. 141.

lectual side, when he declared Kofler to be a representative of an 'unmutilated, living Marxism' and described him as a 'truly obstinate person'.[2] Negt perceived the core of Kofler's 'living dialectic' to be its ambition – with its theoretical work, with its work on perception – to not only serve as a guide to research, but also as a guide to action.

As a matter of fact, the Marxist theorist Leo Kofler was also, at the same time, a political intellectual. His theories and analyses were always theory intended for practice, i.e., a theory that does not conceal its desire to be a guide to action, to getting involved and taking sides, despite Kofler largely keeping contemporary day-to-day politics at arm's length. Like many others, Kofler did not consider himself as an explicitly political thinker and mostly downplayed or even denied this aspect of his work. So, for example, in the foreword to one of his main works he emphasised in connection to his theory of the progressive elite that his remarks should

> not inspire the illusion that the work at hand is a political one. Nothing would be more erroneous. Its concern is of a theoretical nature, as was its origin.[3]

Such passages need to be well understood, since they only make sense for an unmutilated, living Marxist if they are understood strictly in the context of day-to-day politics. For classical Marxism, theory was always a form of practice and theoretical critique was no passion of the head, but rather the head of passion. That this never meant that theory and critique are only a question of political position is as often emphasised as it is forgotten. If one breaks away from the level of immediate day-to-day politics and reads Kofler with an historicising approach to his work, it quickly becomes apparent how and to what extent Kofler was a markedly original and topical political theorist. In the following, I would like to highlight, in abbreviated form, several of the central aspects of his theoretical work.

Reconstruction of Marxist Philosophy

As a social philosopher and theorist, Leo Kofler was first and foremost an innovator of Marxist thought – an innovator who himself grew up in the milieu of

---

2 Negt 2011, p. 189.
3 Kofler 1964, p. 8.

so-called 'classical Marxism', i.e., in the Marxism at the turn of the twentieth century. It was the 'Red Vienna' of the interwar years, the Vienna of the 1920s and 1930s, this last refuge of the classical workers' movement, where he lived and learned until the age of 31. As an organic product of this milieu, Kofler became an enthusiastic student of the left socialist Austromarxist Max Adler (1873–1937), who, in some respects, was one of the last thinkers of 'classical Marxism' and, in other respects, went beyond this legacy. At the very beginning of Kofler's theoretical work, however, is his break with this legacy. He broke away from Austromarxist social democracy in 1933–4, after its capitulation to nascent Austrofascism, and from his theoretical foster father Max Adler when he fled, alone and destitute, into Swiss exile after Austria's *Anschluss* with fascist Germany. Detached from and disappointed in old political and social contexts, Kofler found himself to be flotsam in a world collapsing into terror and blood, and began his theoretical settling of accounts. Though his work of reconstruction, in the vein of Georg Lukács, of a Marxist sociology as subject-object theory – laid down in his debut work, *Die Wissenschaft der Gesellschaft*, in 1944 – Kofler became a typical representative in many respects of 'Western Marxism' as a specific current of intellectual renewal in the 30s and 40s.[4]

This 'Western Marxism' – called by some neo-Marxism, neo-Hegelianism, or intellectual Marxism – is distinguished by its intensive recourse to Hegel and the young Marx. Whether Ernst Bloch or Herbert Marcuse, whether Max Horkheimer or Theodor W. Adorno, whether Henri Lefebvre, Jean-Paul Sartre or other comparable thinkers: these intellectual renewers, mostly independent of each other, draw on Hegelian subject-object theory, in order to free themselves from the mechanistic and deterministic tradition of thought that underlay social-democratic Marxism as well as Stalinist-deformed Soviet Marxism in the 1920s and 1930s. In Kofler's words, the subject-object dialectic is understood as a relationship 'in which subjective activity is as much the condition for the emergence of objective and law-bound conditions as, conversely, the objective laws are the condition for subjective activity'.[5] For Kofler it was also a question of the so-called subjective factor, the role of consciousness in social being.

Consciousness, theory and ideology were in this way decidedly revalued – and thereby also the meaning of a Marxist criticism of ideology, of a view of individuals, strata, and classes living in ideological delusion. An overcoming of this ruling alienation was only possible through conscious being, through enlightened, conscious action. Even if, for Marxists, socially determined pro-

---

4 See Anderson 1979 and Jünke 2007a, pp. 169–70.
5 Kofler 2004, p. 120.

cesses take place, it is still not determinism. The history of humanity is not a natural process and man himself is fundamentally free to act consciously. Kofler also represents this theoretical return to Marx that took place in the 1930s and 1940s and he applied significant labour and energy in this context to criticise, above all, the mechanistic vulgar Marxism of actually existing socialist provenance:

> The mechanistic interpretation of historical materialism overlooks that despite ideology's determinacy through the economy, the entire historical process cannot complete its motion otherwise than *by means of ideology* – that precisely constitutes an essential moment of this process according to its own laws (whereby it does not mean there is any contradiction to concede at the same time that numerous elements of ideology can be of a coincidental nature, i.e., not necessary in its particular manifestation).[6]

We are dealing here with a dialectical relationship of ideology and economy methodically proceeding from the entirety of occurrences, and only understandable on the basis of this observation of the whole that 'overcomes the yet-to-be eradicated theoretical habit of the merely external and mechanistic coupling of the ideological and economic "factor", two structurally opposed conditions'.[7] As much as theory and practice appear, on the one hand, to fall apart and, on the level of social practice, mostly really do fall apart, just as much, on the other hand, are they a unity, theoretically as well as practically.

> Theory and practice are only two sides of one and the same concrete social occurrence, of the history that, once looked at intentionally from the perspective of the whole, allows itself to be grasped as an intrinsic unity of theory and practice. The relationship of theory and practice does not epistemologically let itself be measured by the criteria of greater or smaller dependence, as it is a fundamental relationship contained in all social life.[8]

With this basic epistemological position, the hitherto broadly dominant mechanistic division in Marxism between base and superstructure, between economics and politics, of spirit and power, tends to be overcome: theory and

---

6   Kofler 2004, p. 192.
7   Kofler 2004, p. 62.
8   Kofler 1971, p. 88.

practice are two sides of one and the same social occurrence; social life regards itself in the ideological itself – and independent, in fact, of whether this thinking is correct or false consciousness.

What we have before us is the recapture of that which one can call the 'relative autonomy of the ideological'. This idea of a relative autonomy of the ideological later experienced its by no means unproblematic renaissance in the 1970s, before it was completely perverted in the almost organically ensuing postmodernism of the 1980s.[9] Kofler, as a Marxist, naturally did not take this path of separating ideology off into a world of free-flowing discourse. Despite this, he can be considered a progenitor of this theoretical discussion. For him, theory was also a form of practice.

Every thinker of Western Marxism made their own mark – including Leo Kofler. The distinctiveness of his own understanding of Marxism is a direct legacy of his intellectual teacher, Max Adler, and is founded in the specific role that human consciousness plays for Adler and Kofler. 'Man engaged in practical activities', according to Kofler, 'cannot be thought of differently than as a more active, i.e., more consciousness-endowed, man with the aid of his mind. The capability to act through consciousness does not, however, mean anything other than the capability to set particular goals for oneself and work towards the accomplishment of these goals'.[10] If the idealistic tradition of thought assumed that history is shaped by consciousness, the materialistic dialectic considered history as essentially shaped through consciousness. Work, activity, practice – all these functions of practical processes of life cannot be conceived of without the quality of consciousness, without the dialectical unity of being and consciousness. For Kofler 'there can be no part of social life, no relationship and no activity that does shape itself through consciousness throughout ("throughout"!)'. When this is viewed as a regression into idealism, vulgar mechanistic materialism celebrates 'its lightly achieved triumph'.[11] The main achievement of historical materialism therefore lies in 'having recognised and, at the same time, materialistically explained' the role of social consciousness, hitherto reclaimed by philosophical idealism and neglected by philosoph-

---

9   'By "postmodern", I mean, roughly speaking, the contemporary movement of thought which rejects totalities, universal values, grand historical narratives, solid foundations to human existence and the possibility of objective knowledge. Postmodernism is sceptical of truth, unity and progress, opposes what it sees as elitism in culture, tends towards cultural relativism, and celebrates pluralism, discontinuity and heterogeneity' (Eagleton 2004, p. 13; for more detail, see Eagleton 1996 as well as Wood and Foster 1997).
10   Kofler 2004, p. 107.
11   Kofler 2004, p. 120.

ical materialism.¹² Thus history, for Kofler, is not made and shaped *by* consciousness, but *by means* of consciousness, through consciousness *throughout* [*hindurch*] – a small yet excellent distinction that Marxist theoretical discussion had great difficulties with for over a hundred years.

In 1896 the Italian Marxist Antonio Labriola already felt himself forced to make this the basis of his preliminary remarks concerning historical materialism as a philosophy of practice, when he wrote:

> We hold this principle to be indisputable, that it is not the forms of consciousness which determine the human being, but it is the manner of being which determines the consciousness (Marx). But these forms of consciousness, even as they are determined by the conditions of life, constitute in themselves also a part of history. This does not consist only in the economic anatomy, but in all that combination which clothes and covers that anatomy even up to the multicolored reflections of the imagination. In other words, there is no fact in history which does not recall by its origin the conditions of the underlying economic structure, but there is also no fact in history which is not preceded, accompanied, and followed by determined forms of consciousness, whether it be superstitious or experimental, ingenuous or reflective, impulsive or self-controlled, fantastic or reasoning.¹³

Nevertheless, 'misunderstandings' not only remain, but rear their head again and again. Even 100 years after Marx's death, one of the great Marxists of his time, the British cultural theorist Raymond Williams, felt compelled to defend the basics. The danger still existed, he wrote in an essential contribution to the 1983 volume *Marx: The First Hundred Years*, of separating human thought, imagination, and concepts from 'men's material life-process' and human consciousness from 'real, active men'. Like Kofler, Williams refers back to, amongst others, Marx's famous architect bee quotation in his powerful rebuttal of this bad habit and emphasises the specifically human features of foresight and decision-making capability, of conscious setting of goals and control.¹⁴ Even Marx himself at times occasionally worked with a reduced and criticisable concept of consciousness and set little store by what humans said, imagined and conceived. But,

---

12   Kofler 2004, p. 105.
13   Labriola 1966, p. 113.
14   Marx 1996, p. 188.

The persuasive philosophical presupposition that we must begin from active human beings, in all their evident social and cultural diversity, rather than from some abstractly imagined and conceived concept of Man, must not be weakened by what would in the end be the philistine dismissal or relegation of what actual people, in definite material conditions and by unarguably material processes – writing, printing, painting, sculpting, building – said, imagined, and conceived. Thus, at the root of the problem of Marx's contribution to a theory of culture, and with critical effect on the subsequent development of a Marxist tradition, we have to restore the practical activities which we now generalise as culture to the full social material process on which he insisted.[15]

Humans have always, as Kofler puts it, also produced according to beauty, and consciousness [*Bewusstsein*], per Marx, cannot be something different than conscious being [*das bewusste Sein*], than their real life-process.

Kofler's methodologically-central emphasis on consciousness, more exactly the *endowment of consciousness*, would finally become the basis for his actual theoretical originality, and for his epistemological groundwork (developed at the end of the 1950s) for a Marxist anthropology. His philosophical anthropology as a 'doctrine of the unchanging requirements of human changeability' conceives of itself as a *formal* anthropology, because even though it makes human history formally possible, it does not determine the content. For Kofler, it is *not* an immediate guidance for action, but rather a type of *ancillary discipline*, a type of *metatheory*, that makes a criterion available for us of what the self-realisation of man *can* be and thus precisely what emancipation cannot and should not be. The double function of a philosophical anthropology, in Kofler's sense, thereby becomes, on the one hand, a defence against those repressive conceptions of man that still necessarily prevail in bourgeois, capitalist society (above all necessary for this reason, because all class society – regardless of what cynics say – must obfuscate their own class character, in order to legitimate themselves). On the other hand, the humanist conception of man posited by Kofler in opposition provides an ethical criterion not only for the assessment of actually existing society, but also a political-ethical scale for emancipatory practice and concrete utopia. This could hardly be more current today (see Chapter 4).

Kofler's attempt at the epistemological groundwork for a Marxist anthropology should be read as such here, i.e., not as a worked out, mature theoretical corpus, but rather as *groundwork* – no more, but also no less. His central

---

15   Williams 1983, p. 29.

emphasis here on consciousness and endowment of consciousness is, in my assessment, an apt and *necessary* challenge for all structural and post-structural currents of thought in our time.[16] Due to this emphasis on consciousness, Kofler was unjustly accused of idealism early on. It indeed remains questionable in my eyes whether this emphasis is also *sufficient*. For essence and appearance require, as is well known, a concretising mediation. The nearer we come to social practice, the less helpful the general insight into the subject-object dialectic and the anthropological foundations of human action becomes. Epistemology, which Kofler is also engaged with here, serves as the defence against false theoretical as well as practical approaches, not, however, as direct guidance for action. Kofler admittedly cheated a little bit regarding the problem of the mediation of goals, ways, and means that grows out of this when he somewhat uncritically took recourse in his theoretical solution to two terms from the Marxism of the Second International, the Marxism of his teacher Max Adler, which has not entirely unjustly received a bad name.

Where man is anthropologically defined through his endowment of consciousness, he is, according to Kofler, also capable by means of his consciousness of orienting himself towards goals and pursuing them in activity. Man thereby

> by virtue of his ability to think and act with consciousness (i.e., to be a subject), reaches ever higher forms of freedom and thus remains the true subject of history. History appears here as man's self-realisation on the path of realising ever higher levels of freedom. With this Hegel founded the historical concept of progress, which Marx adopted.[17]

Here the principles of telos and practice are interlaced for Kofler into a concept of progress that is admittedly aware of the snares of the classic, all too vulgar concept of progress, but which, in my view, does not theoretically get to grips with them. In fact, social and political action without a teleological aspect cannot be understood nor thought. As, for example, the Russian Marxist and revolutionary Leon Trotsky wrote in 1924:

> Politics is embodied teleology. And revolution is condensed politics, bringing into action a mass of many millions. How, then, is revolution possible without teleology?[18]

---

16   It would therefore be of particular interest to place Kofler's theory in dialogue with present-day discussions around neuroscientific research on the brain.
17   'The Concept of Society in Historical Materialism' in this volume, p. 192.
18   Trotsky 1957, p. 107.

However, just as important are the material and social conditions and impediments with which the teleological posits inevitably collide. Here Kofler was also a pioneer in his time when he pointed out that Marxist materialism derived less from a concept of matter than from social materiality in the sense of social reality. What is decisive with these anthropologically conceived concepts of teleology and progress is namely the question *whether, and in what manner* a shift from the telos of an individual to that of a whole society is possible; *whether, and in what manner*, what is individually possible is also possible for the human collective. The concepts of teleology and progress, championed by Kofler throughout his life, are only usable within narrow limits here, yet are historically and philosophically overloaded [*geschichtsphilosophisch überladen*] in Kofler's work.[19]

Does the human species-being actually realise itself *in ever higher degrees of freedom*? The Marxist concept of progress has, as is well-known, two components. On the one hand, it denotes the increase of material productive forces for the attainment of more means of subsistence and more existential security for humans. In this sense, there is obviously a progression in history and it has demonstrated itself repeatedly to be exactly the decisive factor in political practice to point out that humanity has at present already, more than ever, accumulated the material conditions for universal human emancipation. There is, however, a second component of the concept of progress, since progress for Marxists above all mean progress in the quality of social relations (made possible, but not inevitable, through the development of material productive forces), or an 'advance from lower to higher forms of human socialization'.[20] One really cannot say that the twentieth century has resulted in such a progression. Auschwitz and the gulag archipelago are the writing on the wall to the contrary. On the other hand, however, there is the fact that neoliberalism, confidently pushed through for over 30 years worldwide, hardly represents a higher form of human socialisation. Whether we achieve this breakthrough is a thoroughly open question/task.

Kofler made it difficult for himself with the stubborn emphasis on these concepts in a time that, after fascism and Stalinism, didn't much want to hear about the teleological conception of history and the old belief in progress. That these concepts nevertheless retain their albeit limited validity can perhaps be discussed more impartially again today. What is decisive for the currency of Kofler's understanding of Marxism is the question, however, if elements of his

---

19 For a more extensive discussion, see Jünke 2007a, pp. 333–4.
20 Fleischer 1973, p. 68.

theory, despite their fundamental character for him, are nevertheless a part that can be reformed without bringing the original structure as such crashing down.

Considered in this way, there are indeed, in the specific execution or details, some questionable or problematic things in Kofler's understanding of Marxism, but by and large, in my view, it has withstood the gnawing criticism of mice quite well. Considering it against the background of the new German Marxism discussion, it is difficult to free oneself – also in relation to its strongest representative – from the impression of a race between the hare and the hedgehog, in which one can exclaim with Kofler: 'I'm already here!'[21]

Historian of Bourgeois Society and Its History of Ideas

Marxist methodology is one thing, its application to practical history famously another. Leo Kofler was not only a Marxist philosopher, but also a Marxist historian, and his monumental *Zur Geschichte der bürgerlichen Gesellschaft* became, after all, his most well-known work – despite being his most untypical.

The question of how one can understand the historical process equally as human action [*Tathandlung von Menschen*] as well as the logic of a historical process is also the central question that connects the Marxist methodologist with the Marxist historian. As a continuation and clarification of his methodological study on *Die Wissenschaft von der Gesellschaft*, Kofler dedicates himself to these questions in his foundational work, *Geschichte und Dialektik* [History and Dialectics]. Proceeding methodically from the whole of events, he deepens his insight here into the dialectical relationship of ideology and economy, only understandable on the basis of a consideration of the whole. For this self-driven historical research as a continuation of his dialectical social science, this means 'the method of comprehending revelation of the historical substance (*Wesenheit*) by means of the "mediation" of aspects within the concrete totality'.[22] History as the concrete thinking of totality fulfils itself within the subject-object dialectic, 'through consciousness and act of will ..., albeit through one that does not always understand itself, doesn't truly grasp reality and, therefore, through "false" consciousness and an act of will corresponding to it'.[23] Because of this, everything depends on not merely narrating and describing history, 'but rather

---

21 This is a reference to a fable from Lower Saxony, 'The Hare and the Hedgehog', which is similar in many respects to 'The Tortoise and the Hare' (trans. note).
22 Kofler 1992, Vol. 1, p. 30.
23 Kofler 1992, Vol. 1, p. 33.

explaining it by means of its comprehensibility as totality and through the constant placing of all historical aspects in relation to this totality'.[24]

Considered in this way, the apparently 'false' consciousness of historical actors has an eminently practical effect and meaning (and, thereby, 'truth'), for such an ideology is a 'form of society becoming conscious of itself. Without it, even if, up to now, it has overwhelming taken effect as false self-awareness, as "false consciousness", the respective next step in the historical process cannot even become a possibility'.[25] Thus, as Kofler formulates his credo regarding the science of history, 'it cannot solely come down to dispelling appearance in favour of knowledge of the essence, but equally to explaining it as appearance in its historical functionality and, thereby, its necessity'.[26]

History, as it actually was [*wie sie eigentlich gewesen*], is thus more than merely the action of principals and states, more than merely politics and economics, is not only social, gender and cultural history, but also always the history of ideas, the history of thinking and struggling human beings. The methodological particularity of Kofler's *Zur Geschichte der bürgerlichen Gesellschaft* therefore lies in its tight interleaving of ideology and economy, since in his most influential work, he is not writing a political or state history, nor economic or trade history, and also no history of class struggle. Yet all these aspects are subsumed (*aufgehoben*) and held together by a fascinating history of ideas that is essentially a critique of ideology (*ideologiekritisch*). His history of bourgeois society is in substance a history of the critical subject: the critical, humanist bourgeois. Kofler writes, as Ulrich Brieler trenchantly formulates it, a 'genealogy of the critical spirit'.[27] It is the history of the bourgeois capitalist spirit that we can see in his historical work. Above all, it is the involved and contradictory history of early bourgeois humanism that he follows from its medieval beginnings through the Renaissance and Enlightenment until the imperialism of the commencing twentieth century.[28]

This bourgeois humanism was, for Kofler, connected to a real world-historical advance, since: 'We shouldn't fool ourselves: There is no social freedom without freedom for the individual, who strives for self-determination and independence, and who, as long as there is human history, has understood,

---

24 Kofler 1992, Vol. 1, p. 29.
25 Kofler 1992, Vol. 1, p. 36.
26 Kofler 1992, Vol. 1, p. 19.
27 Brieler 2001.
28 It would thus be of particular interest to integrate Kofler's historiography of bourgeois society into the contemporary and present-day discussions regarding the transition from feudalism to capitalism, the so-called *transition debate*. A first attempt in this regard was offered by Michael Krätke in 2001.

understands and will understand by freedom the greatest possible freedom from all barriers and bonds'.[29] Yet that very same humanism already has an immanent contradiction of its own, whose structural limits Kofler trenchantly works out in *Zur Geschichte der bürgerlichen Gesellschaft*. For, in general, the blind spot, also of Enlightenment humanism, is its uncritical, affirmative attitude to bourgeois, capitalist private property. The structural barriers of bourgeois thought are therefore the barriers of capitalist private property, as Kofler demonstrates for diverse philosophers and thinkers from the early bourgeois period. This bourgeois humanism believed that a harmonious social process operating in the interest of all was possible, as soon as it took place on the foundation of private property and complete individual freedom. Yet such an ideal burst asunder against the capitalist reality beginning to establish itself in the nineteenth century. The new political freedoms soon demonstrated themselves to be thoroughly compatible with the social unfreedom of the new capitalist class society. This contradiction came to be theoretically glossed over in humanist thought by the bourgeois conception of man as structurally coupled to ownership and to property. One first acquired the full use of bourgeois rights and liberties, and became a full bourgeois legal subject through possession. The possessionless, in contrast, was deemed to be only half a person. In bourgeois thought there could be property without freedom but never freedom without property. Bourgeois freedom is accordingly constitutively bound up in bourgeois thinking with property. Bourgeois ideology could conceive of the true and complete individual only as a propertied bourgeois individual.

In the historical moment where this bourgeois becomes politically challenged by the impinging strata and classes, he lets his humanist ideal of the all-sided development and unfolding of man fall away and parts with his old radical democratic demands. He becomes a mere liberal and cedes the task of the further democratisation of society henceforth to the, in the bourgeois sense, non-bourgeois classes. While the nascent nineteenth-century workers' movement becomes the heir of these radical democratic and humanist demands, bourgeois thought degenerates into an empty competitive individualism with a pessimistic, decadent conception of man that considers man by nature a predator who pursues his own individual interest. He propagates henceforth a state of society in which might makes right takes effect and this might makes right is understood as the right of the owner. The individual man becomes in this way a 'lonely predator restlessly roving between individuals who remain permanently alien and constantly looking for prey'.[30]

---

29 'On Freedom' in this volume, p. 149
30 Kofler 1992, Vol. 2, p. 304.

Even today that structurally broken relationship between liberalism and democracy is once again intensively discussed and researched, a relationship that Kofler illuminated in such a pioneering way almost 70 years ago, by demonstrating that liberalism and democracy structurally diverge, and how. Bourgeois liberalism is indeed rooted in early bourgeois humanism, yet neither historically nor conceptually can it bring this to completion, because this bourgeois liberalism remains structurally bound to bourgeois property, which always means: to the immanent limits of class society. The bourgeois class's concept of freedom, according to Kofler,

> is thus definitely not as consistent as the idea of popular sovereignty advocated in a general and abstract form for centuries by bourgeois ideologues would have one think. The ultimate reason for this contradictory behaviour is definitely not always to be found in any consciously willed inconsistency or dishonesty or even, as some reckon, in the fear of the misuse of the uneducated masses by reaction, but rather mainly in the contradictoriness of the bourgeois perception of man, resulting necessarily from their existential position [*Seinslage*], and the closely related idea of freedom.[31]

Even today intellects – not only leftist ones, but including them – chafe against the (apparent) contradiction between a political democracy that accommodates capitalist economy and life, and insofar conforms with it, and the historical fact that this political democracy was not struggled for and implemented by the capitalist bourgeois, but on the contrary was stubbornly insisted on and struggled for by the impinging classes and layers and must be defended up to the present day. For Kofler, in the understanding of this process lay the central key to the understanding of the eternal struggle for freedom and democracy, his emphasis on the irresolvable [*unaufhebbar*] class character of bourgeois freedom, the class-bound essence of bourgeois democracy and freedom. He thereby coherently updates the old socialist recognition that the liberal democracy wrung out from this bourgeois class is not enough, and that the work has just begun:

> The contradictory character of bourgeois freedom is an expression of the contradictory character of bourgeois class society in general. It is based on the fact that *on the one hand* the individual – *each* individual – appears

---

31   Kofler 1992, Vol. 2, p. 225.

in bourgeois society as a completely autonomous and equal owner of commodities (owner of shoes, intellectual products or labour power) and thus as a completely autonomous and equal contractual partner, but *on the other hand*, the one-sided ownership of the means of production, i.e. excluding whole classes, simultaneously abolishes this autonomy and legal equality of individuals. The contradiction expressed by this fact is the contradiction between the merely de jure (formal) and the de facto (social) state in bourgeois society, which is based on the distribution of property. ... The abolition of the contradiction between formal freedom and social unfreedom means the abolition of bourgeois society in general; it is not possible *within* this society.[32]

With his analyses concerning the historical relationship in the history of ideas between democracy and liberalism, between humanism and property, Kofler still offers a convincing alternative both to the diverse variants of a German left radicalism – whether it stems from critical theory or critical criticism, outmoded dogmatism or undogmatic emotion – that still believe they can, or even must, leave radical democratic theory and practice to the right, as well as to the diverse variants of a left reformism that believe it is already enough only to evolutionarily expand the principals of ruling political democracy in order to satisfy the project of a universal human emancipation.

Critique of Neo-capitalism and Its Late Bourgeois Ideology

Kofler was not only a Marxist methodologist and critical historian of bourgeois society. He applied and expanded this critical historical and methodological perspective to his contemporary 'late bourgeois' society. He was one of the first Marxists after the Second World War to grapple intensively with analysis of the structures, contradictions and snares of this emerging social state capitalism – this alleged affluent capitalism (*Wohlstandskapitalismus*) – starting in the mid-1950s. His primarily socio-psychological analysis, realised in multiple works by the end of the 1960s, directed its attention to the novel integration processes of late bourgeois class society. According to Kofler in his work *Staat, Gesellschaft und Elite zwischen Humanismus und Nihilismus* [State, Society and Elite between Humanism and Nihilism], published in 1960, post-war capitalism, tamed by the social state, was still an antagonistic class society charac-

---

32 'On Freedom' in this volume, p. 149.

terised by exploitation, injustice, and dominance, in which some have what the others lack. There was still master and servant, bourgeois elite and proletariat – and if the latter had become materially better off in the meantime, economic dependence and insecurity remained along with the class consciousness of one's own social inferiority, the knowledge of the gulf between top and bottom.

Nevertheless, the mechanisms of domination had deeply changed. Repression, according to Kofler at the end of the 1950s, had increasingly internalised itself; domination 'intellectualised' [*vergeistige*] itself (a vintage term of his teacher, Max Adler). With the ideological overlaying the social as a means of societal integration, liberalism finally suppressed all radical democratic and humanist demands of the early bourgeois period and became nihilistic: freedom was only conceived of negatively, as *freedom from*, no longer as *freedom to* – at best the freedom to consume as much as one could afford. Undoubtedly, according to Kofler, this form of society had a great deal to offer its members: more political freedom, more income and free time, more security and fewer taboos. Yet at the same time these new freedoms and possibilities shackled the individual more than ever to an, in principle, irrational form of society. Hunger had indeed disappeared, but not deprivation. Consumption was possible, but only by means of an asceticism prior and, once again, subsequent to it: 'Doing without in order to be able to afford something and affording something with the consequence of subsequent doing without belong to the self-evident behavioural patterns of our time'.[33] The apparent de-ideologisation proves itself to be, according to Kofler even then, total ideologisation, individual rationalism as a corollary of collective irrationalism, the democracy of the market as the obfuscation of the despotism of factory and office:

> The truly novel in the modern stage of oppression is the seeming voluntariness with which the individual subjects himself to the repressive demands, a voluntariness, however, that he does not comprehend as an instance of general oppression, but rather the other way round, as the necessary result of freedom gained, particularly in erotic things, for which the order which this freedom grants rewards with loyalty and affection.[34]

What Kofler is trying to theoretically understand here, in his writings of the 1950s and 1960s, is nothing less than the altered relationship of consensus and

---

33   Kofler 2007, p. 129.
34   Kofler 2007, p. 121.

coercion in the neo-capitalist form of society – that relationship that since the 1970s has been understood with the concept of ideological hegemony. Ideological consensus was admittedly always a proven and indispensable means of social integration, yet nowhere had its role become so encompassing as in neo-capitalism at that time. This consensus is, for Kofler, certainly an essentially negative one that at best holds society together in the absence of a common positive goal. In such a form of society, the spiritual [*geistigen*] ties of its members increasingly dissolve, as it were. If the early bourgeois striving for human perfection was directed towards the 'outside world' through enlightenment, education and pedagogy, today it is instead directed 'inwards', into the individual. Everyone becomes his own fellow man and freedom turns 'into an esoteric and self-centred involvement with the spiritual "interior"'.[35] This esotericism takes on traits in the subject of 'fanatical monomania' and becomes elitist. The isolated individual feels, in an elite manner, to be subjectively free and elevated above 'the masses', while, however, pessimism and lethargy alone condense 'into a type of nihilistic *Weltschmerz* ... that encamps itself over the whole of society like a multi-armed polyp'.[36] Late bourgeois ideology therefore made a virtue out of a necessity, 'out of the mark of Cain, of defeat, the emblem of human existence', in which the 'chaotic and meaningless "nothingness" of what exists ...' is exalted 'into an existential of all being', into the eternal human situation.[37]

Kofler here accuses late bourgeois society of having structurally jettisoned its early original early bourgeois ideas of enlightenment and, in this manner, of having intellectually given up. The bourgeoisie threw itself into the arms of pessimism and hostility to progress, and thereby inadvertently conceded the impossibility of the realisation of humanist goals within the bourgeois order:

> The world, for the bourgeoisie, only remains 'useful', bearable for profit, otherwise it has become empty and meaningless. The remaining 'freedom' is no longer the freedom to realise ideals and elevate man – whoever still wants to do this becomes suspect! – but rather the freedom of competition, of the jungle. Basically, everything has been achieved, there was history, but there won't be in the future.[38]

---

35 Kofler 1960, p. 43.
36 Kofler 1960, p. 46.
37 Kofler 1960, p. 47.
38 Kofler 1960, p. 150.

Kofler writes, in the 1950s and 1960s, a critique of bourgeois freedom in neo-capitalist consumer capitalism primarily from a socio-psychological perspective. He thereby avoids the ideological snares, dominant at the time, of an allegedly 'administered world', a 'one-dimensional society' or even an 'integral statism' – without, thereby, ignoring the social phenomena at the base of these ideological constructs ('consumerism', 'bureaucratisation', 'nationalisation', 'lack of opposition'). That he, while doing so, used allegedly outdated terminology ('decadence', 'nihilism', 'irrationalism', etc.) had long made him suspect in the eyes of his young bourgeois leftist critics. Yet here too it appears to me that the present triumphal procession of a postmodern cynicism, penetrating polyp-like into all seams of society, has ensured that the rational kernel of Kofler's critique is revealed in a new manner. The political blockages that such destruction of language and conceptual taboos have imposed on the left are as lasting as they are problematic: 'One may, by and large, speak of human culture but not human nature, gender but not class, the body but not biology, *jouissance* but not justice, post-colonialism but not the petty bourgeoisie'.[39] For Kofler, in any case, the postwar capitalism tamed by the social state was, first and foremost, a *class society* – an antagonistic form of society characterised by exploitation, injustice and domination, in which some have what is withheld from others, in which some deem that they must and may elevate themselves over others. In contemporary postmodern capitalism there still continues to be master and servant, or 'more scientifically' expressed: bourgeois elites and wage-labouring classes, middle classes and new precariat, and so on and so forth. The old analyses of the Marxist tradition are thus not amiss, they must 'only' be thought through, supplemented and reformulated in accordance with today's conditions.

Even if this task of an up-to-date reformulation might be approached differently today than in Kofler's time, it remains, looking backward, to recognise, and looking forward, to proceed from the fact that Kofler was already rightly emphasising that the new consensus had not abolished the old coercion. Today, after neo-capitalism has transformed itself into neoliberalism, and in times in which the ruling globalisation, i.e., the globalisation of the rulers, has armed itself and trumpets the 'war on terror', this insight should also have become more evident. As Werner Seppmann recently wrote:

> It would do well for a left that talks a lot about a universalisation of power entanglement of the subject in nexuses of power, but avoids concrete ana-

---

39   Eagleton 1996, p. 26.

lysis of power structures, to at least allow itself to be inspired by Kofler's sociological view of the ruling class, his theoretical grappling with the actors in the power system and hegemonic thought, as well as his analysis of the structures of mediation of economic position, social power, cultural influence and civilisational determinants of repression.[40]

Critique of the Workers' Movement

Comparable only to the contemporary analyses of Herbert Marcuse, Kofler was thus already working out the new processes of neo-capitalist social formation in the second half of the 1950s – earlier than Marcuse – and insisted – unlike Marcuse – that the class antagonism particular to bourgeois society in the late capitalist situation of reification and alienation was also reflected in the consciousness of wage workers and, if appropriately and consistently pushed ahead, was also politicisable. The bourgeoisification of the working class as such is not, for Kofler, the cause of the dominant misery. Far more to blame was the theory-hostile practicality of the labour bureaucrats of social-democratic as well as Stalinist provenance.

Kofler answered the major social and political question, emphatically posed since the 1950s, regarding the objective as well as subjective role of the wage-labouring class in the contemporary socialist movement with a shifting of the planes: It is not what the actually existing proletariat and its class organisations do in practice, but rather it is what they are forced do on the basis of their social position that socialists must base their politics on. If there is in Marx's Marxism a development from a philosophical into a historically concrete concept of class, without thereby giving up the philosophical concept, this argument in Kofler turns back and he draws on an, in essence, philosophical concept of class.[41] Kofler placing his hope in this class has less to do with the fact that the proletariat is the central class for the functioning of capitalist society and the fact that in its proletarian class struggle, it accumulates the practical and theoretical, the organisational and ideological prerequisites in order to abolish class society as such with its own class position. Both aspects indeed remain correct, albeit losing their historically concrete efficacy. Kofler's contemporary hope in the proletariat is instead once again nourished by a discourse of immiseration. This discourse of immiseration is, however, not one of economics, but rather

---

40 Seppmann 2012, p. 65.
41 See Mandel 1971, chapter 1.

of consciousness: the new pauperism is, for Kofler, a synonym for sociopolitical impoverishment [*Armseligkeit*], for 'the being of man that is remote from the development and realisation of human powers, abilities and talents, namely, the being of man that is subject to human misery'.[42] What the modern proletariat therefore lacked above all was less the material – although this also left something to be desired – than, to a greater degree, the consciousness of its social and spiritual misery. For him, this historical process is, however, neither inevitable nor irreversible: this is far more the historical consequence of the political 'failure' of the two main currents of the organised workers' movement, social democracy and Stalinism.

Specifically in the left Austromarxist tradition and despite ingrained anti-Stalinism, the Kofler of the 1930s and 1940s retained a fundamental political sympathy for the Communist anti-fascism of the Popular Front period. His reform-communist hopes for de-Stalinisation and debureaucratisation in the socialist and Communist movement in the post-fascist period caused him to go to the 'Soviet occupation zone' in Germany in 1947. With its re-Stalinisation at the beginning of the Cold War, however, he had broken from this political commitment and, as a harsh critic of Eastern bureaucratisation tendencies, had to flee to West Germany at the end of 1950. In multiple short pieces, he promptly formulated one of the first Marxist critiques of the Stalinist bureaucracy in Germany. The Communist wing of the international workers' movement had been seized by a structural bureaucratisation and loss of democracy, in his judgement, and should be structurally abolished. Under the pressure of a bureaucratic ruling caste, socialist freedom in actually existing socialism had been reduced to an anti-humanist economic fetishism of the productive forces in the service of a novel bureaucratic rule – structurally incapable of emancipatorily renewing itself.[43]

Even if in West Germany Kofler, as a political intellectual forcefully thrown out of the Communist movement, from then on worked again on the left margin of social democracy and in the respective labour circles, his criticism of their increasing abandonment of Marxist principles and insights was no less sharp. The SPD at the time indeed still referred to the wage-labouring class and was also anchored in this milieu, yet its theory and politics were already increasingly developing in a different direction. Under the guise of a new freedom of the social state and as an alleged lesson from Stalinism, social democracy, according to Kofler's critique as early as the beginning of the 1950s, no

---

42 'The Concept of Society in Historical Materialism' in this volume, p. 204.
43 See Chapter 3.

longer fundamentally questioned the logic of the capitalist social system, but rather merely attempted to technocratically tame it. In this manner of turning away from a Marxist view of society, socialist ideology and practice were also increasingly driven back in their own ranks and only remained tolerated as 'ethical socialism'. However, social democracy thereby increasingly laboured under the external appearance of capitalist reality and became permeated by a bureaucratic functionary consciousness that necessarily separated 'is' and 'ought' from each other. Neverthless 'the kingdom of "pure" "ought" indeed imparted a whole system of the good, just, beautiful and true, in addition to, at best, of the right of man to "self-determination", but not one sentence that allowed one to conclude how one should correctly act in a socialist manner'.[44]

Kofler's critique of social-democratic ethicism is thus no critique of the ethical as such, but rather a critique of the political and conceptual division of 'is' and 'ought', as the farewell to socialist theory and practice it was commonly made to be by social democrats and other leftists. The practical and philosophic critique of the 'ethical realism' theorised by leading social democrats on their way to Bad Godesberg is one of the many remaining merits of Kofler's work in the 1950s. In saying this he would remain painfully correct: 'Where theory and philosophy are separated from politics, there they will be detached or self-contained'.[45] The Social Democrats accepting socialism in the 1950s and 1960s only as an ethics detached from political practice, excluding their traditional supporters at the same time (by means of decisions against 'incompatible' dual memberships [*Unvereinbarkeitsbeschlüsse*]) ever more from their own political world, resulted, in the end (after the detour of a left infusion during the 1970s conditioned by '1968'), in the arrival in the 1980s and 1990s of the new social-democratic credo borrowed from the conservatives: 'There is no alternative'. At the end of this long road, one finally broke even the military taboo, defending Germany's neoliberal freedom in Southeast Europe, North Africa and in the far east Hindu Kush (from 1998 onwards), and flanking this freedom internally with the greatest attack to date on the German welfare state (Agenda 2010). The foundation of this apparently inevitable path is, for Kofler, the extensive bureaucratisation and sociopolitical integration of the organised workers' movement in social state capitalism, a movement that once strove for a fundamental overcoming of the capitalist market economy:

> In the place of theory is the bureaucracy, the place of enlightenment and humanistic education having been trodden on by worry over the 'func-

---

44 Kofler 2000b, p. 82.
45 Cardorff 1980, p. 150.

tioning' of what exists. Minds should no longer be illuminated with philosophy but rather be 'won' through accommodation – after the acknowledged model of market advertising. The 'expert', entangled in the reified process, has supplanted the teacher. This is how one wants to persist against Communism and fascism – no longer, and that for quite some time, against the bourgeois world as a whole, whose alienation and decadence one believes through ignorance and, if one is a bit cleverer due to certain traditions, through passing over it in silence, to have 'overcome'.[46]

With his firm critique of both contemporary currents of the socialist left, essentially concluded in the mid-1950s, this border crosser between the currents was once again a homeless leftist falling between the cracks. He thereby once again moved away from the position laid down in 1944 in his first work, *Die Wissenschaft der Gesellschaft*, one of self-criticism in the tradition of Otto Bauer's 'integral socialism', over to a fundamental critique of both currents. This development reflected the contemporary 'de-social democratisation' in the West and the failed destalinisation in the East, or, in the words of Henri Lefebvre: the 'ghost of the Revolution which never happened over here, ... the ghost of the Revolution which was never completed over there'.[47] Thus 'the spiritual corruption' of a 'general bourgeois decadence' tended to capture all strata of workers and no longer only the old labour aristocracy. 'Even if in good faith', these strata affirmed the bureaucratic structure and are successfully activated by the bureaucracy in a bureaucratic sense. Yet 'the cat catches its own tail: the condition of demoralisation amongst the workers fosters bureaucracy and the bureaucracy fosters the demoralisation of the workers'.[48] Precisely because social democracy and Stalinism, with their positivistically-constricted, bureaucratic thought, were no longer capable of thinking outside the actually existing capitalist as well as actually existing socialist boxes, both currents would capitulate to the dominant alienation. For Kofler, they are henceforth and, each in their own way, two sides of the same coin – the expression of a comprehensive bureaucratisation of the workers' movement hindering universal human emancipation.

Here also little has changed since then. Without having dissolved themselves, both main currents have undergone a progressive process of internal erosion in the subsequent decades – political, ideological, and social. The old

---

46   Kofler 1964, p. 7.
47   Lefebvre 1995, p. 236.
48   Kofler 1960, p. 328.

social democracy is just as irrevocably dead as the old Communist movement. Yet the positions in the history of ideas they once held – 'ethical', 'technocratic' and 'despotic' socialism – have not disappeared from the historical scene. Stalinism may barely exist today as a political formation, but certainly remains as influential political thought.[49] Even if the number of declared socialists in the SPD has become vanishingly small, ethical socialists are quite numerous in other social and political milieus and institutions.

Theory of the New Left and Their Progressive Elite

With this we have finally arrived at the last set of issues in Kofler's thought to be highlighted here, his theory of a 'third way' – not a third way beyond capitalism and socialism, but rather *within* the socialist movement. The comprehensive bureaucratisation of the contemporary workers' movement diagnosed by Kofler in the mid-1950s had, according to him, to be rolled back. This, however, would no longer be immanently possible from inside, no longer possible only through that 'self-criticism' he propagated in 1944. Only the advent of a new (at the moment, barely organised and moreover, only organisable with difficulty) vanguard of workers, citizens and intellectuals could turn this around again and change the 'historical failure' of both main currents of the international organised workers' movement for the better. This terminology already makes Kofler's commitment and his normative standpoint clear. What protagonists of both currents, each in their own way, had already glorified as a success story – the actually existing 'socialism' over there, the actually existing 'welfare state' over here – Kofler still measures according to the criterion of an emancipatory socialist goal that he recognises in radical socialist humanism, and no longer sees preserved [*aufgehoben*] in both main currents of the organised workers' movement.

He shared this assessment with several others in the 1950s and 1960s. What, however, makes him stand out from most of them was his answer to the question of what to conclude from it. Is socialism passé with this historical failure? What comes now? Who embodies the practical advance if forces historically responsible for it have failed in such a manner? History, according to Kofler's hegelianising answer, did not let itself be deceived, and created a replacement, 'to whom the task falls to ensure the transition', as he writes in the last chapter of his work, *Staat, Gesellschaft und Elite zwischen Humanismus und Nihilis-*

---

49   See Jünke 2007b.

mus, published in 1960.⁵⁰ Since he first theorised this in 1957, he terms this replacement 'the progressive', or at times 'the humanist elite', and emphasises that in choosing the term 'elite' he is not using it as an evaluative term but rather as a sociologically descriptive one. 'Elite', for Kofler, is present anywhere where out of the masses in a class society being kept immature [*unmündig*] – unconscious – individuals distinguish themselves through their 'higher', more critical consciousness. This progressive 'elite', for Kofler, characterises all those individuals who are in fundamental opposition to late Stalinist as well as late bourgeois anti-humanism and nihilism. Be they dissident communists fighting against the half measures of destalinisation, or oppositionist social democrats and trade unions fighting against bureaucratisation and accommodation, be they radical democratic bourgeois, or socially engaged Christians – they all turned, willingly or unwillingly, into a distinct political and sociological stratum under the novel historical conditions of a bureaucratically blocked workers' movement, into an 'amorphous elite composed of progressive elements of socialist and non-socialist origin' that, superficially observed, does not exist at all.⁵¹ It was no particular and closed group, no homogeneous part of a certain class or stratum, thus not purely bourgeois or proletarian or petit-bourgeois and so on. The progressive elite was instead an amorphous, i.e., formless mass with strongly heterogeneous and fluctuating tendencies, heterogeneous in its social and political composition, heterogeneous in its social and political views, heterogeneous in its habitus. It fell between the cracks, was contradictory and volatile, socially powerless, and 'yet it was there and not without significance'.⁵² When it comes to these progressives, we are dealing with individuals from all political and social milieus, with individuals who stand socially and ideologically askew to the traditional front of socialism and non-socialism, and lead a kind of pariah existence on the margin and in the niches of social organisations (in parties, groups, cultural and religious associations). What distinguished them was not a question of a rosette in the button hole: nothing that automatically suited them based on creed. It was rather a question of their humanistic sensitivity, their practical attitude, and it therefore had to be consciously wrested anew again and again from the ruling powers.

Kofler thus recognised in this progressive, humanist elite – and herein lies the originality of his theory – a historically independent force that should be treated politically as well as analytically with appropriate seriousness. This new elite, the convinced Marxist and socialist Kofler was quick to append, could 'not

---

50 Kofler 1960, p. 347.
51 Kofler 2000c, p. 141.
52 Kofler 1960, p. 346.

replace the workers' movement historically appointed to society's transformation. They remain a mere and transitory replacement for this movement in the interim periods of its torpor'.[53] However, so long as this workers' movement was bureaucratically torpid, it was 'an *indispensable* fermenting agent ... who safeguards society from rigor mortis' (my emphasis) and called to 'one day play an important role' – precisely because these progressives take the old humanist promises seriously and would consciously turn, sometimes more, sometimes less, against the 'decadence' phenomena of late bourgeois society, against alienation and reification.[54]

Yet *precisely because* they were not socially, politically and culturally consolidated, precisely because they are *not* an integral part of a stable sociopolitical countervailing force like the old classical workers' movement, these humanist individuals are not only inclined to revolt against that which exists. According to Kofler, their incorruptible desire for humanist freedom not only cast their thought into the emancipatory future, but also broke against the nihilistic realities of the time and their own powerlessness. Given the increasing alienation and accommodatory practice, the progressive elite's typical move into the utopian (a move also justified by Kofler) consistently threatened to tip over into an unrestrained utopianism out of touch with everyday life. The individuals of this progressive humanist elite are otherwise permanently inclined to succumb to the compulsion of the dominant alienation and establish themselves in temporising passivity, at times pessimistically despairing, at times resignedly cynical. Torn between optimism and pessimism, their humanistic idealism thus experiences that 'peculiar refraction that one best characterises as irony [*Ironisierung*]' and can be seen, for example, in the art of the late Bert Brecht: 'In this view, not only is the optimist ideal ironic, but also, in dialectical interaction, the irony coming out of the desperation is optimistically refracted'.[55]

Kofler's analysis of the progressive elite not coincidentally recalls his interpretation of the early bourgeois sectarian movements of the Middle Ages and the early bourgeois period in *Zur Geschichte der bürgerlichen Gesellschaft*.[56] These diverse sectarian movements are also carriers of radical social critique. These also manifest an inner contradiction between revolutionary rationalism and mystical acquiescence to what exists. They are products of a historical situation of the objective impossibility of revolutionary social transformation:

---

53   Kofler 1960, p. 348.
54   Kofler 1960, p. 348; Kofler 2000, p. 143.
55   Kofler 1960, p. 356.
56   Kofler 1992, Vol. 1, pp. 199–200.

individual revolts and small group movements are structurally incapable of overthrowing a class society and establishing a new one. The knowledge of these structural limits of the medieval and early modern sectarian movements, however, did not hinder the historian Kofler from understanding them as 'forward-pointing factors in modern history'.[57] Similarly the modern 'progressive elite': with the decomposition of the classical socialist mass movement, more specifically their extensive accommodation, the movement for human emancipation in the middle of the twentieth century was thrown back once more to individuals and small groups. Differently, however, than in the early modern period there was, for Kofler, still convinced of socialism, nevertheless a contemporary perspective of radical change in alliance with a renewed workers' movement.

What Kofler was one of the first to historically describe and analyse here at the end of the 1950s was nothing other than the rise of the 'New Left' in the 1960s and 1970s. This New Left, understood in the broadest sense, comprised socialists and democrats, men and women, young and old, workers, intellectuals, and citizens, the anti-nuclear movement as well as the peace movement, artists, scientists and trade unionists, internationalists and liberation theologians and so on. This New Left was anything but homogeneous, yet nonetheless an identifiable hodgepodge – an amorphous mass with strongly fluctuating tendencies, arising out of a political constellation of 'old' left defeats, and thus a product of historical transition. Kofler's theory of the progressive elite gives these colourful movements a political and theoretical conception, and a structure. It works out their essence and their contradictions, their size and their limits, and sees in the progressive humanistic vanguard a historico-philosophical, or more precisely, a historico-sociological necessity in the time of a world-historically blocked transition, without thereby falling for those myths of the new that so many members of the New Left would fall for in the 1960s and 1970s.[58] As much, however, as he considered this progressive elite collecting itself in the New Left as historically justified and shared many of the 'new' left objectives, he adhered just as much, in the 'old' left tradition, to the idea that the progressive elite could only be a transitional community, whose historical and political task is *not* the founding of a new social movement, but rather the reconstruction of an anti-bureaucratic, revolutionary class movement. In order to arrive at this reconstruction, it required, according to Kofler, a new alliance between intellectuals and the social movement, an association of

---

57   Kofler 1992, Vol. 1, p. 62.
58   See Lefebvre 1995, pp. 184–5.

the progressive elite with those wage earners stuck in a politics of accommodation. Only the common struggle for the recapture of these trade union and political organisations could show a way out of the dominant alienation. Such a perspective of alliance, however, required, as he so picturesquely describes in his 1968 work *Perspektiven des revolutionären Humanismus*, the 'abolition [*Aufhebung*] of the separation of the two groups', 'according to their respective origins, critical and oppositional worlds'. It required the world of the factory, i.e. the world of 'vulgar and stubborn practicality', and the world of the university, i.e. the world of highly developed abstraction and a self-satisfied intellectualism, to again mingle with and influence each other. Such a goal, in fact, demanded a lot from the progressive elite, since both worlds 'jealously guard their existence, as a further connection is only possible with a destruction of both silos, only with the overcoming of practicality on the one side and self-criticism of the half-nihilist nonconformism on the other', yet: 'The destruction of both silos, which have become ideological prisons, forms the precondition for the recovery of revolutionary humanism'.[59]

Such a recovery of revolutionary humanism certainly required intellectuals and activists getting involved and taking sides. Precisely because this new historical stratum was structurally unstable, and precisely because it was under permanent threat of sliding into despairing pessimism and nihilism; because its historical and political task was the self-transformation, the destruction of both silos – precisely because of this, Kofler considered the clarification of its principal ideas as his personal contribution to the development of a new revolutionary socialist humanism. Above all, Kofler considered intellectual contestation with nihilistic tendencies within the progressive elite, but also with liberal, Christian, and other (including leftist) tendencies of humanism as his urgent task. For only through such a self-criticism transitioning into self-enlightenment could the progressive elite fulfil their historical task, and thereby avoid becoming a figleaf for regressive tendencies.

What Kofler, admittedly, too little accounted for is the question of to what extent the particular character of the progressive elite also required a particular culture of debate. For if the progressives are in the historical right, but politically are often only fracturedly humanistic, then one can barely criticise them and their fracturedness from the revolutionary humanist perspective in the same manner as one did earlier, in the classical period of socialism, in discussions between socialists and non-socialists. A purely polemical and debunking critique obviously disregards the historical necessities. Yet precisely

---

59   Kofler 2007, pp. 73–4.

in his sharp reckoning with, for example, the 'Marxo-nihilism' of the Frankfurt School, Kofler inclined to such a partially one-sided polemic.[60]

The originality of Kofler's theory of the progressive elite also consists in it doing two things at the same time that otherwise are generally separated. On the one side, Kofler justifies, in a downright historico-philosophical manner, the historical, political and sociological rise of the New Left. This distinguishes him from many other leftists. Some, the 'traditionalists', veered to the left from these movements, because they were allegedly petty bourgeois, 'moral', and not oriented to the 'real revolutionary subject', while others, the 'modernists', elevated them to an allegedly new historical subject that replaced the working class in their appointed role to overcome capitalism. Kofler, in contrast, made himself into a forward thinker of these movements and told them at the same time that it could not be about the founding of an entirely new social movement, but rather about the reconstruction of an anti-bureaucratic, revolutionary class movement. He demanded the bridging of the humanistic vanguard and the organised workers' movement; of the 'old' and 'new' social movement for common self-transformation. As there could be no talk of overcoming the capitalist class society, so nothing could fundamentally change in the Marxist analysis of bourgeois capitalism. The currency of classical socialism could indeed be suspended for a time – but not for good. As much as the new movements thus contributed to historical progress, they could not structurally attain a post-bourgeois society. This assessment of Kofler's differs markedly from that of a Herbert Marcuse on the one side or social-democratic and Communist Party thinkers on the other – to say nothing of a Theodor W. Adorno. This, however, also distinguishes him from Wolfgang Abendroth, who practically assisted the anti-authoritarian '68ers, the second generation of the New Left, but did not have much idea of how to theorise about them. Kofler's stance here is interestingly most closely comparable with that of Peter Brückner, yet Brückner again is more of an elder brother of the anti-authoritarians, more a theoretical child than a theoretical father of the movement.[61]

---

60 See chapters 5 and 6.
61 In his *Attempt to Explain the Federal Republic to Us and Others* [*Versuch, uns und anderen die Bundesrepublik zu erklären*, Berlin 1978, p. 140], Peter Brückner later writes in an entirely Koflerian manner 'that there was a particular opposition in the FRG, that – barely organised and spread over *many* strata and classes – in essence had the student protest movement of 1967–68 to thank for its precarious existence. Its "project", which stands askew to German traditions and the general climate, is perhaps altogether rather a method of political action, a way of perceiving social relation that turns up in various oppositional currents, than, say, the ideological basis for a party'.

Kofler's theory of the progressive elite accounts for the structural heterogeneity of the historical phenomenon of the events of 1968, allows us to see the largely student-based New Left as such in a larger historical context as the most effective expression to that point of a historically necessary and justified Third Way, not between the bourgeois and socialist way, but rather between or beyond two 'socialist' ways (social democracy and 'actually existing' socialism). It allows us to recognise that both are required for the renewal of the socialist movement, the yeast as well as the dough, the intellectuals as well as the workers' movement, and that it comes down to their mixture. It allows us to explain why, from the beginning, the movement was inscribed by the two poles of opportunism (i.e., the inclination to re-accommodation in the social and political institutions of late bourgeois society) as well as sectarianism (i.e., the inclination to political and/or cultural self-ghettoisation), to which the movement should not be reduced. Additionally, it allows us to understand why the progressive elite is in the position, under specific historical conditions, to develop a considerable social breadth and utopian depth that stands in peculiar contrast to their inability to form lasting structures of their own kind.

A Grand Narrative

Kofler's theory of the progressive elite, which remained fragmentary, is not only a politically original theory of the 'third way'. It also focuses his essential theoretical achievements to practical purpose and offers, at the same time, a thread by which to understand his own biography. It takes the critique of the Old Left extremely seriously and segues to a critical defence of the New Left. It thereby connects theory and practice, the work for a renewal of the dogmatic bureaucratised Marxist thought with the call for a renewed socialist movement that, in principle, belongs to all, the 'old' as well as the 'new' left – insofar as they are ready to really begin anew. Finally, Kofler's theory of the progressive elite allows us a politico-theoretical as well as historico-philosophical perspective on the socialist left in the second half of the twentieth century, and puts an interpretive key to the history of the post-fascist left in our hands – from the homeless left of the 1950s and the '68ers' movement to the failure of the New Left in the 1970s, the new social movements of the 1980s and the postmodern, cynical decomposition processes of the early 1990s until the globalisation critics of the turn of the millennium, and the new Left Party or Occupy – that allows us to better understand their strengths as well as their weaknesses: as specific forms of breaking free from the world-historical dilemma of fascism, Stalinism, and the bureaucratically blocked workers' movement, from the collapse of the classical socialist mass movement, specifically its extensive absorption into the institutions and value systems of the capitalist bourgeoisie.

The movement for universal human emancipation is again returned to the actions of individuals and small groups. The new nonconformists (comparable to the medieval and early modern sectarian movements), structurally incapable of the revolutionary transformation of late bourgeois class society, fluctuate back and forth between a heaven-storming optimism on the one hand, and a sorrowful pessimism on the other, between times of an explosive awakening on the one hand and times of a long decay. Accordingly, the generally articulated hope in 1966–8 to focus the new leftist movements on an emancipatory and socialist transformation of society had already collapsed in 1969–70. The two silos of which Kofler wrote were not destroyed. On the contrary, they began to increasingly seal themselves off from each other. The movement broke into many individual parts that admittedly, as new social movements, experienced quite a flowering. A new focus for these movements, however, did not pan out, just as there was no incursion into the institutionalised world of the West German workers' movement worth mentioning. The fall was correspondingly deep – deeper than in other countries of the metropole, where this convergence of the radical Left and the new workers' movement at least partially succeeded.

The New Left of the 1960s and 1970s neither managed to destroy both silos nor to focus social discontent politically and strategically into a social revolutionary movement. As Peter Cardorff wrote in 1980:

> Not only the euphoria of an ultra-left actionism and the eccentricities of M-L recourses to the Stalin period have proved themselves to be untenable ... but also the serious attempts to draw on the revolutionary traditions of Marx, Engels, Lenin, Trotsky and Luxemburg and connect them with various newer theoretical currents have not resulted in the envisioned successes. The political hegemony of the social-democratic and Communist parties in the decisive social layers has not been broken up.[62]

The New Left, according to Cardorff, was pulverised between technocratic reformism and the irrationalist cult of immediacy. Out of the ruins of this New Left emerged in the second half of the 1970s and during the 1980s the so-called 'new social movements', which were given focus by the Green alternative party.

---

62   Cardorff 1980, p. 160.

For Kofler, these alternative Greens were a typical new example of the progressive elite, albeit one that in many respects again fell behind the level already attained with the old extra-parliamentary opposition (APO). In his work *Zur Kritik der 'Alternativen'* [On the Critique of the 'Alternatives'], published in 1983, he lamented their 'being mired in practicality, economism, biologism and reformism' that expressed itself in lack of theory, leading to intellectual constriction and thus a conditioned 'incapability for education and reception of a theory that breaks through the empirical surface appearance and, through many channels of popular communication, embraces decisive sections of the people', surrendering the 'alternatives' to bourgeois nihilism.[63] If Kofler still massively supported the progressive elite of the 1950s and 1960s, he no longer found a real approach in their newest embodiment in the 1980s. Although he attributed 'unreservedly' to the Green-Alternatives the merit of 'having rediscovered the everyday in its erotic meaning and as a starting point for political action', he otherwise picked them to pieces and invoked Marx's critique of 'true socialism' against them.[64] If he had already polemicised against the New Left of Frankfurt provenance in 1964 that they could be best characterised with the old song lyrics 'Half-left, half-right, straight ahead!', the Green-Alternatives now explicitly understood themselves as 'not right, not left, but forward'.[65]

Kofler's now changed and deeply pessimistic dealings with the newest form of a progressive elite were accompanied in the middle of the 1980s by a just as changed assessment of the, at that time, still 'actually existing socialism'. The nominally socialist Eastern Bloc led by the Soviet Union, according to Kofler, against the backdrop of the general loss of Marxist ideology in the West, became the guarantors of ideational socialist common interest, and Kofler placed all his hopes in the new Soviet general secretary, Mikhail Gorbachev, who had stepped up to reform Soviet society. The time of world-historical transition, according to Kofler, was over. Yet the price that Kofler would pay for this illusion – an illusion that was widespread at the time – was great. He diluted his anti-Stalinism into a mere critique of Stalinoid remnants and blamed it less on the Soviet bureaucracy than on the traditions of Asiatic despotism. As his reform socialist hopes finally shattered in 1989–90, Kofler was not preserved from a certain elitism and cynicism that he had criticised throughout his life, culminating in justifying the bloody suppression of the Beijing Spring in his lectures.[66]

---

63 Kofler 1983a, p. 9.
64 Kofler 1983a, p. 61.
65 Kofler 1964, p. 9.
66 See Jünke 2007a, Chapter 7.

That this elitist cynicism was also not untypical at the time is, if nothing else, made clear in those discussions of political restructuring in 1988–9, when other parts of the West German left responded to the upsurge in leftist ideas triggered by 'Gorbymania' with the formation of a 'radical Left'. This attempt at consolidation also failed in 1990–1, in light of the annexation of the GDR to the FRG, pathetically and momentously. A greater section of the West German left retired into postmodern private life, another gave up its independence by subordinating themselves to the import from the East, the Party of Democratic Socialism (PDS). The rest formed that milieu of a new cynical intelligentsia that would set the 'leftist' tone for an entire decade.[67] In 1967, Kofler had already warned the progressive elite against getting stuck in such a manner of 'marxo-nihilist' negation in his work *Der asketische Eros* [The Ascetic Eros], even seeing a possible development into a self-reinforcing system of negation.[68] A quarter of a century later it had finally reached that point. The 'force of negation' [*Kraft der Negation*], as the radical Left called itself, revealed its nihilistic cloven hoof.

'None of the political currents that set out to challenge capitalism in this century', wrote Perry Anderson in his summation of the socialist movement at the beginning of the 1990s, 'has morale or compass today'.[69] What was specifically German in this development was, at most, the thoroughness of this enclosure. Yet 'the left' may be ever so shattered and demoralised, capitalism lives on and it even keeps producing the structural contradictions as well as hope for its alteration. This is the root of those resurgences of movements critical of capitalism that one, more or less correctly – emphasis on the less – calls the 'anti-globalisation movement'. These new social movements that have arisen since the end of the 1990s have become a contentious object of public discussion. What actually moves there, why does it move and to what end? My thesis, first advocated in 2002, is that, following Leo Kofler, we are dealing with a typical form of a progressive elite construct.

The characteristics with which we are confronted in discussion of the new movements are the same as those of the 'progressive elite'. We are once again dealing with an amorphous mass with strongly fluctuating tendencies, which distinguishes itself above all through its programmatic breadth and vagueness as well as its social, political and cultural heterogeneity. We are once again dealing with a movement that is essentially oriented towards radical democracy and humanism. The more radically its activists and supporters scrutinise those phenomena of reification and alienation, against which they revolt ('The world

---

67 See Jünke 2014, Part III.
68 Kofler 1967, p. 325.
69 Anderson 1992, p. 358.

is not a commodity!'), the more they are open to emancipatory and socialist beliefs and positions. Only they want nothing to do with the mostly ossified political forms of the 'old' and 'new' left and one of their greatest fears is the fear of the bureaucratising power of integration into the dominant system. Against this contemporary form of incapacitating representative politics, they place what one earlier called self-activity, which deposits itself in various – and anything but new – forms of direct action. They make a political virtue out of historical necessity, and propagate network-type forms of organisation oriented to permanent movement and action. Even that which is seemingly most original, their practice of internationalism, is nowhere as new as it initially appears. That '1968' was also, from the beginning, a deeply international event has been all too quickly forgotten. Yes, even more: even the classical workers' movement was in its beginnings, the First International, and later, an eminently international phenomenon. As a matter of fact, social movements in history confront the question of how they can durably organise themselves, above all nationally, at a later phase. The New Left of the 1960s and 1970s shattered against this task, and the idea of a green alternative anti-parties party connected with the new social movements of the 1970s and 1980s did not really fare any better. They indeed successfully grouped themselves, but then fairly quickly also accommodated themselves.

As much as the newest social movements also represent a new attempt at emancipatory criticism of society, it will be difficult for their protagonists to cite a criterion in terms of content that would not already be known in some manner or another. For example, Pierre Bourdieu considered the essential foundations of this new European social movement to be the struggle against the theory and practice of neoliberalism; and the international and internationalist character of this struggle, the radically democratic network structures and their strongly symbolic forms of action, as well as solidarity to be its goals and attitudes.[70] For Naomi Klein, the Canadian activist and journalist, it is also primarily about direct action and decentralised, non-hierarchical movement structures, in order to face the crisis of representative politics, precisely also that of traditional left party politics. They don't want to wait for the abstract revolution, but would rather recapture communal values and institutions and collective spaces to manoeuvre.[71] Not only the spirit of such declarations of self-conception, but even its terminology, for the most part, turns up in the corresponding texts of the 1960s. With protagonists like the French farmer leader

---

70   Bourdieu 2001.
71   Klein 2001.

José Bové, the Filipino NGO activist Walden Bello, or the Mexican guerrillero Subcomandante Marcos, the relation to the events of 1968 is also biographically distinct. The Mexican Zapatistas are a paradigmatic example in our context: their specific mixture of radical democracy and anti-capitalism is as fascinatingly successful as it is powerless to decide the societal struggle in their favour. The struggle against representative politics and vanguard aspiration can hardly be fought more sharply than here. Yet this struggle is led by a vanguard, even by a progressive elite.

The contradiction appearing here is one of formal logic and can only be understood and resolved dialectically, i.e., historically. Kofler's theory of the progressive elite allows us access to such a dialectical interpretation. It gives us insight into the scope and limits of the new movements and understanding of why the movements embrace, on the one hand, not only a powerful social breadth and utopian depth, but also why they will always fail to develop forms of social revolutionary organisation oriented for the long-term and political efficacy. It allows us, in short, to appreciate the historical significance of these newest social movements without falling into their self-delusions as an allegedly new world-historical subject. Be it an Immanuel Wallerstein, who attempts to theorise the anti-globalisation movement as an expression of a world-historically novel 'anti-systemic' collective subject in line with '1968' that transcends the old workers' movement left, knowing full well that it has 'not offered a fully coherent alternative strategy'.[72] Be it the successful authorial duo of Michael Hardt and Antonio Negri who grandiloquently and irrationally elevated Kofler's 'amorphous mass with strongly fluctuating tendencies' to a 'multitude', a crowd with agency.[73] These and other 'ideologues' of the new movements confuse the surface of a new capitalism and the countermovements brought forth by it with their unchanged essences.

That the newest social movements are also programmatically vague and draw on democratic beliefs and demands like democratic control and participation, recognition and appropriation, etc., is thus neither coincidence nor new. That they want to follow through with certain values of the dominant society such as justice and prosperity, freedom and democracy and the like is not their weakness, but rather their strength. At the centre of the new movements is the protest against profit and the competition economy pervading society; the protest against reification and alienation. Measures are taken quite practically against central institutions of the capitalist world economy, and against those

---

72 Wallerstein 1989, p. 448. Wallerstein 2002.
73 Hardt and Negri 2000, and 2004. With regards to the critique, see Balakrishnan 2003.

predominant parties that subordinate themselves to the same in world politics. Instead, the aim is to participate, to have a say, to change – and this in the spirit of humanism and international solidarity. It is hardly to be seriously disputed that the new social movements are revolting against the current constitution of neoliberally dominant capitalism and that they are thereby, according to their objective logic, anti-capitalist, without this having subjectively expressed itself in each participant. Behind the predominance of the apparently new beckons the unsatisfied legacy of classical socialism. 'A civilization based on solidarity is a socialist civilization', write Michael Löwy and Frei Betto – and the fate of movements critical of globalisation will not insignificantly be determined by how much they make this recognition their own.[74]

Kofler's theory of the progressive elite proves itself thereby as a 'grand narrative' in times of a renunciation of grand narratives, as a socialist principle of hope in a time of left scepticism. It not only assumes that we live in a world-historical stage of transition, in an epoch of transition, in which the factors pointing forward are inhibited and detours have to be accounted for. It is in its unimplemented fragmentariness itself the expression of this transitional situation, in which the international proletariat has proven itself, on the one hand, as a transformative social and political force of historical magnitude, but on the other, has shown itself to be unable to prevent fascism and Stalinism as well as successfully use the emergent social welfare state for social revolutionary goals or exploit the collapse of the pseudo-socialist state bureaucracy for a breakthrough to true socialist democracy.

Kofler himself, beginning in the mid-1980s, thought that, after the collapse of the New Left in the West and with the rise of Gorbachev's reform Communism in the East, this period of a blocked world-historical transition was over, and that we were returning to a 'classical' socialist transition. He erred in this, as did many others. The period of blocked world-historical transition instead persists – and it poses the question: transition to where? The dependent working class has still not fulfilled the hopes placed in it by socialists and others – just as, conversely, the political left has not fulfilled the hopes placed in it by the working and marginalised classes. Only in historically exceptional situations have the class and their left come together, the class 'in itself' becoming a class 'for itself'. Yet all alleged alternatives to class politics have proven themselves equally unstable and less enduring. Sociopolitical opposition is still strongest where it – like 1999 in Seattle or 2005 in Paris – brings together an alliance of 'new' and 'old' social movements. The 'old' social movements, the organised

---

74 Löwy and Betto 2015, p. 337.

workers' movement in its trade union and political currents, are still extensively caught in their socioeconomic and sociopolitical integration in bourgeois capitalist relations. Additionally, the emancipatory left has still not found any convincing way to deal with the confounded dialectic of reform and revolution. Whoever does *not* want to take this as an occasion for bidding farewell to the left thus has reason enough to take note of and discuss Kofler's theories and propositions.

That this has so far occurred so little, and Kofler has become one of the most strongly suppressed thinkers of the German left and so far remained so, has primarily to do with those impertinent expectations he presented to the German left. His 'dismal radicalism needs to be endured. The solitude of such fundamental critique may itself be too severe for some committed "leftists"', wrote the then still young psychoanalyst, Tilmann Moser, in the conservative *Frankfurter Allgemeine Zeitung*.[75] Kofler's impertinent expectations are, however, due to the consequences of the general fate of that German left socialism that was successfully smashed by the double onslaught of fascism and Stalinism in the 1930s and 1940s and whose new restructuring in the 1950s, 1960s and 1970s was successfully blocked and mutilated – partly through its own weaknesses and mistakes, but not least because of a holy alliance of technocrats in the West as well as the East. Kofler's life and work is therefore, with all of its individuality, an exciting reflection of the transition from the old socialist classical period of the previous turn of the century – in Kofler's case in the form of Austromarxism – to the Western Marxism of the middle of the century, the New Left of the 1960s and 1970s and the postmodernism of the 1980s and 1990s up to a neo-socialism of the twenty-first century, for which no reclamation of any historico-philosophical certainty applies, but which nonetheless is more urgent than ever.

75   Tilmann Moser, 'Der asketische Eros: Leo Koflers neues Buch', in *Frankfurter Allgemeine Zeitung*, 19 December 1967.

CHAPTER 3

Kofler's Critique of Stalinism

The political spring of 1967–8 was not only a time of lasting politicisation, not only a time in which the incursion of subaltern strata and classes in everyday political and social life moved the social balance of power globally to the left. An integral part of this process was also the sharpening of theoretical wits. For those who want more than merely to flee the earthly vale of tears of the here and now, those who want to set off for new shores, also want to know from where the journey starts. The question of Stalinism at that time stirred the passions, since it weighed like a nightmare on the brains of the living. But not only that, since it was more than just a question of history, as the violent suppression of the Czechoslovakian 'socialism with a human face' in autumn 1968 made painfully clear.

In this time of a tumultuous expansion and politicisation of necessities, the demand for reading material was immense. Many authors critical of society, who until then had been leading a ghettoised social life, now became much sought after authors with mass appeal. Leo Kofler also 'profited' from this, the pioneer of a non-dogmatic postwar Marxism suppressed from all sides, who, in the German-speaking world, was only comparable in diversity of topics and radicalism of content to Adorno, to whom, however, he was far superior in the courage of his socialist convictions. In any case, the anti-authoritarian revolt and its need for theory allowed Kofler to reissue one or two of his old writings. The one that is to be discussed here is his 1970 publication, *Stalinismus und Bürokratie* [Stalinism and Bureaucracy], in which Kofler published two of his old essays critical of Stalinism, already published in 1952, together with new material.

Kofler's old analyses of Stalinism were of particular significance, because they marked the first systematic attempt in the German-speaking world after the Second World War to criticise Stalinist theory with Marxist means – and this at a level that many of the later, similarly grouped works of other authors barely approach.[1] Even if Kofler's critique of Stalinism trod on historical new ground at the beginning of the 1950s, it was also deeply rooted in that socialist classical period of which Kofler was also a child.

---

1 See Linden 2007.

A   Laying the Cornerstone

Kofler was a child of Austromarxism, a particular variant of international social democracy between the world wars, which was decidedly radical and Marxist in orientation compared to the European social democracy of the time. He stood on its left wing and was strongly influenced by Max Adler, perhaps the most important representative of left socialism at the time, who saw himself as an alternative to both Leninist Communism and social-democratic revisionism. The young Kofler accordingly criticised his party from the left at the beginning of the 1930s and – like most of the Austromarxist left at the time – wished for a stronger orientation by social democracy to the Bolshevik model of Soviet Russia. This closeness to the Soviet Union, however, never went so far that Kofler or the other Austromarxists became blind apologists for the Soviet system. The criticism of the Stalinist terror of the 1930s was widespread in the Austrian workers' movement and a matter of principle; Kofler also shared this approach. In spite of all the sympathy for Moscow, he was never uncritical, and massively doubted, for example, the legitimacy of the Moscow show trials during his Swiss emigration at the end of the 1930s.

This tension between political closeness and intellectual distance was also reflected in his first work, *Die Wissenschaft von der Gesellschaft*, written during his Swiss emigration and published there in 1944. In the last pages of this 'methodology of dialectical sociology' (so runs the subtitle), dedicated to practice, Kofler detected in the 'carriers of the correct consciousness', i.e. amongst contemporary Marxists and Communists, a 'propensity to bureaucratism' that originated in the fact 'that the reification structure of the environment still perpetually projects into the thought of individuals who are already, in general, standing on the ground of correct consciousness'. Bureaucratism here is thus conceived of as 'that form of retreat behind the actual awareness that sociologically has its cause in the not overcome influence of the environment on the carrier of the correct consciousness, and therefore appears ideologically as the rigid mediation of knowledge and its application'.[2] If he explicitly disassociates himself in the last paragraphs of his book from the 'tendency of a fundamental opposition' and from 'destructive criticism of bureaucratism', Kofler adopts the position of the reform Communist Georg Lukács and implicitly distances himself from the left Communist, i.e., most notably the Trotskyist critique of Stalin. This meant that he – in the tradition of the 'integral socialism' of Otto Bauer – demands a 'self-criticism' of the socialist Marxist movement, which he

---

2   Kofler 1971, p. 150.

consciously places in quotation marks, since he obviously claims such a self-criticism not in the Stalinist sense, but against the same.

In typical reform-communist manner, he also lamented 'vulgar mechanistic thinking' and its 'smart alecks', that is to say, the socialist bureaucracy, in his second work, *Zur Geschichte der bürgerlichen Gesellschaft*, published in 1948 in the not-yet-GDR. He emphasises that he agrees with both Stalin and Lukács on this, but implicitly questions Stalinist propaganda concerning the socialist character of the USSR when he points out, among other things, that due to the conditions of primitive accumulation, 'a certain restriction in the consumption of consumer goods is inevitable'.[3] He reacted to the fact that the SED guardians of pure doctrine at the time, the 'intellectual bureaucracy', the 'inquisition', as Kofler will soon say, make precisely such references the reason for his condemnation, with a detailed theoretical critique in 1950 of Marxist bureaucratic mechanism in the fundamental work *Geschichte und Dialektik*, which was written while still in the GDR but only published in the West in 1955. Here, in continuation of the *Die Wissenschaft der Gesellschaft*, he calls the 'mechanistic vulgar sociology' a tumour within Marxism, a product of the failure to overcome being mired in bourgeois reification:

> The conscious or unconscious notion in the vulgar Marxist conception that history follows economic legalism, without ideology, which has grown up out of the soil of economic being, playing an essential role here, tears up the historical process in the exact same way as the old materialism, which had humans clutching the apron strings of 'nature' (geography and climate). Here, as there, man remains ultimately at base only a *passive* appendage of a law *external to him*, here, as there, the *dialectical relationship between activity and passivity* is alien to thought.[4]

With the loss of the dialectic, Marxist bureaucratism also lost the horizon of individual and social practice. For without the Marxist subject-object theory, only a flat historically-determinist materialism remained.

As open and unmistakable as this methodological critique of Stalinist bureaucratism is on the theoretical level, Kofler gave no account, up to this point, of the historical conditions and continuous forms for the implementation of Stalinist theory and practice. Only when he finally had to give up the hope of being tolerated as a reformer within 'actually existing socialism', only after his

---

3 Kofler 1992, Vol. 2, p. 319.
4 Kofler 2004, p. 192. Kofler's emphases.

flight to West Germany at the end of 1950, did he also reflect on this side of the Stalinism complex.

In both the years 1951 and 1952 Kofler wrote five small pamphlets on Stalinist theory and practice. The first – a treatise on the Stalinisation of the East German universities – was highly personal and not published. In the second (*Marxistischer oder stalinistischer Marxismus? Eine Betrachtung über die Verfälschung der marxistischen Lehre durch die stalinistische Bürokratie* [Marxist or Stalinist Marxism? An Observation on the Falsification of Marxist Teachings by the Stalinist Bureaucracy], Cologne 1951), he places Marxist and Stalinist Marxism against each other with pointed political emphasis. In the third (*Der Fall Lukács: Georg Lukács und der Stalinism* [The Lukács Case: Georg Lukács and Stalinism], Cologne 1952), he defends Georg Lukács, and in the fourth (*The Essence and the Role of the Stalinist Bureaucracy*, Cologne 1952), he takes up the second pamphlet in a more sober and comprehensive manner. In the fifth and last (*Marxism and Language: Regarding Stalin's Investigation 'Marxism and Problems of Linguistics'*, Cologne 1952), he deepens his critique, with reference to Stalin's influential work on linguistics. The last two essays are those that he eventually collected in his book *Stalinismus und Bürokratie*, published in 1970 by Luchterhand.

B   Expansion

Kofler's critique of Stalinism worked out in the early 1950s differs substantially from both of the two predominant explanatory models for historical Stalinism. He rejects the bourgeois critique that first and foremost attributes Stalinism to Marxist theory, in the same fashion as he rejects those allegedly leftist theories that attribute Stalinism to crimes, cult of personality and excesses, in order to maintain a 'socialist' kernel of the same. Against both he argues that Stalinist practice was no product of Marxist theory. Rather, it was their 'Marxist' theory that was the product of a blinkered bureaucratic practice, the product of a 'narrow and mindless practicality' of a bureaucratic stratum that sought to defend their privileges.[5] Stalinism, for him, is no historically inevitable phenomenon. It is rooted far more in specific historical conditions of societal backwardness. It could, however, successfully spread, because it provided an answer to objective problems of each and every transitional society from capitalism to socialism. The specifically Stalinist answer to the general transition problem was,

---

5   Kofler 1970, p. 77.

however, a deeply inhuman anti-humanist one, and had set back the socialist movement for at least several decades. The political aim appearing here in his radical anti-Stalinist critique is that of democratic socialism: It will 'prove that every genuine socialism must be fundamentally democratic, or it won't be at all'.[6]

1   Critique of Bureaucracy

At the centre of Kofler's typical left socialist critique of Stalinism is the role of the bureaucracy as a ruling stratum. His theoretical point of departure is a fundamental critique of the same. For Kofler, Marxism was always and inherently anti-bureaucratic, as bureaucracy is always a sign of the formalism of bourgeois conceptions of equality. Bureaucracy could only exist where the measuring stick of formal equality of individuals was applied. Historically, the bureaucracy may have been indispensable, even progressive and revolutionary (primarily in the early bourgeois period, when the liberation of the individual was at stake), however, it was always a fundamental evil. While the bureaucratic habitus fundamentally expressed 'indifference and unfamiliarity towards life', and was inclined to encroach on all social spheres, and subjugate individuals and their thought, socialism was per se a break from this essentially formal bourgeois equality based on market and commodity relations.[7] In principle, bureaucracy was therefore also surmountable. First, through a rationalisation and simplification of administration and, second, through its democratisation. Such a democratisation would be made possible above all through education and cultivation for the purpose of taking over bureaucratic work: 'The democratisation of bureaucratism turns, at a certain height and breadth, into its abolition [*Aufhebung*]'.[8]

Since Kofler shares the Marxist theory of a necessary transitional society, in which new relations of production are still coupled with old maxims of distribution, he considers the bureaucracy in the phase of historical transition to be unavoidable. He does not see in this assessment any justification of the Stalinist bureaucracy. To be sure, every transition to socialism has to struggle with bourgeois and bureaucratic habits and mentalities, but the concrete point of departure for the question of bureaucracy in Soviet Russia was the specifically Russian conditions: first, the lack of consumer goods conditioned by industrial underdevelopment, which made a 'primitive accumulation' necessary; second, the missing democratic tradition and the depletion of democratic forces dur-

---

6   Kofler 1970, p. 106.
7   Kofler 1970, p. 28.
8   Kofler 1970, p. 18.

ing the Russian civil war; third, the 'additional entrusting to the bureaucracy of the direction and supervision of the economy'.[9] For Kofler, the mixture of the tsarist legacy and the post-revolutionary planned economy is therefore causally responsible for the degeneration of the structures, and not the planned economy as such, which is possible in democratic as well as non-democratic forms. Under democratic conditions, he writes, the formalistic technicism of the plan was only a normal problem of arithmetic: 'Without the direct participation by the democratic forces of the people in the government and without direct democratic control through the people, every planned economy must bureaucratically degenerate; with the presence of these forces and such a control, the planned economy cannot bureaucratically degenerate'.[10]

With regards to the practical means for a democratic demarcation against post-revolutionary bureaucratism, Kofler refers to Lenin's remarks in *State and Revolution*, advocates for bureaucrats to be subject to recall at any time, to have a worker's wage, a constant changing of function, cultivation of workers for administrative work, amongst other things, and considers the retention of a free market compatible with the democratic self-administration of the shop floor. Against this theoretical backdrop, Soviet Russian bureaucracy is, for him, a historical phenomenon of degeneration in which there was explicitly *no* inherent historical necessity and, therefore, 'sooner or later it will be overcome'.[11] There is, for Kofler, no excuse 'for the Stalinist degeneration of Russian socialism ... since, first, the degeneration of bureaucratism in Russia into an utterly terroristic dictatorship was avoidable and, second, it was thoroughly possible to gradually dismantle this instead of increasing it'.[12] This incremental dismantling was and is possible, as '[a]ll observations teach us that the masses of the East will not voluntarily agree to any restoration of capitalist private enterprise; they want to take their fate in their own hands on a democratic basis. They want socialism'; to this end, 'a reasonable and sympathetic leadership and education of the people' is needed so that the development 'in regards to economy and culture can take place on liberatory ground'.[13]

In summary, Kofler sees the dynamic element in the socioeconomic relations of Soviet Russia, because with material development, the material basis of the bureaucracy waned. The solidifying ideological relations are, for him, in

---

9   Kofler 1970, p. 51.
10 Kofler 1970, p. 33.
11 Kofler 1970, p. 104.
12 Kofler 1970, p. 34.
13 Kofler 1970, p. 48.

contrast, the static, the inhibiting element of a de-Stalinisation that was essentially anti-bureaucratic.

2 Critique of Bureaucratic Ideology

The bureaucratisation and the dehumanisation organically connected with it – and in this Kofler is in agreement with all contemporary Marxist critiques of Stalinism – is the product of the interests of the bureaucracy as a social stratum, which 'essentially revolves around the fear of a possible democratic resistance and the defence of the privileges of the bureaucracy'.[14] At the same time, Kofler shifts and presents his own main points in the contemporary context, against a reduction of the problem to bureaucratic privileges. 'From "interest" alone it is, for example, impossible to understand the specifically vulgar Marxist and mechanistic mode of thought in Stalinism', he writes.[15] Whoever thinks too much in categories of bureaucratic conspiracy will find no explanation of the subjectively honest mental state [*Befindlichkeit*] of Stalinists. The mode of thought and being of the socialist bureaucracy would be torn asunder, and their strength in regards to intellectual hegemony – to use a newer term – thus not understood. The bureaucratic ideology, Kofler insists on this, was not merely pure cynicism, but rather an objective self-delusion, namely ideology.

Kofler correctly sees his originality and his main merit less in the historical analysis of Stalinism and more in its ideological critique. Stalinism solidified itself as a bureaucratic ideology, distorting and falsifying Marxist theory not only beyond recognition, but also to a point of leading an independent existence. It was therefore pertinent to theoretically confront this falsification that had taken on a life of its own, and to work out Marxism anew as something anti-dogmatic and liberatory. A de-dogmatisation of such a kind, brought about through enlightenment and critique – de-dogmatisation is understood here, in opposition to the bourgeois critique of dogmatism, as an explicit return to the Marxist sources – is, for Kofler, a decisive means for the de-bureaucratisation of the socialist movement and thereby also a piece of political practice. What historical critique is for an Isaac Deutscher, critique of Marxist theory is for Leo Kofler.

Kofler identifies three characteristic forms of Stalinist distortion of Marxism. First, Stalinist thought eliminated the dialectic from Marxism. Second, it

---

14 Kofler 1951, p. 10. For a stimulating overview, besides that offered by Linden 2007, see Ahlberg 1976. Kofler does not join the discussion then taking place about whether this bureaucracy involved a new class or merely a new stratum, but it is clear that he inclines to those who understand the bureaucracy not as a new class, but as a stratum.

15 Kofler 1951, p. 10.

reduced historical materialism to a flat, mechanistic economism. Finally, Stalinism 'forgot' Marxist humanism which seeks to free man from every form of alienation. All three distortions are neither coincidental nor marginal. They concern Marxism as a whole, concern those three core elements of Marxism that Kofler considers fundamental. For him, Marxist theory is essentially based on three pillars. In that the limits of consciousness are nowhere exceeded, the Marxist search for the historical laws of motion stood in contrast to the natural scientific concept of law and could only be grasped as a dialectic of subject and object, as thought in totality. It is the subject-object dialectic, mediated by human consciousness, that made Marxism a philosophy of practice. If this dialectic is removed, as became clear in the Stalinist condemnation of the Hegelian legacy, one thwarted the recognition of the social and practical side of Marxism, and fell back into a 'stupid' materialism based on the methodology of natural science. This persistence in bourgeois reification was promoted through the new, mechanistically misunderstood methods of economic planning, and solidified itself into a bureaucratic formalism, which was compelled to violate humans in their real existence.

> The 'egalitarian' formalism, which is therefore hostile to quality, not only blindly passes by the distinctness and variety of individual abilities, needs and fateful experiences; in the condition of this contempt for the human and qualitative, it is also incapable of grasping the complicated social process, whose essence exists in the social relationality between the individual and the universal, the subjective and the objective, and in the constant changing of the one into the other ... Only seeing through the character of reality as essentially being dialectical totality, makes practice possible as a form of a fully consciously aware action resting on a correct knowledge of the elements of real events. Where this cognitive condition is not fulfilled, there thought clings to itself and activity in its own jurisdiction determined by it, so that it rationalises in an extreme fashion with respect to the entire social world, as it is sinking at the same time into an abstruse irrationalism (of either mechanistic or metaphysical character).[16]

Bureaucratic thought fell prey in this way to specialism and fetishism of facts, to positivism and vulgar materialism, sharing the bourgeois materialist misunderstanding of Marxism. As in bourgeois thought, such a mechanism was

---

16   Kofler 1970, pp. 56–7.

supplemented by a voluntarism that is in principle unbridled and unmediated. Subject and object fell apart just like objectivism and subjectivism. If Stalinism in sociopolitical practice is primarily subjectivist and voluntaristic, in theory it is primarily objectivism, naturally and mechanistically passive, 'biased to vulgar Marxism', 'sensualistically blind', in short, it is 'the most visible and, at the same time, most extreme exponent of unmarxist Marxism in our time'.[17]

Kofler repeatedly illustrates this with two important examples: Stalinist historiography, and its theory of aesthetics.

Due to the flattening of historical materialism into vulgar economism, Stalinist historiography is capable of achieving little more than an elaboration of sources and the compilation of an external body of facts. They hunted in a purely outward fashion for the economic factor in history, but did not advance to an 'interpretative understanding of history', an organic integration of the struggles in the history of ideas. Thus they continued to cling to the bourgeois overestimation of the study of source material, to 'flat empiricism', i.e., to a 'descriptive representation of history', without advancing to that 'narrative representation of history' that one could occasionally admire, in isolated bourgeois historians mostly coming out of idealism.

Since the stupid, flat materialism did not understand the dialectic of the individual and universal, it was also incapable of understanding art, which is essentially concerned with the totality of the individual. Because 'the bureaucratic consciousness is not capable of truly grasping the individual and his problems, it imputes a mental and psychological development to him that conforms in a stereotypical fashion to a preconceived outlook'.[18] This led ultimately to flattening, distortion, depletion and stereotyping. The form of socialist realism thoroughly defended by Kofler became reduced in Stalinism to a naturalistic and positivistic 'romantic realism', to a sensualistic theory of reflection, that degraded the active individual into a passive object. This peculiar mixture of the flattened naturalism and idealising romanticism ultimately condensed into the inability to sensibly divide the worldview of the artist and his artistic product. Incapable, in this manner, of understanding practice and individuality in history and the present, Stalinism also found no access to the understanding of Marx's revolutionary humanism.

> Stalinism changes the individual in his traditional onesidedness, imperfection, misery and inner strife only insofar as it must restlessly subjugate

---

17 Kofler 2000a, p. 42.
18 Kofler 2000a, p. 53.

him to its bureaucratic needs: it gives him education, insofar as it needs 'intellectuals'; it gives him idealism, insofar as it needs this idealism in service of the 'fatherland' and 'construction'; it makes him familiar with the theories of Marx, insofar as he needs these theories to be a blindly credulous servant of the state – but it leaves him unchanged at the core, so that he can do all this![19]

On the one hand, one emphasised in recourse to Marxism a fundamental historical optimism, on the other, one pessimistically accepted man 'in his so-being'. The specifically Stalinist ethic was accordingly also a markedly contradictory mixture of 'exaggerated morality and abysmal immorality' that found its cause in the typical Stalinist inclination to 'impinge educationally on man via disciplinary intent'.[20] Thus, the mental elite of Stalinism, the 'mental bureaucracy', acquired the character of 'Stalinism's inquisition'.

Kofler's ideological critique of the Stalinist bureaucracy proves itself here to be a typical exemplar of the philosophy of praxis, a critique of Stalinism situated in the context of 'Western Marxism'. Western Marxism as a philosophical current, however, took no unified political conclusions from its approach. Correspondingly, Kofler also emphasises his own accents here.

3   *Perspectives of De-bureaucratisation*

It is a feature of Kofler's approach that he attributes a revolutionising role to ideology, and consciousness, once it is enlightened and de-dogmatised. Because the social antagonism in the East was fundamentally different than in the West, because the dominant bureaucracy there was 'not capitalist, but rather an exponent of transformed, namely – at least formally – socialist relations', it could not 'divest itself of that consciousness of socialist responsibility that flows from the commitment to the socialist humanism of Marxism'.[21] The unveiling of Stalinist thought is therefore, for Kofler, an eminently practical act.

With his dialectic of norm and reality, he aligns himself with the reform Communist position that sees its hope in de-Stalinisation and anti-bureaucratic democratisation, primarily in a transformation of the political superstructure. After all, according to Kofler at the time, the Yugoslav party leader Tito had shown 'that with a correct leadership and education of the masses, the same result can be achieved without forcing things and terror'.[22] In this sense,

---

19   Kofler 2000a, p. 65.
20   Kofler 2000a, p. 71.
21   Kofler 2000a, p. 64.
22   Kofler 1970, p. 46.

Kofler would side with all reform Communist aspirations in the Eastern Bloc, from Tito to Dubček. However, the case was different with the USSR. The Soviet Russian bureaucracy, Kofler assessed in 1952, 'defends the interests of accumulation against the interests of the masses, whereby it shies away from no means to defend this against them, along with their uninterruptedly increasing power to subjugate ever more domains, including the cultural and intellectual'.[23] Thus, historical Stalinism until the middle of the 1930s, i.e., until the outbreak of the Great Terror, was 'from the Historian's [!] point of view ... perhaps [!] still bearable' – 'But, in the meanwhile, the completed [!] bureaucratisation of the whole social life of the Soviet Union, which can only [!] be reversed by the people itself and its intellectuals, no longer permitted this turn of its own accord'.[24]

Yet even in Russian Stalinism he sees the dialectic of norm and reality fundamentally at work, since 'many indications speak for the contact of the great masses, especially students and intellectuals, with the critical and humanist theories of Marxism having awakened an oppositional and anti-bureaucratic consciousness, which, if even only to be hoped for in the long-term, must end in a democratic explosion and socialist democratisation of the East'.[25]

Kofler's position on de-Stalinisation exhibits distinct ambiguities at this point. He gives no definite account about *how*, i.e., in which way the state socialist bureaucracy will disappear. His partiality for reform Communist currents and his insistence on a dynamic contradiction of norm and reality immediately suggest a evolutionary process from above. His argument, by contrast, that precisely such a revolution, fed by the contradiction between norm and reality, amounted to a new revolution in thought, and would displace and dissolve the bureaucratic stratum, emphasises the revolutionary character and has a markedly left Communist slant. It was these theoretical ambiguities and latent contradictions – reflections of a historically open situation – in which shifts in position in later years can be found with Kofler.

C Renovations

Kofler returns repeatedly to the topic of Stalinism after 1952, but only in passing – especially whenever new movement and new debates arose on the

---

23 Kofler 1970, p. 38.
24 Kofler 2000a, p. 64.
25 Kofler 2000a, p. 65.

political left. In the middle of the 1950s, with the emergence of the non-aligned states, the breakup of actually existing socialist relations and the Social Democratic path to Bad Godesberg, for example, a consequential restructuring debate, largely repressed today, also happened on the West German left. Khrushchev's 'secret' speech at the 20th Party Congress of the CPSU in February 1956, in particular, posed the question of the dynamics and perspectives of the increasingly widespread de-Stalinisation. In the *Andere Zeitung*, the 'central organ' of this first generation of the 'New Left', radical democrats, socialists and Communists discussed these questions. Kofler actively intervened with his anti-Stalinist reform Communism in these discussions, and radicalised himself, when he recognised that after the suppression of the uprisings in Hungary and Poland, a lasting re-Stalinisation was also coming in Western leftist thought.

He thus criticised, for example, the 'orthodox clericalism' of an author of the *Andere Zeitung* in sharp and decidedly current tones. According to Kofler, the 'reactionary orthodoxy' could be recognised after the 20th Party Congress by the fact that the author placed Stalinism and the Stalinist bureaucracy in quotation marks, thereby blatantly justifying their crimes with, yes, all the important figures of history were likewise criminals, and polemicised against allegedly bourgeois humanism. With all due sharpness, Kofler polemically responded:

> There is no question whether Stalinism with its methods has done more good or harm to Russian and international socialism, whether or not a way without shameful show trials with inhuman self-accusations, without the murder of renowned Bolsheviks, without the degradation of Marxist science and the arts into a farce, without bureaucratic insanity and without Stalinist narrowness, even if a more deft and milder way ... would have been possible. Instead, the cold-blooded answer is given: They were all thus, therefore ...! Does the author of this thesis know that without Stalinism we would have had a socialist country or countries in the West long ago, namely there where socialism, as a result of more mature economic conditions, would have allowed experimentation with vastly more ease, and where even reformism itself could not have prevented it, if Stalinism and its satellites had left behind anything other than a disappointing impression to the nations? He considers this question, despite his so self-confident appeal to his *concreteness* that has degenerated into an empty phrase, with not a word.[26]

---

26 Kofler 1958.

Against the 'orthodox platitudes', Kofler polemicised that Stalin's terror as well as 'Ulbricht's method of demoralising the masses of supporters of the SED and pushing them down into the anti-socialist opposition with a methodical stamina that no capitalist opponent would have ever managed' was not to be explained rationally with reference to the allegedly colossal tasks – we instead are dealing here with 'phenomena of socialist suicide'.

> Only the modern unorthodox and truly Marxist humanism [understood] that *consciousness is an element of practice* [and had the strength] to *work from the ground up revolutionarily on the consciousness of man*, to awaken in him, precisely due to its rational rigour and consistency, the *belief* in the future, to teach him to be deeply steeped in the *dreaming* of the truth of a higher and freer future order, as Lenin demanded ... Only when this caricature has disappeared, i.e., has been overcome through the 'third way' beyond capitalism and Stalinism, only then will the ideological reflection of Stalinism, reactionary orthodoxy, disperse into nothing.[27]

In 1965, with the first tender sprouts of a renewed left-wing formation, Kofler returned anew to the question of the significance of the socialist block for Marxists. He warned the young student left that an exact analysis of Stalinism proved 'that a humanist regime would have shown at least the same economic success with, at the same time, vastly greater political, cultural and educational successes at home and abroad. Stalinism has set back the international development of socialism half of a century'.[28] In the same text he highlights as positive that the dismantling of Stalinism achieved up to that point 'has resulted in a considerable strengthening of the left currents in Italy, France and England', while 'its relative further existence in East Germany conversely represents a strong impediment for the everyday primitive and passive class consciousness in the proletarian masses, documented many times in the literature, changing ... into an active one'. The 'success or failure of humanist democratisation of the Eastern countries' depended ultimately on 'whether a decisive historical step forward in the bourgeois countries is achieved'.

Another two years later in 1967, he analysed Maoism in an article (incorporated into the Stalinism book of 1970), 'From Stalin to Mao Zedong'. Kofler did not fall for the anti-bureaucratic habitus of Maoism. He sensitively registered the bureaucratic puritanism becoming apparent in the Chinese Cultural Revo-

---

27   Kofler's emphases.
28   Kofler 2000d, p. 163.

lution, 'which compels the masses, entirely following the bourgeois model, to asceticism and sacrifice', and characterises it as an – even if mild – 'act of 'cultural revolutionary' re-Stalinisation of China'.[29]

> The form of this act is certainly more impressive and makes use of the 'democratic' plebiscite of the skilfully called-upon youth. But what is obviously repeated is the anti-bureaucratic argumentation on a totally bureaucratic basis. It also repeats the effect of deintellectualisation [*Entgeistigung*] – the canonisation of the writings of Stalin and the writings of Mao Zedong as sacrosanct guidelines for all other judgements in politics, art and science – under the intrusively propagated slogan of creativity ('creative Marxism' under Stalin). It repeats under the slogan of the struggle against dogmatism the total dogmatisation of socialist theory.[30]

Finally in 1970, in the topical foreword to *Stalinismus und Bürokratie*, he unreservedly defended the ousted Czechoslovakian reformer Alexander Dubček, since all the accusations against Dubček were 'consistently slanders'.[31] Once again Kofler sees Eastern Communism '[moving] towards one of its nadirs that repeatedly interrupt its path to de-Stalinisation'.[32] Yet he somewhat alters his emphasis, when he indicates directly afterwards that despite the suppression of the Prague Spring, much has changed in the meantime. The Prague Spring in particular had proved that the historical process of de-Stalinisation, to be understood as the 'replacing of terrorism with a democratic dictatorship ... is unstoppable'.[33] It would, above all, have confirmed that this de-Stalinisation 'was led *from above*, i.e, without a revolution from below, which was held in many circles to be the only path to the democratisation of the Soviet Union'.[34] It would also, however, have confirmed 'the fact of the emergence of a market as central to the turnover of the commodity economy on the base of the planned economy, pointed to many years later by ignorant critics as a convergence with capitalism'.[35]

For the first time in 20 years, Kofler here opposes a revolutionary de-Stalinisation from below and stands up for an evolutionary de-Stalinisation from

---

29 Kofler 1970, pp. 108–9.
30 Kofler 1970, p. 110.
31 Kofler 1970, p. 8.
32 Kofler 1970, p. 7.
33 Kofler 1970, p. 8.
34 Kofler 1970, p. 7.
35 Ibid.

above – a conception that he had last formulated in the 1940s in his first two works, but which he had not advanced since his practical experience with 'actually existing socialism'.

D   Collapse

Differently therefore from, for example, Isaac Deutscher or Georg Lukács, the far more radical Leo Kofler before '1968', in his theoretical foundations and practical consequences, appears after '1968' to evolve to the 'right', that is, towards those ruling in the Eastern Bloc states. This shift in position, however, only became apparent in the 1980s, as a result of his political and personal disappointment in the fate of the New Left, and a changed global political situation. The ascension of Margaret Thatcher in Great Britain (1979) and Ronald Reagan in the USA (1989) marked the global political transition to both the so-called Second Cold War and to neoliberalism. In its wake Kofler was early to register the resurgence of a radical social Darwinist 'Manchester liberalism' after the end of history ('*posthistoire*'). However, he no longer saw a left response to it.

Kofler had drawn the strategic consequence from the failed de-Stalinisation at the end of the 1950s that a new 'progressive elite' was needed, reflected in the rise of the New Left, in order to dissolve the deadlocked world-historical situation of a 'ghost of the Revolution which never happened over here, ... [a] ghost of the Revolution which was never completed over there' theoretically as well as practically.[36] Accordingly, he had detected the spirit of revolt early on and was all the more disappointed as this markedly 'decomposed' (Peter Brückner) itself after 1969. After the obvious disintegration of the New Left at the end of the 1970s and its transition to the new social movements and the green alternative party, he saw this New Left, which he had justified historically and philosophically, ultimately pass over into irrationalism and sectarianism. His historico-political view also shifted, however, to 'actually existing socialism'. If he had previously always emphasised the character of the inadequately de-Stalinised Eastern Bloc as an obstruction to emancipatory thought and action and the forces of historical progress, he now saw this force of progress only in the East and adopted the Stalinist theory of camps in terms of a theory of the new form of class struggle. He saw the world split anew into two internationals, 'who however no longer faced one another as two hostile brothers, but

---

36   Lefebvre 1995, p. 236.

rather are clearly split in a recently founded capitalist international here, and in a socialist one there'. The industrial world was divided, according to Kofler, in radical antagonism 'according to markedly class struggle perspectives' with the consequence that the Soviet Union-led 'socialist bloc *as a bloc* put socialist interests in the place of national interests and, so to speak, made the *socialist common interest* into its political domain'.[37]

He did not hold domestic conditions in the USSR responsible for this lasting change in perspective, but rather the new global political conditions. The political situation of the Second Cold War was quite comparable to the first Cold War in the 1950s. Kofler's answer, however, was not. If he had then belonged to the sharpest critics of Stalinism on the left, now the apologetic tendencies were overwhelming. Though he continued to criticise the historical crimes of Stalinism, he exonerated and excused the Stalinist system. In his 1986 work, *Aufbruch in der Sowjetunion? Von Stalin zu Gorbatschow* [Awakening in the Soviet Union? From Stalin to Gorbachev], he adapted his old essay on the essence and role of the Stalinist bureaucracy, albeit framed with newer articles that spoke a markedly different language. The bureaucracy no longer stands as a ruling anti-Marxist stratum in the centre of the analysis of Stalinism. He now regarded the 'main problem of the construction of socialism' to be its 'entrance into the stage of *primitive accumulation*'.[38]

From this perspective, it is consistent to assume that with the obvious end of this *primitive accumulation*, historical Stalinism had also lost its virulence. Kofler associates the phase of *primitive accumulation* with the transitional society and this with 'what Marx understood under the stage of socialism, in contrast to that of subsequent communism' and recognises in the USSR of the 1980s 'substantial tendencies of loosening up, though without being able to speak of a final overcoming of the Stalinoid remnants'.[39] The Stalinoid remnants here, however, signify nothing other than that the social foundations for an organic development towards socialism and communism have been laid and that it comes down to consciousness alone to develop them accordingly. In 'the question of the de-dogmatisation and humanisation of the socialist ideology, in some quarters decisive steps have already been taken' (that is, for Kofler, under Gorbachev as an educated 'charismatic personality' committed to humanism), so that 'the process in this direction – when looked at in the long-term – is unstoppable'.[40] In this manner the 'incremental turning away from Stalinism

---

37 Kofler 1983b, pp. 25–6.
38 Kofler 1986, p. 15.
39 Kofler 1986, p. 17.
40 Kofler 1986, p. 101.

... [becomes] likewise a major step on the path of the construction of a new ... social order. Gorbachevism provides a reliable guarantee for it'.[41]

Just as he recognises the essence of socialism 'chiefly and precisely as the consequence of a properly wielded planned economy ... in seeing through the secrets in which capitalist reification expresses itself', Kofler's anti-Stalinism reduces itself completely into an enlightened educational dictatorship from above, because 'extremely alienated people are not at all capable of the true use of their democratic rights'.[42] Socialism and communism here is, for Kofler, no self-acting *free association of producers*, but rather 'a clever interplay of the central political control ... and the extensive autonomy of enterprises and other institutions'.[43] A comparison with what is depicted above makes clear that this is at best a wicked caricature of Kofler's old critique of Stalinism. Suppressing his words from 1958, he now claims – in a typically neo-Stalinist manner – that the USSR, 'due to these certainly inexcusable abuses under Stalinism, does (not) need to feel ashamed in front of the capitalist countries, who with fondness call themselves *democratic* and *free*', after all, their relations under conditions of *primitive accumulation* were in no way better.[44]

Yet the logic of apology drove Kofler even further. The difficulties that Gorbachev's Perestroika in the USSR would run into, he explained at the end of 1989, had to do with the 'Asiatic mentality', hence, everything would already be better 'if the Russian individual, who owing to a long-lasting historical tradition is only ready to fulfil his obligations to the public under the knout, had not used the freedoms granted to him under Gorbachev for sabotage'.[45] That he himself earlier thought and argued differently becomes clear in his 1952 pamphlet, *The Case of Lukács*, where he writes:

> It was thus not so much, as many claim, 'the Russian Asiatic tradition' and the influence of the 'Asiatic Stalin' that are at fault for the peculiar structure of Russian Bolshevism, but rather a good deal more the depicted aspects that also threaten a future European socialism, if the engagement of the democratic assistance of the people and the deepening of socialist theories do not put it on the right track.[46]

---

41   Kofler 1986, pp. 104–5.
42   Kofler 1986, pp. 11–12.
43   Ibid.
44   Kofler 1986, p. 19.
45   Kofler 1989. Regarding criticism of Kofler's conception of 'Asiatic despotism', see Kößler 2001.
46   Kofler 1952a, p. 10.

At the beginning of 1990, he called the 'democratic elections [in the still existing GDR], based on the model of bourgeois formal conceptions, problematic' since they 'could lead to historical disaster'.[47]

Such thought is a break not only with his own earlier critique of Stalinism, but also a break with that understanding of freedom for which he was a lifelong advocate – thus, for example, in a programmatic article of 1951, 'On Freedom', that begins with the words:

> We shouldn't fool ourselves: There is no social freedom without freedom for the individual, who strives for self-determination and independence, and who, as long as there is human history, has understood, understands and will understand by freedom the greatest possible freedom from all barriers and bonds.[48]

This turn of the late Leo Kofler may only be understood biographically against the backdrop of his disappointment in that 'progressive elite' who Kofler saw as a backbone of his historico-philosophical theory of a transitional historical epoch, who did not, however, meet his expectations. Yet what does this mean for his theory of Stalinism?

E   Measurements – Beyond Kofler

Kofler's critique of Stalinism as a critique of bureaucratic ideology is in itself consistent and belongs in its systematisation to the best that the Marxist left contributed to the critique of Stalinism. It shows in detail how Stalinist 'Marxism' is a fundamental and sustained falsification of Marx's theory. Kofler manages to reveal a theoretical grammar of pseudo-socialist Stalinoid thought (undialectic, mechanistic, anti-humanist and anti-emancipatory) that is in the position to approach the posthumous survival of Stalinism. He manages it not least because he understood that the consciousness of an active person is enrolled in an active, fact-creating role, and because he understood that Stalinism was also more than only a specific Russian derailment and that this, to a far greater degree, drew its dynamic from the objective problems of each and every transition to planned economy socialism. So in this sense, Kofler's theory of Stalinism is a radical critique of the bureaucratism of every educational

---

47   Kofler 1990.
48   'On Freedom' in this volume, p. 149.

dictatorship that retains its currency until the historic moment in which the free association of producers and consumers – if it can ever be won – has cultivated self-sustaining institutions and human beings.

Yet it is precisely here that a central lacuna (not the only one) in his criticism, which Kofler never really reflected on, becomes clear, since he barely reflected on the question of how these socialist and democratic self-supporting human beings and institutions could establish and stabilise themselves. His emphasis on consciousness for the processes of socialist emancipation, carried over from classic Austromarxism, while as apt as ever, was just the one aspect. It could additionally serve to gloss over this lacuna in political practice with the philosophy of consciousness. Kofler tended to that which Henri Lefebvre had criticised in Hegel. Proceeding from the recognition that action has specific laws and that practice is creative, Lefebvre formulated the following against Hegel and his 'Hegelianism':

> True, Hegel did give action a part to play; he saw the absolute idea as a unity of practice and knowledge, of the creative activity and thought. Mind transcends the immediate; it modifies the object, transforming and assimilating it. ... But Hegel did not elucidate action in itself, inasmuch as it comes up against an object which it cannot cause to disappear more or less '*spiritually*'. Hegel did not develop Kant's analysis of the specifically practical Reason. He determined a concept of action, and *confused action with the thought of action*.[49]

This lacuna of political theory and practice that naturally is indebted to a fair degree to the world-historically novel conditions of a socialist revolution and its ensuing 'socialist' bureaucratic planned economy, led Kofler, who substantially focused on consciousness and reform of consciousness, to position himself in the current of reform Communism. If one thereby compares him with other reform Communists, not least naturally his guiding star, Georg Lukács, it becomes clear that Kofler, on the left edge of reform Communism, far more radically revealed and attacked the systematic character of Stalinism. Despite this, he remained volatile. If he began in the 1940s with an evolutionary de-Stalinisation *from above*, in the 1950s he emphasised antagonistic de-Stalinisation *from below*, and fell back in the 1980s to the position he advocated in the 1940s, which with the obvious implosion of actually existing socialism at the end of the 1980s, took on marked features of the educational dictatorship.

---

49 Lefebvre 2009, pp. 38–9. My emphases.

However, the conceptually central emphasis on the reform of consciousness, the hope in an objective dynamic of de-Stalination mediated through intellectual contestation, not only characterised Kofler. Rather, it was central to the whole of reform Communism and hegemonic in the anti-Stalinist left in the twentieth century, even in the Trotskyist camp. Through his prominent emphasis on the role of correct consciousness for emancipatory tranformations, Kofler gave particularly incisive expression to this hope. If reform Communism in general already suffered from the inability to show the institutional foundations and paths of a socialist democratisation, this applied all the more to the Austromarxist Kofler, deeply influenced by its socialist pedagogy. The liberalisation of the markets and the autonomisation of the enterprises, propagated by him and others, were only makeshift solutions, nothing to do with socialist institutions, and became – hardly disputed from the historical vantage point – gateways for bourgeois capitalist logic. In this likewise objective as well as subjective dilemma, the hope in leadership 'from above' was always latently present.

From today's vantage point, i.e., after the collapse of 'actually existing socialism', it is clear that the majority of the left, along with Kofler, erred. If the hope of a more or less harmonious de-Stalinisation had been deceptive from the beginning, this does not mean that the dialectic of reform and revolution was condemned to impossibility. The reform movements and uprisings 'within socialism' were, in any case until the Prague Spring of 1968, demonstrably and explicitly pro-socialist. This was valid even for the Polish Solidarnosc movement and Soviet Perestroika, at least in their beginnings. That leftist hopes of reform had lastingly cooled since the Soviet invasion of Czechoslovakia may also have to do with Kofler's dialectic of norm and reality obviously waning within the nominally socialist countries, after the ruling bureaucracy had again proved itself to be unwilling to reform – indeed incapable of reform.[50] The global political changes of the 1970s and 1980s, however, likely just as much played their – as of yet little addressed – role. The demise of Western socialism, the disintegration of the New Left, and the loss of Marxist ideology contingent on it, on the one hand, as well as the rise, subsequent to this collapse as well

---

50 Boris Kagarlitsky has strikingly described this historical turning point: 'The invasion of Czechoslovakia and the restoration there of the old political and economic system meant the end of the Soviet economic reform and also of hopes for a new wave of liberalisation. ... Market socialism had not suffered an economic defeat, only a political one. ... But before new democratic ideas began to spread there was disappointment at the fate of the reforms, loss of confidence in Leninism, Communism, socialism – everything one had so naïvely believed in during the 60s. As usually happens, the baby was chucked out with the bath water' (Kagarlitsky 1989, pp. 199–200).

as deepening it, of social Darwinist neoliberalism in the Second Cold War, on the other hand, led to all potential attempts at breaking out of the Stalinist and post-Stalinist system being isolated – and this under conditions of a profound economic crisis and the intellectual hegemony of the 'idol of the market'.

Leon Trotsky's much maligned prediction that the new 'socialist' bureaucracy – out of fear for their social position and of those ghosts they would be compelled themselves to awaken if Soviet society aspired to reform – would rather seek to close ranks with the international 'class enemy' than cede their power to a renewed council democracy, proved itself more powerful in reality than the common hope of most reform Communists and left socialists that such a world-historical about-turn would not occur – at least we would be dealing with the social relations of a 'declared transition to socialism', with the objective substance of an allegedly socialised economy, which nevertheless had to inevitably bring about the corresponding subjective consequences.

How profound this illusion was historically can also be precisely observed where one would have expected a socialist alternative. So, for example, Ernest Mandel's Perestroika writings belong to those which, in my estimation, have best stood the test of historical practice. I am naturally thinking here primarily of 1989's *Beyond Perestroika* and 1991's *Power and Money*.[51] In them is found an analysis of the scope and limits, the successes and contradictions of the Soviet reform process, which contributes more to an understanding of the actually existing socialist implosion then most writings of other socialists and Marxists – not least because he proceeds from the sociopolitical and material interests of the persons, groups, strata and classes involved. In (re-)reading them, however, it is striking how the discussion of the perspectives of a revolutionary overcoming of actually existing socialism's reform dilemmas is shielded from the global economic and political context that, however, was of central importance to Leon Trotsky for the future of the socialist world revolution.

The likelihood of a political anti-bureaucratic revolution, writes Mandel, for example, in his last great work, hinged 'on several questions: the depth and explosiveness of the systemic crisis; the extent of the antagonism between the toiling masses, essentially the working class, and the bureaucracy or its top stratum, the nomenklatura; the relationship of forces between the major classes and class fractions; and the capacity of the nomenklatura for self-reform, pointing in the direction of its own suppression'.[52] Yet what of the

---

51   Mandel 1989 and 1992.
52   Mandel 1992, pp. 195–6.

worldwide relationship of forces between the forces of progress and of reaction? What of the hegemony of a neoliberalism based on coercion and consensus, so strong at the end of the 1980s, and the notorious weaknesses of Western socialism as well as that of the liberation nationalism in the countries of the so-called Third World? Against this backdrop, was anti-bureaucratic revolution at all conceivable in a country in which that the working class, on whom this transformation depended, had 'unlearned' to act politically independently and class consciously? Certainly: the dialectic of reform from above and revolution from below was also present in the 1980s in the Soviet Union, though it was plainly too weak under the corresponding global political conditions to change the global political course, and to be able to successfully take 'the mighty leap into the realm of socialism freedom'. As Lucio Colletti wrote at the end of the 60s:

> This historical defeat of Stalinism, in all its forms, has only one positive outcome. It restores to the internationalist theory of Marx and Lenin a sense of truth and actuality. For this theory, the socialist transformation of the world was unthinkable without the determinant contribution of revolution in the West, that is in the heart of capitalism itself.[53]

'We have to admit', writes Mandel in the introduction to *Power and Money*, 'that revolutionary Marxists seriously underestimated the disastrous long-term effects of Stalinism and bureaucratic dictatorship on the average level of consciousness'.[54] The disastrous long-term effects – these were exactly those subjective consequences of a decades-long educational dictatorship congealed into a new objectivity that systematically destroyed and impeded that which actually matters to socialists: 'the transformation in the consciousness and organisational level of the international proletariat'.[55] This concerns not least precisely the socialists and Communists beyond the borders of the Eastern Bloc, who attempted to compensate for their sociopolitical powerlessness with dependence on the enlightened absolutism of the 'big brother'.

---

53   Colletti 1970, p. 81.
54   Mandel 1992, p. 5.
55   'The most important criterion of politics for us is not the transformation of property in this or that piece of territory [or, as it were, the mere development of productive forces; CJ], as important as it ever may be in and of itself, but rather the transformation in the consciousness and organisational level of the international proletariat and the increasing of their capability to defend old achievements and make new ones. Under this decisive aspect alone and seen as a whole, Moscow's policy is, now as before, reactionary and remains the main obstacle on the path to international revolution' (Leon Trotsky 1988, p. 1292).

Already in 1935 Trotsky had written in his work *The Revolution Betrayed*:

> As a conscious political force the bureaucracy has betrayed the revolution. But a victorious revolution is fortunately not only a program and a banner, not only political institutions, but also a system of social relations. To betray it is not enough. You have to overthrow it. The October revolution has been betrayed by the ruling stratum, but not yet overthrown.[56]

A year later he came back to this:

> If the proletariat drives off the Soviet bureaucracy *in time*, it will still find the nationalised means of production and the basic elements of the planned economy after its victory. That means that it does not need to begin again from scratch. Only radical snobs, who are accustomed to hopping carefree from branch to branch, can frivolously ignore this advantage. The socialist revolution is too great and difficult a task, that one can frivolously do without its invaluable material achievements and begin again anew.[57]

At the end of 1939, he explained what he meant by this:

> If a nervous mechanic inspected a car, in which – let us say – gangsters had fled on poor roads from police pursuit, and determines that the body is dented, the wheels are buried and the motor is partly damaged, he is fully justified in saying: 'This is not a car, this is a devil knows what!' A definition of this kind has no scientific or technical character, but expresses the justified indignation of the mechanic at the work of the gangsters. Let us now imagine that the same mechanic were forced to repair the thing that he just called a 'devil knows what'. In this case he would indeed have to proceed from the recognition that he has a demolished car in front of him. He would have to determine which parts are damaged and which are whole, in order to be able to decide where he should begin with the work. A responsibility-minded worker should relate similarly to the USSR. He is completely justified to say that gangsters of the bureaucracy have changed the workers' state into 'devil knows what'. But if he passes over from this outburst of indignation to solve the political problem, then he

---

56   Trotsky 1972, pp. 251–2.
57   Trotsky 1988, p. 1131. Trotsky's emphasis.

must concede that he has a demolished workers' state in front of him, whose economic motor is admittedly damaged, but that can continue to work and be completely restored, if one only switches out some parts. This is obviously nothing more than a comparison, nevertheless it's worth thinking about.[58]

Not least owing to the decades-long destruction of socialist (class) consciousness through historical Stalinism and Stalinism in theory and politics, there were simply no longer enough technicians and responsibly minded workers to handle this colossal work in the 1980s. At least since then, it should have been clear to the socialist left that, in fact, it had to be about a real 'new beginning'.

Unfortunately, however, this is hardly the case. With the final collapse of reform Communist hopes in the epochal rupture of 1989–91, a large part of this left turned away from socialism in frustration and towards the bourgeois West and its promises of freedom. Another part paid for its refusal to do likewise by turning to cynicism and/or new forms of sectarian existence and thought. Another, in turn, surrendered itself to a neo-Stalinism, only hidden with difficulty, the core of which consistented of the sometimes more, sometimes less open defence of historical Stalinism and/or its nature of an educational dictatorship. Against this backdrop, Kofler's critique of bureaucratic, pseudo-socialist thought in particular gains relevance – even if directed against himself.

Moreover: precisely because Stalinism is more than a historical occurrence; because it expresses a political thought that certainly need not have to do with the specific national conditions of a Soviet Russia during the 1920s; because it signifies a specific methodology of political theory and practice that always becomes virulent if processes of emancipation and transformation are to go beyond the ruling capitalism – because of all this, we won't be rid of it too quickly. Only after the illusions have collapsed that Stalinism was merely a historical degeneration (which, do not misunderstand me, it certainly also was, but not only), will it become evident that the best analysts of Stalinism not unjustly referred to the clearest parallels, brought Stalinist thought and action into relation with the thought and action of people in the bureaucratic labour organisations in the bourgeois capitalist form of society (compare, not least, Ernest Mandel's comprehensively developed theory of the labour bureaucracy in his last book, *Power and Money*).

Leo Kofler also had a specific intuition for this, when he emphasised that it was impossible to make the specifically vulgar Marxist and mechanistic mode

---

58   Trotsky 1988, p. 1297.

of thought of Stalinism comprehensible from the 'material interests' of these people alone (see above). In a quiet moment, he carried this thought further. As he worked in the first half of the 1960s on the volume, *Der proletarische Bürger* [The Proletarian Citizen], which encapsulated his sociopsychological studies of neo-capitalist society, he developed once again his original theory of education as the theory of three class ideologies.[59] In the all-around alienated consciousness there were, loosely speaking, three levels of knowledge: the proletarian, the bourgeois and, as the third, the dialectical Marxist level abolishing both. If bourgeoisie and petty bourgeoisie had the illusion of a subjective freedom, independent of active practice, and therefore oriented themselves primarily to subjective education, in order to redeem themselves, education for the contemporary dependent worker was 'nothing other than a practical tool. He troubled himself about it only as far and only in those times that he was able to practically and politically exploit it, and he turned resignedly away in times of the failure of his *movement* or of historical stalemate'.[60] If the educational aspirations of the bourgeoisie distinguished itself through a contemplative and freer attitude, the modern proletarian consciousness was more reified and oriented towards a narrow practicality, although exactly because of this it boasted an element of truth, precisely because it acknowledged no fundamental difference between being and thought and faced the ideological heaven of the capitalist world with strong distrust. If one compared these two levels of knowledge and education and placed them in relation to the third, to the Marxist 'self-knowledge of the identical subject-object and its processual positing through this self-knowledge', the formal closeness of the first, the proletarian level, to the third, the Marxist, is apparent, since dialectical thought is, as something scientific and philosophical, a non-contemplative one, 'an aspect of the essence of the practical process itself ... a reasoning of reality'.[61] 'Perhaps it was exactly the vulgar misinterpretation' – Kofler is referring here to that vulgar materialist mode of thought that consistently struck a chord with the proletariat – 'which at the same time presented something like a popular version of Marxism, through which the thinking worker could get an understanding of this theory, just as it probably conversely contributed much to the in-itself reified proletarian mode of thought, lending it a vulgar materialist appearance'.

---

59 In German *Bürger* can mean bourgeois, citizen, burgher, etc. The wordplay in Kofler's title indicates his discussion of the *Bürger*, as a participant in civil society, taking on features of the proletarian, who, in turn, takes on features of the *Bürger*. (trans. note)
60 Kofler 1964, p. 171; see, at length, Jünke 2007a, pp. 502–3.
61 Kofler 1964, p. 173; 1967, p. 226.

Here, a look at Stalinism suggests that its vulgar material thought in East *and* West derives less from the not-overcome remnants of bourgeois ideology, as Kofler and many other Marxists suggested in their critique of Stalinism, but more from the specifically proletarian situation of the workers, from their theory and practice. Considered in this way, Kofler's emphasis on a necessarily transformed ideology in the process of de-Stalinisation loses its limitation as an ideological critique (and thereby also its illusions related to ideological critique), and constitutes itself much more strongly as an emphasis on radical change in the practical proletarian situation, and thus refer back less to questions of ideological education of the proletarian class than to questions of economic and political forms of work, organisation and life, that is, to political and social practice! In this way, it opens a provocatively fresh perspective on Stalinist vulgar materialism as an expression also of a proletarianly-reified, i.e., half-emancipated consciousness, a conformism cloaked in non-conformism, which under certain historical and sociological conditions forms a backbone of labour bureaucratic 'degeneration', and shines another, interesting light on Trotsky's theory of politbureaucratic socialism as 'degenerated workers' states'.

CHAPTER 4

Socialist Humanism, Human Nature and Marxist Anthropology

> In a sort of way, it is with man as with commodities. Since he comes into the world neither with a looking glass in his hand, nor as a Fichtian philosopher, to whom 'I am I' is sufficient, man first sees and recognises himself in other men. Peter only establishes his own identity as a man by first comparing himself with Paul as being of like kind. And thereby Paul, just as he stands in his Pauline personality, becomes to Peter the type of the genus homo.
> KARL MARX 1867 (Capital)

⋯

> Human beings have to work fairly hard to become human beings.
> TERRY EAGLETON 2004

⋯

Whoever would like to speak about socialist humanism and about the necessity of grappling with questions of human nature, and the contours of a specifically Marxist anthropology is confronted, as a rule and from a long tradition, with a strongly defensive attitude in his enlightened and progressive audience. It is still, to put it diplomatically, abundantly disputed on the political and intellectual left whether socialism as an idea and movement was and is a form of humanism, and what such a socialist humanism could or should be. There are remarkably many for whom socialism, in theory as well as in practice, would be better off having little or nothing to do with an explicit humanism. That may lie in the fact that humanism in the twentieth century was co-opted by every conceivable political current, but that this century was at the same time a century of the most terrible crimes against humanity. The defensiveness with regards to the concept of humanism may also relate to the fact that allegedly humanist motives even today time and again must serve as a philosophy justifying and uplifting an opposite practice of the rulers – let us think only of the talk of humanitarian interventionism, of the allegedly humanitarian war against terror. However, one could just as rightly object here that the political or intellectual resistance against such a 'humanism' is often also carried out in the name of humanism.

Let us thus attempt to bring some clarity into the discussion and first question the central political and theoretical arguments of a left anti-humanism. In my assessment, we are dealing with three main objections.

First, it is argued that every form of socialist humanism always partakes in something deeply normative, something ethical, and that this has its own extensive problems. To speak of the humanist content of a theory or worldview always also means speaking of an ideal that does not really exist, of an in-itself abstract idea, which needs to be put into practice. Thus, one speaks not only materialistically of a real being of humans, but also of an 'ought', of a type of imperative – humans ought to be one way or the other! Between 'is' and 'ought', between 'idea' and 'reality', however, a deep gulf of antagonisms [*Gegensätzen*], of antagonistic interests [*Interessens-Gegensätzen*], has always opened up in historical reality. The idea, according to Karl Marx, always disgraced itself where it was divorced from interest. How does one thus, one must ask, come from 'ought' to 'is' and from 'is' to 'ought', how does one connect the idea with the interest?

The second major objection ties in directly with the first, since on account of this obvious difference between 'is' and 'ought', 'idea' and 'interest', the humanist idea as something isolated, something abstract, can also become a philosophy of consolation and uplift for entirely different purposes. Most of the history of humanist ideas is characterised by the fact that its representative not infrequently became ideologues of actual historical oppression, that is, their humanism became used by those ruling and governing as a gentle form of oppression. Where the direct, naked repression against impinging classes and strata did not function as frictionlessly as before, one resorted to the humanist goal idea as a justifying philosophy for the exclusion, exploitation and oppression of parts of the population. Precisely because abstraction is inherent in the humanist idea, it can serve as the legitimation of actual oppression.

The third objection of a left anti-humanism is ultimately closely related to these other two. Since humanism would always like to signify a certain idea of man 'in itself', of human essence, it provides a good foundation for argumentation in order to explain the factual difference between 'is' and 'ought', between 'idea' and 'reality', and to justify actual historical oppression. Such is man – it is then said. Because man was such and such, one had to act in such and such a way. Yet what is man actually, ask the critics not unjustly? Can one ascertain and determine the essence of man once and for all? And hence, if one can define no such human essence, is not every basis for a humanism of any kind whatsoever destroyed?

Those are the three major, traditional objections against humanism in general, which are also brought forward again and again explicitly against a *socialist* humanism. It must be readily conceded that they are eminently serious and, as a rule, trenchant objections that should be kept in mind. Yet they do not exhaust the topic, since they speak against every conceivable variant of socialist humanism only if every form of humanism is declared in principle impossible and counterproductive. Whoever would like to speak, as I do in the following, of the necessity of a theoretical and practical humanism, must therefore not only say what he understands by such a socialist humanism. He must also justify why such a humanism is practically as well as theoretically needed, and how such a humanism relates to the three central objections.

Contours of a Socialist Humanism

That socialists have some reason to speak of a specific socialist humanism finds its cause above all in the history of the socialist left in the twentieth century. This quickly becomes clear if one considers the historical conditions of the emergence of socialist humanism as an identifiable movement of political thought, and if one asks how its leading thinkers themselves justified the necessity of such a socialist humanism.

Socialist humanism as an independent current in the history of political thought is a product of the second half of the 1950s, a code word of the movements for de-Stalinisation at the time in both the West as well as the East, which argued as a socialist opposition inside and outside the politically erupting Communist Parties for a renewal of leftist politics.[1] There were already initial left attempts in the 1930s to position a socialist humanism against the emerging Stalinist socialism. For example, the Left Oppositionist Victor Serge composed a sort of political testament at the beginning of 1933, in which he drew out the three central political consequences of the Stalinist degeneration, namely that from now on it was above all necessary to defend, first, free thought, second, the truth, and third, respect for man:

> Man must be given his rights, his security, his value. Without these, there is no Socialism. Without these, all is false, bankrupt, and spoiled. I mean:

---

1 See Soper 1990.

man whoever he is, be he the meanest of men – 'class-enemy', son or grandson of a bourgeois, I do not care. It must never be forgotten that a human being is a human being. Every day, everywhere, before my very eyes this is being forgotten, and it is the most revolting and anti-Socialist thing that could happen.[2]

Georg Lukács also attempted in the 1930s to emphasise the humanist content of Marxism, but turned this only implicitly, not explicitly, against historical Stalinism, to which he remained loyal in a historico-philosophical manner. It was precisely in this Popular Front tradition of the Communist movement, favoured by Lukács and others, that an implicit, humanist opposition to Stalinism was to be found – which was at least powerful enough that in 1946–7 the French Marxist Maurice Merleau-Ponty insisted, as this Popular Front thinking received new historical sustenance, on publishing a critique of this socialist humanism that was as learned as it was influential.[3]

However, not until the second half of the 1950s did these individual approaches to a socialist humanism receive a systematic, politically and publicly articulated expression in the form of an identifiable, independent intellectual current. Essentially triggered by Khrushchev's disclosures of Stalinist crimes at the 20th Party Congress of the CPSU at the beginning of 1956, this de-Stalinisation from above also sparked a powerful anti-Stalinism from below. Inside and outside of the Communist movement, socialist opposition movements erupted worldwide, arguing for a renewal of leftist politics and coalescing with the then incipient emergence of a New Left. What was common to this in itself heterogeneous movement was that it accused both Stalinist Communism and reformist social democrats of having betrayed the emancipatory and communist impetus of the socialist tradition, and of having failed to exhaust the possibilities that were anchored in this tradition for humans to be capable of mastering their own lives. In doing this, socialist humanists propagated a political and conceptual return to man, counting on the active, self-active element, on autonomy and subjectness, and broke with the conventional determinism of the Marxist base-superstructure schema, with Stalinist as well as reformist technocratism, and emphasised creativity, morality and practice.

To illustrate this, let us take one of their leading British thinkers, the historian and leftist activist, E.P. Thompson, who made socialist humanism the subject

---

2 Serge 2012, p. 327.
3 Merleau-Ponty 1969.

of an influential 1957 essay.[4] In socialist humanism E.P. Thompson saw first and foremost a revolt against the dogmatism and inhumanity of the Stalinist bureaucracy as a new ruling stratum that had transformed itself from a formerly revolutionary elite into a bureaucratic ruling stratum with a bureaucratic ruling ideology – Stalinism. Unlike many other leftists of his time, Thompson did not see Stalinism as a transitory accident or mere mistake that would historically sort itself out. It was instead a form of false consciousness, an ideological system. To view it as mere deviation or hypocrisy, for Thompson, reduced Stalinism to individuals and, in this way, underestimated its strength, inner logic and consistency. Second, such a view overlooked the fact that many aspects of Stalinism were already established many years before Stalin, before the Russian revolution and before the rise of the Soviet bureaucracy. Third, neither did it explain how Stalinist concepts and practices could gain a foothold in other countries and amongst non-Soviet Communists, who reaped only ostracism, hardship, prison or death, without benefiting from the privileges of the bureaucracy. Last but not least, such an approach, for Thompson, tended to be infected by one of the worst mistakes of Stalinism – the attempt to derive the analysis of political phenomena all too directly and simplistically from economic causes, and thereby to minimise the part that human ideas and moral stances play in the historical process.

We must thus, according to Thompson, *also* view Stalinism as an ideology, as a constellation of certain attitudes and false or partially false ideas. Stalinists act or write in certain forms, not because they are subjective fools or hypocrites, but because they are objectively prisoners of their false ideas. Even if this does not subjectively exculpate them, Stalinism is rather the false consciousness 'of a revolutionary elite which, within, degenerated into a bureaucracy … Stalinism did not develop just because certain economic and social conditions existed, but because these conditions provided a fertile climate within which false ideas took root, and these false ideas became in their turn a part of the social conditions'.[5] As ideological practice, Stalinism had outlived the social context in which it arose, and this helped to clarify the character of the Communist dissidence. It was namely a matter of 'revolt against the ideology, the false consciousness of the elite-into-bureaucracy', 'a revolt against dogmatism and the anti-intellectualism which feeds it' and

> a revolt against inhumanity – the equivalent of dogmatism in human relationships and moral conduct – against administrative, bureaucratic and

4 Thompson 2014.
5 Thompson 2014, p. 52.

twisted attitudes towards human beings. In both sense it represents a return to man: from abstractions and scholastic formulations to real men: from deceptions and myths to honest history: and so the positive content of this revolt may be described as 'socialist humanism'. It is humanist because it places once again real men and women at the centre of socialist theory and aspiration, instead of the resounding abstractions – the Party, Marxism-Leninism-Stalinism, the Two Camps, the Vanguard of the Working Class – so dear to Stalinism. It is socialist because it reaffirms the revolutionary perspectives of Communism, faith in the revolutionary potentialities not only of the Human Race or of the Dictatorship of the Proletariat but of real men and women.[6]

The first characterisation of socialist humanism is thus a certain, expanded interpretation and opposition to Stalinism as a novel form of aristocratic and elite rule and ruling ideology. The second characteristic is a certain 'humanist' interpretation of Marxist theory. For Thompson and other socialist humanists Marxism is an approach to thought; to think actively as well as passively of the dialectical relationship of social being and social consciousness. Marx's socialist humanism was the first to declare, as Erich Fromm said, that theory cannot be separated from practice, knowledge from action, spiritual aims from the social system.[7] And for E.P. Thompson it was 'of first importance that men do not only "reflect" experience passively; they also think about that experience; and their thinking affects the way they act. The thinking is the creative part of man, which, even in class society, makes him partly an agent in history, just as he is partly a victim of his environment'.[8]

Socialist humanism here combines a deeper and more radical critique of Stalinist theory and practice with an elaboration of human freedom of action within Marxist social theory. It is thus no coincidence that the late Thompson was so polemically and sharply critical of Louis Althusser's thesis of Marxism as a theoretical anti-humanism. Both Stalin as well as Althusser, the one practically, the other theoretically, '[stink] of inhumanity', because they have found ways 'of regarding people as the bearers of structures [*kulaks*] and history as a process without a subject'.[9]

Socialism as a comprehensive, radical anti-Stalinism and Marxism as a theory of human agency – these are two main components of socialist humanism

---

6   Ibid.
7   Fromm 1965, p. viii.
8   Thompson 2014, p. 57.
9   Thompson 1978, p. 140.

as a historically identifiable current of the history of political thought. There are, however, further components. For a systematic and sustainable theory of socialist humanism we must go further, to one of the most systematic theorists of socialist humanism at that time, to one of the most important Marxist philosophers of postwar Germany, to Leo Kofler.

In Kofler's first works, works on Marxist methodology published from the mid-1940s to mid-1950s, we find the same insistence on and the same development of human freedom of action and human consciousness in theory and history as with E.P. Thompson – though in a philosophically more systematic and detailed version. We also find in Kofler, several years before Thompson, the first systematic critique of Stalinist theory and practice in German. Comparably to Thompson, we are thereby dealing with a systematically developed critique of Stalinism as the ideological system of a bureaucratic caste that emphasises the non-dialectical, mechanistic, economistic and anti-humanistic character of Stalinism.[10] In two central aspects, however, Kofler's socialist humanism already goes beyond that of Thompson's. On the one hand, Kofler expands the range of socialist humanism, in that he uses it for a developed critique of bourgeois humanism. On the other, he undergirds this humanism with the development of a specific philosophical anthropology.

With regards to the first: in his book on the long history of bourgeois society, first published in 1948, Kofler traces the historical development of the emerging bourgeois class from its medieval beginnings to the Renaissance and Enlightenment until the imperialism at the start of the twentieth century. He traces the intellectual (socio-philosophical) path of bourgeois humanism, which breaks away from the centring of God dominant in the Middle Ages by declaring the real man and no longer the abstraction, God, to be the measure of all things. In the Enlightenment humanism of the eighteenth century, this is radicalised in considering man as a man, who develops himself in a process of education and cultivation, and in this way is convinced of the unending possibility of the development and unfolding of human personality and reason.

Kofler, on the one hand, clarifies the world-historical advance connected with this bourgeois humanism, and on the other also works out its inner contradictoriness, its structural limits, as the bourgeois ideologue is trapped in a methodological individualism and can only 'imagine the true and complete individual as a bourgeois one, and that means only as a property-owning individual'.[11] If elements of a critique of the approaching bourgeois capitalist form

---

10   See Chapter 3.
11   Kofler 1992, Vol. 2, p. 218.

of society are to be found in Enlightenment humanism – primarily in those places where the market economy-based division of labour is accompanied by a social division of labour, leading to a return of the ideal of the 'whole man' – the blind spot inherent in it is the generally uncritical, affirmative attitude to bourgeois capitalist private property, as Kofler demonstrates in various bourgeois thinkers and philosophers. Early bourgeois humanism indeed believed that a harmonious social process in the interest of all men was possible on the basis of private property and complete individual freedom. Yet this bourgeois ideal was broken by capitalist reality, as it developed in the nineteenth century. This contradiction is theoretically glossed over in humanist thought, in which the bourgeois concept of man becomes ever more openly coupled to ownership and property. One came to the full use of bourgeois rights and freedoms, to being a full bourgeois legal subject, in the bourgeois self-conception, through property, while in contrast the propertyless was only half a man. In bourgeois thought there could indeed be property without freedom, but no freedom without property.

Thus, in the historical moment where the new political freedoms prove themselves to be compatible with the social unfreedom of the new capitalist class society, and therefore become politically challenged by the impinging strata and classes, bourgeois thought lets its old, humanist ideal of all-rounded development and the unfolding of man fall to the wayside, and separates itself from its old radical democratic demands. The task of the further democratisation of society is henceforth left to the, in a bourgeois sense, non-bourgeois classes. While the workers' movement became in this way the heirs of the radical democratic, humanist demand, bourgeois thought deteriorated into an empty competitive individualism with a pessimistic and decadent conception of man, viewing man as by nature a predator pursuing his own individual interests (Hobbes), and propagating a state of society in which 'might makes right' prevailed and understood this 'right' as a right of the owners. The individual person thus becomes a 'predator restlessly roaming between the remaining individuals, who remain alien to him, and constantly lying in wait for prey'.[12]

A decade later, from the mid-1950s onwards, Kofler deepens his critique of bourgeois thought by examining the specific contradictions of the neo-capitalist social state in articles and in several books. Comparable to other interpreters of the 'affluent society', Kofler also examines the historically new forms of alienation and their prevailing social philosophy, and comes to the conclusion that in neo-capitalism the world was merely still 'useful' for the

---

12   Kofler 1992, Vol. 2, p. 304.

bourgeoisie, i.e., profitable, otherwise it had become empty and senseless. Contemporary ideas of freedom were no longer about pursuing the old ideal of an all-rounded development of species-being and the raising of the individual in that sense – 'whoever still wants this becomes suspicious!' – but rather solely about the freedom of competition, of the jungle: 'Basically everything has been achieved, there was history, but in the future there won't be any more'.[13] Everyone here is their own neighbour and freedom deteriorated into an esoteric, egocentric preoccupation with the inner workings of the soul, took on fanatical and monomaniacal traits and became elitist. In neo-capitalism the isolated individual felt subjectively free in an elitist manner and elevated over 'the masses', while in reality only pessimism and lethargy condensed – 'into a sort of nihilistic *Weltschmerz* ... which imposed over the whole of society like a many-armed polyp'.[14] The decline's 'mark of Cain' became reinterpreted as an emblem of human existence and the chaotic 'nothing', bereft of meaning, of the existing being was elevated to an existential characteristic of *all* being. The damaged man of today became understood as the eternal situation.

Kofler thus detects a systematic jettisoning of the humanist demands in the contemporary bourgeoisie. The bourgeoisie became *structurally anti-humanist*. This practical as well as theoretical anti-humanism spread under late capitalist conditions piece by piece to the thinking of the whole of society, even to the thought of large sections of the left – which is why it is all the more important to occupy humanism from a left position. In this way, Kofler's critical approach to bourgeois humanism's ideals of freedom draws on the anti-Stalinism described above, and on a renewed understanding of Marxism focused on human freedom of action. This connection becomes the start of a new socialist humanism that Kofler began to explicitly speak of from the beginning of 1951 on, and that culminated in his theory of the three world-historical stages of freedom.

What does he mean by this theory of the three world-historical stages of freedom? In the tradition of classical socialism, Kofler considers the political freedom implemented in the bourgeois revolutions, i.e., the civil and personal freedoms (that is, freedom of association, assembly, religion, expression, universal and equal suffrage, etc.) to be the first world-historical form of a *real* human freedom. The advancement of this political freedom to a social democracy, claimed above all by the protesting and struggling proletariat since the middle of the nineteenth century, is for him, by contrast, the

---

13   Kofler 1960, p. 150.
14   Kofler 1960, p. 46.

second world-historical stage of freedom, economic and social freedom. Yet both forms of freedom, according to Kofler, are essentially conceived of negatively as 'freedom from' – freedom from the feudal bonds, from personal dependence and political paternalism on the one hand, and freedom from material misery, social oppression and disenfranchisement on the other. The world-historical third form of freedom, the actual socialist idea of freedom, is for Kofler, however, a positive freedom. 'Freedom from' is not in the foreground here, but rather 'freedom to', the old humanist idea of a freedom to engage in all-rounded development of personality. For Kofler, this third form, this third stage of a world-historical freedom, is, however, only to be reached if one does not pit the two earlier world-historical freedoms, political and social freedom, against each other, but rather indivisibly unites them on a higher plane. It is precisely such a synthesis of social and political freedom that was not successful in the twentieth century. According to Kofler, the social-democratic left limited themselves to political freedom over the course of the twentieth century, and made the working class into the component of bourgeois capitalist rule that is formally equal before the law. The Communist left, in contrast, brought the working class social freedom, i.e., freed them from material insecurity and immiseration, but only at the price of taking the workers' individual and political freedom away. In this the two main currents of the socialist workers' movement in the twentieth century suppressed the decisive third world-historical stage of freedom and 'forgot' the old emancipatory and progressive idea of the all-rounded and individual as well as collective development of human essential powers.

In Kofler's theory of the three world-historical stages of freedom, first formulated over 70 years ago, we find not only the critique of bourgeois freedom and the critique of actually existing socialist freedom in the twentieth century connected to each other. We also find an actualisation of the early bourgeois, radical humanist representation of the goal for the socialist movement. Every new attempt at socialism could only have majority appeal and be victorious if it practically and politically united political freedom with social freedom. Socialism proved itself in this way as the more comprehensive humanism – as that simple thing which is hard to do.

Contours of a Marxist Anthropology

The historical as well as theoretical critique of early bourgeois humanism, and socialist humanism's claim to the legacy derived from that critique, constitute the first major aspect with which Kofler enriches the socialist humanism of the 1950s. The second is that he not only refers to the right to the free and all-rounded development of human personality, but from the second half of the 1950s begins to give it anthropological content. Whoever would like to speak of the all-rounded development of the personality of man must have a philosophical conception of this man. The all-rounded development of personality contains a certain conception of man, and Kofler begins at the end of the 1950s to develop the contours of such a Marxist anthropology.

Again, he is not the only one in his generation to do so. From the end of the 1950s and the early 1960s, the discussion of a socialist conception of man and a Marxist anthropology gains momentum. Henri Lefebvre and Jean-Paul Sartre, Adam Schaff and Karel Kosik, Erich Fromm and Isaac Deutscher, Che Guevara and Franz Fanon, György Markus and Herbert Marcuse, all of them and many more (including for that matter, E.P. Thompson) set off on the trail of an emancipatory anthropology.[15] Yet once more it appears to me that Kofler was not only one of the first, but also one of the most systematic of these leading thinkers.[16] Where most of those mentioned still wrestled with their own tradition, torn between the recognition of the necessity of anthropological thought, and the fundamental rejection of every naturalism, he already went markedly further, and conceived a Marxist anthropology in thoroughly dialectical form.

The relationship of Marxism and anthropology is not only a problem historically, but above all a methodological problem. If philosophical anthropology in general is about the timeless being of men or man, that is, insight into essences, the Marxist theoretical tradition, in contrast, primarily emphasises historicity – the historicity of its object of knowledge as well as its methodology of knowledge. It is programmatically about the specific, the historically concrete and changeable, and it thereby orients itself primarily against every type of idealist speculation about the alleged essence of things. Marxist social theory is therefore less concerned with the knowledge of the structure and laws of motion of human societies as such, or of man as such, but rather, more particularly, the knowledge of the specific structure and laws of motion of a particular human society, namely the bourgeois capitalist society – under the stipulation of its necessary and possible change. Dogmatisms within Marxism and the deterring experience with a bourgeois anthropology obviously in service of reaction have additionally and lastingly marred this precarious relationship of Marxism and anthropology. So how then do these two different approaches fit together?

---

15 See Fromm 1965; Lepenies 1971; Honneth and Joas 1988.
16 Jünke 2007a, pp. 512–13.

As a rule, Marxists define man, and this is often exactly the point of criticism, by labour. Marx and Engels write in a famous passage of their *German Ideology*:

> Men can be distinguished from animals by consciousness, by religion or anything else you like. They themselves begin to distinguish themselves from animals as soon as they begin to *produce* their means of subsistence, a step which is conditioned by their physical organisation. By producing their means of subsistence men are indirectly producing their material life.[17]

Many Marxists have uncritically adopted this, although there are also other statements and thoughts to be found in Marx. Kofler corrects this traditional Marxist view in one specific aspect. He too proceeds from labour, or more generally speaking, activity, being that which makes the man into man, into a socialised being. Man produces itself in labour – as an active and labouring being. Reification, alienation and exploitation, these three central Marxist theorems of a critique of capitalist societies, find their origin here, in the social division of labour with its structuring of class society. Unlike the Marx and Engels quotations, however, Kofler does not oppose – and this is the initial originality of his approach – labour and consciousness. Kofler emphasises that such a kind of labour/activity is indissolubly [*unaufhebbar*] paired with consciousness, that activity and consciousness are not to be separated from each other.

'The practically active man', according to Kofler, 'cannot be thought of differently than one who is active with the aid of his mind, i.e., a consciousness-endowed man. The ability to act through consciousness means nothing other than the ability to set oneself specific goals and to work towards the achievement of these goals'.[18] If the idealist tradition of thought assumes that history is shaped *by consciousness*, the materialist dialectic considers history as essentially *shaped through consciousness throughout* [*durch das Bewusstsein hindurch gestaltete*] – a fine yet far-reaching difference. Labour, activity, practice, all these functions of the practical process of life are unthinkable without the quality of consciousness, without the dialectical unity of being and consciousness. For Kofler there can be 'no single aspect of social life, no relationship and no activity, that does not shape itself through consciousness throughout ("throughout!")'.[19] Where this is seen as a regression into ideal-

---

17   Marx and Engels 1975, p. 31.
18   Kofler 2004, p. 107.
19   Kofler 2004, p. 120.

ism, the vulgar materialist mechanism, as he says, 'celebrates its lightly won triumph'.[20] The main achievement of historical materialism for him therefore lies in 'having acknowledged and at the same time materialistically explained' the role of social consciousness, hitherto claimed by philosophical idealism and neglected by philosophical materialism.[21] For Kofler, the decisive difference between animal and man is thus human consciousness, or preferably: the human capability for consciousness, for conscious being. Consciousness here is the 'ability to make possible acting in the sense of setting goals'.[22]

With this, a far-reaching difference is posited with all the social scientific or social philosophical theories that essentially reduce man to the natural conditions around and accompanying him. Kofler's concept of man is irreconcilable with any naturalism or biologism. Such a concept of man belongs rather to their opposite pole, the so-called culturalism, i.e., the concept that man is defined through his culture, through that which he makes out of himself. What again distinguishes Kofler from this culturalism, however, is precisely the fact that there is also for him a human nature that forces limits and perspectives on human culture.

We humans are, as the British cultural critic Terry Eagleton once put it, 'cultural beings by virtue of our nature, which is to say by virtue of the sorts of bodies we have and the kind of world to which they belong'.[23] Humans stand, so to speak, between nature and culture, human nature ('communal, somatically based and culturally mediated') is changed through human culture, but not eliminated.[24] This is also Leo Kofler's concept and it is justified at its core, in his view, in that it is consciousness, conscious being, i.e. culture, that distinguishes human nature. It is in the essence of this human nature that it is structurally dependent on one's fellow man and the labour/activity mediated with him.

However, for Kofler, what equally is of the essence of this human nature – and this is his second original shift of emphasis in regards to the Marxist tradition – is that it is not summed up in the cultural achievements of labour and activity. Labour and activity are themselves only the means for a purpose, rational and cultural means for the 'irrational' satisfying of the drives of the natural being man – and these drives are, in the broadest sense, erotic drives, i.e., oriented towards enjoyment and play. Erotic is naturally not understood here in the sense of contemporary erotic categories, but rather in a comprehensive

---

20 Ibid.
21 Kofler 2004, p. 105.
22 Kofler 1967, p. 28.
23 Eagleton 1996, p. 73.
24 Eagleton 2000, p. 99.

sense far beyond sexuality, in the sense of beauty and the free play of essential powers, in the sense of eros. Therefore man is understood by Kofler not only to be defined by transformative doing, and not only by rational activity oriented towards goals, but also by those, in essence, joys gathered up in his expression of irrational eros – today we would say: through desire. Man defines himself for Kofler therefore as a 'man erotically enjoying himself in creative activity, and actively realising himself in enjoyment'.[25]

With these words another concept is placed beside labour, namely that of play. Labour and play have, indeed, for Kofler the same anthropological origin as practical externalised forms of man, but, viewed historically, were divided and went different ways. This division of labour and play is a product of those antagonistic class societies in which humans have moved since their early days. In class societies, characterised by the exploitation of individual labour power and the appropriation of social surplus product, human activity deteriorated into repressive labour based on the repression of the erotic drive, into ascetic discipline, while the originally harmonious play was pushed backed into the recreational and private sphere and degraded into an anarchic and orgiastic principle.

As long as eros and asceticism, repressive activity and free play of essential powers are separated, there was a desire of humankind for a non-repressive, non-alienated unity of labour and play. For Kofler this is the utopian content of a humanist anthropology which must be nurtured, for such a humanist anthropology allowed

> an optimistic prospect on what can become of man and what he, according to his nature, strives for. This anthropologically defined perspective has, however, absolutely no spontaneous influence on the concrete historical event, since as an anthropological perspective it is merely of a formal nature. What will really become of the recognised possibility of the 'playing' man depends on the historical conditions and the realisation of the inherent possibilities in these conditions. Yet it does not remain without significance for the practical effects of critical theory, which 'concept of man' it represents.[26]

An anthropology understood in this way is therefore no theory or concept of history, for it, as mentioned earlier, is not at all able to grasp the historicity

---

25 Kofler 1967, p. 34.
26 Kofler 1967, p. 36.

of man, the historically changeable and changing. For Kofler, an anthropology thus understood is thoroughly a science, to wit, as he says, 'a science of the unchanged preconditions of human changeability'.[27] Kofler recognises eight of these anthropological and formal conditions of any human existences: human reason, human activity, historicity of man and his externalisation, his physical and psychic organisation, his socialisation, as well the subject-object dialectic. For Kofler, these formal conditions only make man into man, make human history *formally possible*, without thereby *determining its content*. This anthropological essence of man thus did not concern the historical and concrete man, who was changeable in the space of history. This historical and concrete man is rather that 'which he thinks, feels, knows, recognises and experiences, in short, what he *became* by means of his historically-shaped consciousness'.[28]

Looking backwards, the changeability of historical man is an affair of historical science and theory, and looking forward, an affair of social and political science. (Philosophical) anthropology becomes, as it were, a metatheory, a type of auxiliary science, which for Kofler is no guide to action and also, by definition, cannot be. Despite this he considers this auxiliary science of anthropology to be theoretically and practically necessary, since the humanist concept of man resulting from this anthropology connects in an organic way anthropological essence and human past with the socialist and humanist goal idea and progressive thinking – yesterday with today, tomorrow, and the day after tomorrow.

The humanist concept of man derived from this epistemological anthropology – which proceeds as such neither from a good or evil man, but rather is to be qualified as a neutral concept of man – therefore does not serve as a direct guide to action, but rather as a defence against false theoretical and practical approaches to action. It has in essence two functions, or tasks. On the one hand, the task of defence against contemporary pessimism and nihilism, 'i.e., the perception of man as a basically negative being incapable of any historical development towards freedom', and on the other, 'the task of the creation of a positive, humanist ideal, a criterion in the assessment of all concrete human situations and all actions, in the properly understood sense of an ethical criterion'.[29] Above all in intellectual struggle against the bourgeois pessimism spreading like an polyp, anthropological thought had to prove itself, for:

> Why, just like fear, desperation, threat of death and guilt, also hope, enthusiasm, zest for action, love, beauty, revelry, striving for truth and so on are

---

27 Kofler 1967, p. 28.
28 Kofler 1967, p. 25.
29 Kofler 1960, p. 309.

not beheld as 'potential' (Tillich) dormant in man remains an eternal mystery of decadent bourgeois nihilism.[30]

It becomes clear here that Kofler's philosophical anthropology relies on a 'neutral' concept of man, which directs the focus once again to those historical conditions that decide which facilities in the human essence are used. Man is not per se good or evil, he has both (and still more) parts. He investigated this in detail in the early 1970s using the example of the bourgeois biological determinism of drives and its leading thinkers, Arnold Gehlen, Irenäus Eibl-Eibesfeldt and Konrad Lorenz, and in doing so, subjected their influential promotion of the 'theory of the ubiquitous and threatening aggression drive, by which all tribulations of human behaviour in social and historical life are accounted for' to a comprehensive critique.[31] There was indeed an anthropological and biological aggression drive of man, yet precisely because this was an anthropological constant, it was essentially *formally* determined, i.e., the historically concrete conditions and thus also humans themselves decided how it was to be handled. Only on historical ground could the formal aggression drive realise itself as a substantial and, accordingly, changeable inclination to aggression. 'Looked at it in isolation, it is not capable of effecting anything historical – i.e., including wars'.[32]

Grappling in detail with this sort of biological determinist neoconservativism at the beginning of the 1970s was, however, not something the left mainstream succeeded in doing. The excessive confidence of the left radicalism emerging out of the revolt of '1968' did not linger on questions of anthropology or humanism. In the dialectic of culture and nature, questions of culture and cultural theory had dominated since the mid-1960s. That phase of high cultural theory began, which Terry Eagleton self-critically characterises as a continuation of modernism by other means, and dates to the period from approximately 1965 to 1980.[33] It was then the height of Louis Althusser, who was able to recognise *solely* an ideological and not a scientific concept in humanism, and asserts the 'rupture with *every* philosophical anthropology or humanism' as one of the centres of Marx's thought.[34]

> Strictly in respect to theory, therefore, one can and *must* speak openly of Marx's theoretical anti-humanism and see in this theoretical anti-

---

30   Kofler 1967, p. 62.
31   Kofler 1973, p. 13.
32   Kofler 2000e, p. 189; see also Kofler 1973, pp. 46–7.
33   See Eagleton 2004, pp. 23–4.
34   Althusser 1969, p. 223. My emphasis.

humanism the *absolute* (negative) precondition of the (positive) knowledge of the human world itself ... [*A*]*ny* thought that appeals to Marx *for any kind* of restoration of a theoretical anthropology or humanism is no more than ashes, theoretically.[35]

Although Althusser himself qualified at the time that with his theoretical antihumanism the historical reality of humanism should not be denied, he still accepted henceforth only a purely *practical* (irremediably contaminated with ideology, i.e., with dirty practice) humanism that had nothing more to do with THEORY. That he thereby also *conceptually* severed theory and practice little irritated his students and sympathisers in the structuralist pull of the time, as they understood how this purely theoretical position was itself only the product of a certain theoretical *practice* – the practical attempt of a theorist to politically and theoretically defend himself against a certain historical form of left thought and action (namely reform Communist and socialist humanism).

That an anti-anti-humanist thinker like Kofler was also largely ignored in the structuralist and poststructuralist 1970s may be understandable against this backdrop.[36] That in the early 1980s, however, he was one of the first who began to combat the then emergent neoliberalism with anthropological arguments – this too has its own logic. The neoliberalism that has been hegemonically established since the 1980s draws a good part of its intellectual strength and hegemony as a social philosophy from an extensively internalised concept of man that one can only consistently face on the same terrain, i.e., when one has one's own consistent concept of man. The ideological model of neoliberalism is famously the flexible, mobile, universally available and alway prepared person, the Me Incorporated, the isolated individual as entrepreneur and lone warrior, who mobilises his individual resources in a race of commodification against others: each is his own neighbour and all becomes a fetish of profit accumulation at any price, of self-valorisation of value as well as universal competition, or more precisely: subjugation to the imperatives of market competition. This neoliberal ideology ('Man, the individual man, is what he makes out of himself') is

---

35 Althusser 1969, pp. 229–30. My emphases.
36 When a small radical left publisher in 1972 set out to publish an edited volume of Kofler's preeminent texts in honour of Kofler's sixty-fifth birthday, they tellingly gave it the title *Zur Dialektik der Kultur* [On the Dialectic of Culture] and furnished the volume with a long introduction by the then still young and radical leftist intellectual Günter Maschke, who echoed the 'new left' culturalist rejection of Kofler's philosophical anthropology (Kofler 1972), before later becoming himself an adherent of Gehlen's right-wing anthropology – and trying to capture Kofler for the ultra-right scene. For a critique of this attempt at co-optation, see Jünke 2015.

thoroughly reactionary, due to its methodological individualism and its blindness to class society, but is not necessarily conservative. It was not infrequently 'progressive' social democrats or nonconformist leftists who helped neoliberal thought to its sociopolitical breakthrough ...

It is to be asserted, not only but also and precisely against this neoliberal concept of man, that man – anthropologically and historically considered – is a collective being, always socialised and structurally dependent on one another, a *species-being, that can only individualise itself in the community and only through the community*. Man inevitably reflects himself in others and is structurally dependent on forms of collective solidarity – everything else, as Kofler never tired of saying, is the predator ideology of market radicals.[37]

On the Necessity of a Socialist Humanism

Socialist humanism *as a historically identifiable, independent current in the history of political thought* is thus a product of the latter half of the 1950s, a code word for the practical as well as theoretical challenges to which the socialist movement was subjected on the basis of the lastingly blocked de-Stalinisation in the Communist movement and the abandonment of socialist theory and practice in Western social democracy (the 'ghost of the Revolution which never happened over here, like the ghost of the Revolution which was never completed over there' as Henri Lefebvre formulated it).[38] Socialist humanism holds fast to the old socialist programme of emancipation and combines a fundamental critique of Stalinist theory and practice with the stronger emphasis of human freedom of action within Marxist social theory. It reformulates the historical as well as theoretical critique of bourgeois humanism under conditions of 'late bourgeois' alienation and reification and derives from that the political as well as theoretical claim to the legacy of a socialist humanism, to which an anthropological foundation should now be given. This elaboration of the historical as well as theoretical content of such a socialist humanism now allows us to formulate several generalisations with regards to its relevance today.

A contemporary socialist concept of man is first necessary as a critical criterion for other social theories and philosophies. Whether conservatism or

---

37 As the economic critic Marx already knew – see the quotation at the beginning of the chapter from Marx in Marx 1996, p. 63.
38 Lefebvre 1995, p. 236.

biological determinism, racism or postmodernism, classical liberalism or neoliberalism, but also the different variants of socialism – they all work, whether consciously or unconsciously, openly or secretly, with a specific concept of man even where they think they reject such a thing. In almost all of them, a mostly one-sided and repressively distorted concept of man is to be found, which is intended to serve the legitimation of different forms of rule and is ultimately pessimistic or nihilist.

Second, a socialist humanism is necessary because only it provides us with an ethical criterion for the assessment of actually existing societies. With what right do we actually reject torture and violence, and why should class societies – rule of humans over humans – have less moral validity than the idea of collective self-realisation and society without rulers and classes? 'We can't get any further without a Marxist anthropology', according to Kofler, expanding on this in an interview: 'There are scholars who believe that it suffices to look into history, how it develops, how it conforms to laws: the problems always gradually solve themselves, etc., so what's the point of adding anthropology? ... Because without anthropology one cannot prove that the one who lives from surplus value, that is, from exploitation, does this unjustly'.[39] At the same time as this interview appeared, a younger British Marxist, Norman Geras, wrote a short, scholarly treatise on the work of Karl Marx, in which he (in critical engagement not least with the then leftist icon, Louis Althusser) debunked the old legend that there was a rejection of universal human nature and a theoretical anti-humanism in Marx.[40] Two decades later, Terry Eagleton comes back to this question, which he formulates as follows:

> It seemed impossible to establish, say, the idea of justice on a scientific basis; so what exactly did you denounce capitalism, slavery or sexism in the name of? You cannot describe someone as oppressed unless you have some dim notion of what not being oppressed might look like, and why being oppressed is a bad idea in the first place. And this involves normative judgements, which then makes politics look uncomfortably like ethics.[41]

Third, a socialist humanism is necessary, so that we affirm an emancipatory goal-idea, a vision of human progress, which has often gone missing. Such

---

39 'The Anthropology of Consciousness in the Materialism of Karl Marx' in this volume, p. 234. Interview in Kofler 1983b.
40 Geras 1983.
41 Eagleton 2004, pp. 148–9.

an anthropological 'utopia' is about the needs and capacities of the species-being man 'to develop himself', grounded not only in his historical, but also anthropological being. Insofar as socialist humanism refers back to the old, early bourgeois humanism, it wants to make the capacity for autonomy of the individual developed there strong in the socialist movement. Insofar as it refers back to the proletarian humanism of the radical tradition, it wants to make the capacity for solidarity of the class collective strong. Accordingly, the socialist left must, if it wants to politically begin anew, learn a capacity for autonomy, not least the individual capacity, which first arose with the early, radical bourgeoisie and latently came up short in the classical proletarian class movement. If they want to begin anew, socialist leftists must, correspondingly, relearn the capacity for solidarity of the class collective that first arose historically with the radical workers' movement. Such a reformulation of a socialist and humanist goal has a further strategic sense, not to be underestimated in its significance: precisely because the emancipation of the species-being man does not automatically follow any historical path, neither automatically predetermined nor automatically taking place, and precisely because the leap into freedom in the Marxist sense is a qualitative break with all human prehistory, the anthropological utopia becomes necessary, to wit, 'because it mobilises man to hopes and actions that exceed their own limits in practice and help to realise ideas that, as laid out in history, would never be realised without utopia'.[42]

Fourth and finally, a socialist humanism is necessary because only it can offer us a political and ethical criterion for the assessment of possible forms of emancipatory practice and concrete utopia. Not all means are permitted on the way to the goal of human emancipation. This is also a comprehensive and complicated discussion that I can only identify but not expand on here. However, it was not a historical coincidence that socialist humanism originated as a reaction to historical Stalinism and its survival even after Stalin's death. Stalinist thought and action is 'only' the extreme variant of authoritarian forms of socialism. Stalinism has been to date the worst and most devastating form of a despotic 'socialism from above', which was shaped by the idea that concrete, actually existing humans, in the name of higher values, may even be treated dictatorially for a more or less long period of time.

Socialist humanism therefore draws its historical, political and theoretical conclusions from the history of the socialist left in the twentieth century. The socialist struggle for emancipation finds its specific ethics in the overcoming of the theoretical as well as practical powerlessness and lack of consciousness

---

42   Kofler 2007, p. 25.

of the majority of the population. All means are permitted that contribute to such a politicisation. All means are permitted, *insofar* as they overcome the powerlessness and lack of consciousness of the wage-labouring class, promote their class solidarity and class autonomy and spur the universal human emancipation of all oppressed and exploited strata, ethnicities, and genders. Conversely, however, this also means that those means that impede, twist or make a mockery of these developmental processes are forbidden. This points to the inherently radically democratic character of every sustainable socialist politics that is based on the premise 'that the development of human capacities can occur only through social practice and that thus points to our need to be able to develop through democratic, participatory, and protagonistic activity in every aspect of our lives', as Michael A. Lebowitz, another contemporary theorist of socialist humanism, formulated it.[43]

After the experiences that people and nations have gained with the once actually existing socialism, it is more essential than ever that socialists and others give account of their visions of the alternative.[44] Criticism, as the young Marx (put in the naughty corner by Althusser) already wrote, is no passion of the head, but the head of passion – and it is not for nothing that Kofler made this sentence the motto of his autobiography.[45] In what can only be understood as a theoretical as well as practical warning against a culture of critique detached from real human life, Althusser and others also suppressed in the young (and most of the old) Marx his understanding of what people are about, those who don't exclusively live at their writing desk or (as critical critics) in their own heads.[46] In the face of postmodernism and neoliberalism, it does contemporaries good to think about specific human needs and capacities, about specific human possibilities and limits, even if concrete answers are not self-evident.[47]

Three Objections and Responses

Let us return in conclusion to the three main objections to socialist humanism. Every form of socialist humanism always had something deeply normative, ethical in itself, while a deep chasm of antagonistic interests opened up between

---

43 Lebowitz 2010, p. 22.
44 See Lebowitz 2010, p. 7.
45 Kofler 1987a.
46 The sharpest and most trenchant critique remains that of E.P. Thompson, Thompson 1978.
47 See Callinicos 1987.

'is' and 'ought', between 'idea' and 'reality'. This obvious difference between idea and interest had hitherto all too often served the purpose in history of using humanist ideals to justify exclusion, exploitation and oppression of parts of the population and correspondingly served as a philosophy of consolation and uplift for actual historical repression, being used as a 'gentle form of oppression'. Every humanist argument with 'man' was ultimately based on an idea of a human essence that was either deterministically and biologically structured or not defined scientifically.

Let us first deal with the question of Marxist anthropology, and the socialist concept of man. Can one speak from an emancipatory, even Marxist, view of a human essence and engage in insight into essences or does one not thereby inevitably fix in place something permanently changing and/or something to change, in an undue and problematic fashion? Are Marxism, socialism and humanism conceptually compatible? That this has its far-reaching (theoretical as well as practical) problems is not to be disputed, but rather to be considered at all times, if one recalls the practical history of the socialist movement in the twentieth century. It is precisely this history that indicates the necessity of such a reflection. For unlike in bourgeois humanism, which beheld the light of the world when the early bourgeoisie and proponents of the Enlightenment in their excessive confidence of their historic mission planted the flag of their radical humanism, socialist humanism only began to take flight as a historically identifiable current of political thought after the onset of the twilight of a despotically degenerated socialist movement. Accordingly the necessity of an anthropological reflection also imposes itself on contemporary Marxists.

In his small piece on Marx's conception of human nature, for example, the aforementioned Norman Geras – not the first and only, but one of the most discerning Marxists of the last decades to strive for a Marxist anthropology – demonstrates that while Marx's theory was not anthropology, it surely presupposes one:

> [I]f diversity in the character of human beings is in large measure set down by Marx to historical variation in their social relations of production, the very fact that they entertain this sort of relations, the fact that they produce and that they have a history, he explains in turn by some of their general and constant, intrinsic, constitutional characteristics; in short by their human nature. This concept is therefore indispensable to his historical theory.[48]

---

48   Geras 1983, p. 67.

This is pure Kofler – without Geras having known Kofler's work – for Kofler also emphasised repeatedly that although no concrete history can be explained from the essence of man, or general human nature, this human nature explains why man has history at all. We are cultural beings due to our nature, as Terry Eagleton aptly formulated it, and he has in recent years focused on formulating a dialectical version of Marxist anthropology that can be found almost entirely in Kofler. It is, as shown, a philosophical anthropology that is neither biologistically nor deterministically structured, but which, as 'the science of the unchanging preconditions of human changeability', satisfies theoretical and scientific demands.

However, the rejection of humanism and anthropology still prevails on the left. How comprehensively such thought has entered into left, including Marxist, common sense is shown by the example of the German Marxist Frieder Otto Wolf, who himself acts in practice as a humanist, and would like to only accept his conceptual humanism as explicitly practical, while simultaneously feeling obliged to fundamentally defend the theoretical anti-humanism of an Adorno, an Althusser, or a Foucault, even as president of the Humanist Association of Germany. Wolf's lectures, published in 2008, on a humanism of the twenty-first century clarify the tenacity of an almost tragicomic left tradition, in which self-declared humanists feel themselves compelled to pay homage to a *theoretical* anti-humanism.[49] If the classic Marxist dogmatism of inexorable progress in history was almost necessarily coupled with its accompanying practical and political voluntarism, *theoretical anti-humanism* in its inevitably apodictic form is just as necessarily accompanied by concessions to a *practical* humanism, which is only able with difficulty to draw its boundaries in relation to 'anything goes' liberalism. Yet, can one really divide theory and practice in that way? Can one really, like Frieder Wolf, publish a philosophical book on the necessity of a contemporary humanism and, in the same book, claim that this necessity would be of a purely practical nature? A nice example of those curiosities of the world spirit that one finds in such numbers amongst the friends of Adorno, Althusser and Foucault. And a nice example of the hegemonic strength of ruling thought that through the structuralist tradition has even implanted itself lastingly in oppositional minds.

As a sad consequence the Marxist Humanist Frieder Wolf explicitly rejects emancipatory concepts of man [*Menschenbilder*] and even demands a complete ban on images [*Bilderverbot*], because he can only conceive of such con-

---

49 See Wolf 2008; though one could also name many others.

cepts of man as comprehensively solidified and deterministic.[50] Yet the rejection of speculative, idealist concepts and images of man cannot, however, be the rejection of non-speculative, materialist concepts and images.

The same questionable apodictics of argumentation, however, also prevail where socialist humanism is countered by the argument that it not only all too often functioned in history as a 'gentle form of oppression', but also that it inevitably did this and also must inevitably do this in the future. That humanism, 'also humanism, the fighter against obsolete or an openly repressive system, is *nothing other* than an instrument of oppression', is one of the many variations in Werner Raith's booklet on *Humanism and Oppression*.[51] According to Raith (by no means the first and only, but one of the sharpest of these critics of a gentle, humanist oppression in the German-speaking world), humanism has a '*constantly and necessarily oppressive, repressive function*' in history and this, for him, is 'not a coincidental ... but rather a *fundamental* characteristic of humanism overall, *how ever* one may define it'.[52]

In this case too, it cannot be about denying how historical humanism (primarily the old bourgeois humanism, but also certain forms of a socialist humanism) contributed to the legitimation of exclusion and oppression by elite rule – the old socialist classics as far back as Franz Mehring or Karl Kautsky (the latter, for example, in his book on Thomas More) repeatedly address this. How near such temptation can be exemplified in Leo Kofler himself. Even at the end of the 1940s he let his early conception of a socialist humanism flow into a (reform Communist) apologia for Soviet Russian socialism, and spoke of marching in lockstep as the sure sign of the progress of humanity to ever higher stages of development.[53] His ensuing anti-Stalinist radicalisation shortly thereafter, however, clarifies not only that conceptually there are other ways, but also how such a consistent anti-Stalinism as is depicted above belongs to the 'essence' of socialist humanism (just like an understanding of Marxism as a philosophy of practice). The possible misuse of such a humanism does not make the matter itself obsolete, only more difficult to deal with. Against the backdrop of red detours in the twentieth century and discussions of possible renewal of socialist theory and practice, however, such difficulty must be endured and accordingly processed. 'Criticism has torn up the imaginary *flowers* from the chain not so that man shall wear the unadorned, bleak chain but so that he will shake off the chain and pluck the living *flower*'.[54]

---

50 Wolf 2008, p. 26.
51 Raith 1985, p. 9. My emphasis.
52 Raith 1985, pp. 17, 8. My emphases in the latter quotation.
53 See Kofler 1992, Vol. 2, pp. 320–1.
54 Marx 1975, p. 176.

We come now to that third great objection against any form of a socialist humanism, which correctly points out that such a conception always has something deeply and inherently ethical and normative about it, while, however, there exists an obvious difference between 'is' and 'ought', between 'idea' and 'interest', which has an abundantly complicating effect here. With some authority and in many respects convincingly, this argumentation runs like a common thread, for example, through the remarkable work of the German researcher of Marxism, Helmut Fleischer.[55]

Yet here again the main objection is one of methodology. In fact, socialist humanism is conceptually about the normative, the ethical, but where is it written that this only works in the form of an ethical *imperative*? The *lived ethos* that Fleischer correctly advocates for, conceptually, against an ethics of the imperative, is a form of ethics and morality. It is not necessarily moralism.[56] If one considers the great questions of our time and the everyday discussions of the humans living in it, it quickly becomes clear how common and central the question of normative coexistence is in these discussions, about what humans can afford to do, what man should or should not be allowed to do. While the world virtually teems with discourses about the ethical and about one's own as well as others' concepts of man, emancipatory forces can hardly stand aside, asserting the fundamental impossibility and senselessness of ethics and concepts of man:

> There can never be any question of denying anything that exists the right to exist. It is the movement within whatever exists which transforms the world, past, present or future, and not theories about what should be rejected and what should be preserved. The essential thing here is to denounce confusion with all its baggage of bad faith, guilty conscience, ideological duplicity, trickery and trumpery. Now this confusion is *lived* – in other words it intervenes in life and in the consciousness of life.[57]

History and politics indeed cannot be derived from the normative essence of man – this basic Marxist position is absolutely correct and important. Kofler himself was one of the sharpest critics of such an ethically conceived socialism. As he wrote in direct engagement with the newly emerging social-democratic theory of so-called 'ethical socialism':

---

55   Fleischer 1973, 1974, 1980, 1987.
56   See Jünke 2007a, pp. 519–20.
57   Lefebvre 1991, p. 193.

> The realm of 'pure' 'ought', to be sure, imparts a whole system of the good, just, beautiful and true, in the best case, also the right of man to 'self-determination', but not one sentence from which one is able to conclude how one should correctly act in a socialist manner. Ethical postulates are indeed 'generally binding', but in fact bind one to nothing as soon as action, practice begins.[58]

Kofler himself also stressed that there was not a Marxist ethics in the sense of a *theoretical system*,

> since inasmuch as theoretical ethics sets itself the goal of shedding light on the principles of individual conduct on the 'ought'. As experienced morally, in its general and i.e. also transhistorical application, it divides – at least in its starting point, in order ideally afterwards to bring the two poles together – the 'ought' (the normative) from the 'is' (the 'causal' or 'legal'). This division, however, contradicts the Marxist idea of the 'unity' of being, more precisely, the dialectical identity of opposites, which does not allow for a division of 'is' and 'ought'. This negation of ethics as a particular system is, however, only one such of the theory or – which here means the same thing – a negation of the traditional individualist and thereby idealist ethics. (Idealist here is equivalent to abstracting from the overall scope of being).[59]

Even if a thinker like Marx detested commonplaces and empty generalities and denied ethics as something abstract, an ethics was nevertheless not only immanently contained in his thought, but also permeated it with an almost 'ethical lustre'.[60] For Kofler, it pertains to the essence of man that

> man, acting in historical and social space and thrust to constant decision, must establish moral norms within his ideal mode of being if action is to be at all possible and meaningful for him. ... It is appropriate to the man endowed with consciousness, not only to strive after simple preservation of life like the animal, but also to make his natural disposition, grounded in the fact of the endowment of consciousness, into an ever advancing (if also never 'finally' attainable), social as well as individual, further and higher development of the impetus of the historical process.

---

58   Kofler 2000b, p. 82.
59   Kofler 2000a, p. 59.
60   Ibid.

> This basic disposition already shows itself in the simplest execution of human 'labour'; man changes not only his materials, but also, in developing his capacities and constantly revolutionising his relationship to his fellow humans in the work, himself, and his ingenuity is individual as well as that of the species, in which he participates in this or that form, even if he 'personally' was not thought to be ingenious. The animal lacking consciousness has only 'development'. Man carries out 'history' in consciousness of his self and in striving to make all the possibilities inherent in him reality, to 'realise himself'.[61]

Such sentences have a programmatic character and hence refer to the vision of a goal immanently inscribed on the human essence, without which the actual emancipation process cannot be established in the long run. Yes, between 'is' and 'ought' lies a gulf of actual history. But does this render untenable the programmatic demand for surmounting such a gulf as much as possible? Yes, the sense of reality of practical humanism is not the ethics of the imperative, but rather a practice-philosophical [*praxisphilosophisch*] deed of lived ethos. This, however, does not mean that one may not conceive this theoretically.

According to Eagleton:

> Because we are labouring, desiring, linguistic creatures, we are able to transform our conditions in the process we know as history. In doing so, we come to transform ourselves at the same time. Change, in other words, is not the opposite of human nature; it is possible because of the creative, open-ended, unfinished beings we are.[62]

Such a view interestingly draws on the socialist beginnings of the nineteenth century, when Moses Hess (even before Marx) spoke of an anthropology of socialism as a theory of the socialisation of man. What Moses Hess meant by this at the time, Eagleton trenchantly encapsulates for today:

> Only through others can we finally come into our own. This means an enrichment of individual freedom, not a diminishing of it. It is hard to think of a finer ethics. On a personal level, it is known as love.[63]

---

61   Kofler 2000a, p. 60.
62   Eagleton 2011, p. 81.
63   Eagleton 2011, p. 86.

For love means creating for another the space in which he might flourish, at the same time as he does this for you. The fulfilment of each becomes the ground for the fulfilment of the other. When we realize our natures in this way, we are at our best. This is partly because to fulfil oneself in ways which allow others to do so as well rules out murder, exploitation, torture, selfishness, and the like. In damaging others, we are in the long run damaging our own fulfilment, which depends on the freedom of others to have a hand in it. And since there can be no true reciprocity except among equals, oppression and inequality are in the long run self-thwarting as well. All this is at odds with the liberal model of society, for which it is enough if my uniquely individual flourishing is protected from interference by another's. The other is not primarily what brings me into being, but a potential threat to my being.[64]

When it comes to emancipation, we are thus dealing with a process of reciprocal self-realisation, a sociopolitical process in which the self-transformation of individuals coincides with the radically-democratic collective transformation of social conditions. That is naturally easier said than done. Socialists and Marxists know that a pertinent portion of instrumental practice also pertains to the realisation of this goal-idea, a radical politics that must not only, but also not least, rely on proletarian class struggle. They should, however, also know that these occasionally authoritarian means must not be allowed to take on a life of their own as a dictatorship of a minority (and this is essentially a question of their own political *forms*). For if there will ever be a socialist society, it will be a society in which each will derive their freedom and autonomy in and through the solidarity and self-development of the other.

Considered in this way, socialist humanism is as much a goal as a form of socialist politics. Yet a socialist humanism, thus understood, is no handbook of political practice, no direct instruction for action, no ethics of the authoritative imperative. It is a philosophy of neither consolation nor uplift, nor a ruling ideology. Such a socialist humanism is first, a powerful means of critique of what exists; second, a political and ethical criterion for the theory and practice of an emancipatory alternative; third, a means against apathy, a principle of hope as exhortation to the practical deed, to sociopolitical practice. Such a socialist humanism is grounded in an anthropology understood in a Marxist sense, i.e., it possesses a specific concept of man that satisfies scientific criteria, without establishing a dogma. Such a socialist humanism is based on a

---

64   Eagleton 2008, p. 97.

certain interpretation of Marx that emphasises the primacy of human freedom of action in the dialectical relationship of subject and object, of structure and human freedom of action, because such a Marxist critique is no passion of the head, but rather the head of human passion.

CHAPTER 5

The Debate over a Marxist Aesthetics: Going beyond Adorno and Lukács with Kofler and Lefebvre

If we consider the debate between Adorno, Lukács and others over a contemporary political aesthetics committed to a political and historical perspective, at the end of the 1950s and beginning of the 1960s, these words of Eric Hobsbawm in his *Age of Extremes* characterising that era are quickly confirmed: 'When people face what nothing in their past has prepared them for they grope for words to name the unknown, even when they can neither define nor understand it. Some time in the third quarter of the century we can see this process at work among the intellectuals of the West'.[1] In the following, the point is to scratch at the dichotomies of this old debate by recalling two other thinkers who intervened in the dispute, and with whom certain blockages can be productively resolved: Henri Lefebvre and Leo Kofler.

Henri Lefebvre and the Transition

One of the contemporaries of the third quarter of the twentieth century, who had already attempted to come to terms with the new historical situation and gave eloquent expression to the unknown, was the French Marxist Henri Lefebvre. In 1962, he published his twelve preludes to the *Introduction to Modernity*, in which he conceived of the 'modernity' that had finally established itself after the Second World War as a situation of historical transition. Considered politically, this transitional situation was the product of a defeated, absent revolution in the capitalist West and a bogged down, incomplete one in the 'socialist' East – the 'ghost of the Revolution which never happened over here, ... the ghost of the Revolution which was never completed over there':[2]

> Man's appropriation of his own nature (desire and sensual satisfactions) and the radical transformation of everyday life (prefigured by morality

---

1 Hobsbawm 1995, p. 287.
2 Lefebvre 1995, p. 236.

or art) were part of the initial Marxist programme for a total praxis, but they have not been achieved ... There is an increasingly intense feeling that the total revolutionary praxis which Marx thought would abolish all alienation has not been achieved ... Freedom remains a shattered ideal, confused, abstract but as powerful as ever ...[3]

Lefebvre conceives of freedom of such a type as a *third way*: 'Faced with a choice between the ultrarevisionism of those who insist that Marxism is exhausted as a current in modern thought, and the ultradogmatism of those who seek to perpetuate the results of the Stalinist period by pretending that its deviations were just a minor hiccup, we can therefore discern an alternative way, the way of dialectical critique, the way of irony'.[4] And this third way is for him more than 'only' an abstract programme – it is real. Writing in the transition of the 1950s to the 1960s, he observed:

> But now, worldwide, avant-gardes are forming again, and making their voice heard. It is an observable fact. But what is happening in these often miniscule little groups. ... How many of them are there? Not many.[5]

Yet the signs of a new 'attitude' already existed in droves:

> ... Acts of verbal or physical insubordination, rebellions, revolts, protests, abstentions, people trying to wipe the slate clean and start from scratch, failures and disappointments understood (as far as possible) and taken on board. There is a growing sense of disorder, and its causes and effects are becoming more and more apparent. Although it is confused, it can be identified. It is youth in ferment – not simply here in France, but on a world scale. As yet the indications are all negative.[6]

Lefebvre distances himself in a correspondingly negative fashion from the specific ideology of 'modernism' – that 'cult of innovation for innovation's sake, innovation as fetish', which he illustrates in central ideologemes such as the 'new life' or the (strikingly current) cult of youth.[7] On the other hand, the opposition still cultivates a cult of the proletariat, to which it is time to say

---

3 Lefebvre 1995, p. 229.
4 Lefebvre 1995, pp. 27–8.
5 Lefebvre 1995, p. 343.
6 Lefebvre 1995, p. 240.
7 Lefebvre 1995, p. 169.

farewell. There is no doubt the working class exists. For Lefebvre, it is also without a doubt, the social and political force of the highest rank, the potentially revolutionary force. However, one must admit and reflect that it had so far shown itself incapable of interrupting history and ending alienation: 'The proletariat is not revolutionary by ontological essence or by absolute structure. It is revolutionary in certain circumstances, but (given favourable circumstances) only the proletariat can be revolutionary right to the end'.[8] He concludes that, if the working class was no longer the solid and certain ground, the absolute criterion of action (the emphasis here lies on the adjectives, not on the nouns!), '[historical development] is a difficult, winding road, much more so than Marx and Lenin ever imagined'.[9]

What Henri Lefebvre formulates here theoretically and politically is the programme of the then powerfully developing so-called New Left, whose first clearly articulated forms and content date to the years 1955–7. It is also no coincidence that the Lukács-Adorno debate takes place in this regrouping phase of the socialist left. It was above all the restalinisation in East *and* West coming with the military suppression of the Hungarian uprising that led to a lasting renunciation of left hopes in the Communist world movement, without those turning automatically towards international social democracy – the 'Godesbergisation' of the latter was only a pointed German expression of general trends of the 1950s, which had little attraction for the disappointed left cadre and the young oppositional generation.[10]

Not only the tone of the debate between Adorno and Lukács, but also its political and aesthetic content was shaped by this historical and political context. Can Adorno and Lukács not stand here as examples of 'ultra-revisionism' on the one hand, and 'ultra-dogmatism' on the other? Is their contestation over the significance of organic (realistic) as well non- or anti-organic (avant-garde) works of art in contemporary society not a contestation over the question of where these transitional societies are going?

For both thinkers, as Peter Bürger trenchantly elaborated in his account of the Lukács-Adorno debate, the modern avant-garde is the expression of late capitalist alienation. For Lukács, however:

> ... it is also the expression of the blindness of bourgeois intellectuals vis-à-vis the real historical counterforces working towards a socialist trans-

---

8   Lefebvre 1995, p. 82.
9   Lefebvre 1995, p. 40.
10 In reference to the Social Democratic Party of Germany's 1959 Bad Godesberg Programme (trans. note).

formation of this society. It is on this political perspective that Lukács bases the possibility of a realistic art in the present. Adorno does not have this political perspective; therefore, avant-garde art becomes for him the only authentic art in late capitalist society ... Adorno not only sees late capitalism as definitively stabilized but also feels that historical experience has shown the hopes placed in socialism to be ill-founded. For him, avant-gardiste art is a radical protest that rejects all false reconciliation with what exists and thus the only art form that has historical legitimacy. Lukács, on the other hand, acknowledges its character as protest but condemns avant-gardiste art because that protest remains abstract, without historical perspective, blind to the real counterforces that are seeking to overcome capitalism.[11]

What we have before us is, in my view, the classic argument about whether the glass is half-full or half-empty. The opinion to which one inclines depends above all on the particular measuring stick. For Lukács the glass of avant-gardism is half-empty, because he believes himself in possession of the correct counter project – actually existing socialism, which he certainly did not consider the optimal possibility, but rather as the uncircumventable necessity and, therefore, historically and philosophically [*geschichtsphilosophisch*] justified. For Adorno and the left avant-gardistes the glass is half-full, because they don't consider actually existing socialism a real alternative. If, for Lukács, a half-empty glass is worthless, for Adorno a half-full glass is the best one can get. So who was, who is, right – Adorno or Lukács? Historical hindsight allows one to state that just as Lukács's historically and philosophically anchored hope in a self-reformation of erstwhile actually existing socialism showed itself to be wrong and fatal for the political left, Adorno's historical and philosophical spectre of an unquestioningly [*widerspruchslos*] administered world was equally wrong and fatal. Adorno's conception must, at the latest in times of societal rupture, be openly positioned against the counterforces working towards the overcoming of capitalism (the extra-parliamentary opposition). If one side of the debate absolutises the goal as the path, with 'socialist realism' the way out, the other dissolves this goal as a power of negation into the movement, into the artistic medium.

The question of who was right at the time was thus essentially a question of the measuring stick used. Just how difficult reaching a decision was is demonstrated by Kofler's intervention in the debate.

---

11   Bürger 1984, pp. 86, 88.

Kofler's Critique of Avant-Gardism

Leo Kofler's *Zur Theorie der modernen Literatur: Der Avantgardismus in soziologischer Sicht* [On the Theory of Modern Literature: The Avant-Garde in Sociological Perspective] was not without good reason considered by many contemporaries as a continuation of the Lukács-Adorno debate. However, they wrongly regarded him as a pure Lukácsian – a misunderstanding to which Kofler himself substantially contributed.

Kofler's treatment of artistic avant-gardism, *from a sociological perspective*, stands in the Lukácsian tradition as a critique of the naturalistic character of avant-gardism, starting from the premise that the bourgeois capitalist commodity society tears apart form and content, subject and object, abstract and concrete, general and particular. Incapable of grasping the totality of social processes, the bourgeois intellectual lapses into naturalism, that is, he transfigures the modern alienation on all sides into an imperishable, thus always existent [*soseienden*] – into a mythological consciousness of destiny. Like Lukács, Kofler also finds evidence of this in modern literature, and, with only very few exceptions, again in modern avant-gardism. He writes: 'Naturalism and expressionism both affix "the pathos of the free man" to an essentially undynamic, mechanical and, thereby, naturalistically understood world. This critique of this world takes place from the outside and not from the inside, not resulting out of the world's own dynamic'.[12] Despite all the intended depths, avant-gardism remained 'in the anarchist variety of expressionism, in depth psychological surrealism', on the surfaces of the poetically shaped subject, though which 'the truly contradiction-filled totality of human existence only barely [shines] through'.[13] The avant-gardist rebellion implies, despite subjective honesty, reconciliation with the bourgeois capitalist world, as the bourgeois flight into irrational subjectivity could not in principal succeed, 'because subjectivity with its differentiated interiority also proves itself under closer analysis to be a poor imitation of the reified external world'.[14]

Kofler shares this analytical approach with Lukács, as he also shares the Lukácsian alternative of a normative return to classical artistic realism, set upon a totality of observation and composition. Yet his concrete approach distinguishes itself lastingly and with decided originality from that of his teacher Lukács – not fundamentally, not principally, but rather in a gradual manner, which yields far-reaching, fundamental consequences. For even if he sided

---

12   Kofler 1974, p. 25.
13   Kofler 1974, p. 24.
14   Kofler 1974, p. 32.

vehemently with Lukács's, it remains unmistakable that Kofler, in purely practical terms, made many steps in the directions of the avant-gardistes. Bourgeois classicism could not, he wrote, be continued seamlessly under modern conditions. Bureaucratic, that is, actually existing socialist realism, was also not an alternative, but rather remained just as inescapably stuck in positivist naturalism. Since one could not get around avant-gardism, this implicitly meant a new synthesis between realism and avant-gardism – on the basis of a fundamentally renewed realism. Here the quantity of Koflerian 'deviation' from Lukács turns into a new quality, which above all expresses how openly Kofler, despite all his criticism, takes the side of a Franz Kafka or, even more, a Bertolt Brecht. Precisely because pseudo-critical nihilists like Nietzsche possessed a keen eye for the weaknesses and contradictions of all that exists, for their unrestrained, animalistic excesses – keener still than most realists – and precisely because avant-gardism had the historical merit of 'having at least energetically posed, in an admittedly false, but still clear manner' the problem of reified life in a nihilistic society; precisely because of this, according to Kofler, one could not get around avant-gardism.[15]

He illustrates this peculiarity of modern 'nihilism' above all with the work of Franz Kafka, who for him remains 'in his most inner core a paradox'.[16] Kafka, according to Kofler, believes in freedom, but mistrusts man. Kafka indeed strove for emancipation and freedom, yet at the time raises the reification *of human relations* to a reification *of man himself*, because he did not want or could not see the active and conscious side in the reification process. Thus he again and again is the creator of that 'twilight condition "between sleeping and waking", that Kafka loved so much as the moment of dawning [*aufleuchtender*] awareness and self-awareness in his depictions'.[17] A modern realism, admittedly, cannot adopt this 'half-nihilist avant-gardism', but it could however, 'still learn much from the seriousness and depth with which the trailblazer Kafka comprehended and treated alienation'.[18] Thus Kafka becomes 'even for those, who cannot befriend him to the last', an original, interesting and 'highly useful' author, who showed 'what today's realists for the most part lack, in order to be modern in the true sense of the word'.[19] That applies above all, but not only, to Kafka: 'Realism can no longer simply pass by the nightmare scenarios [*Schreckensbildern*] of Kafka and Beckett's images of "worldlessness" [*Weltlosigkeit*], if

---

15   Kofler 1974, p. 124.
16   Kofler 1974, p. 245.
17   Kofler 1974, p. 251.
18   Kofler 1974, pp. 255, 252.
19   Kofler 1974, p. 252.

it does not want to lack that self-imposed goal of critically grappling with all manifestations of alienation'.[20]

As much as Leo Kofler made himself into an adherent of aesthetic realism, to the same degree he knew that what went under the name of 'socialist realism' at the time was barely more than an undialectically flattened, out and out bureaucratic pseudo-realism. Therefore he avowedly relies on the 'cunning of reason', on 'the unintentional aid of nihilistic art in service of the assertion of the humanistic'.[21] The aim was to raise both decisive poles of realism and avant-gardism to a new level, to a renewed realism. The way there entailed the retention of classical art's essential features and the preservation of the humanist and dialectical conception of man as well the adoption of avant-gardism's formal techniques of tableau and representation. The only one who had at least begun to explore this path was Bert Brecht: 'Only in Brecht, who remains essentially realist, do [realism and avantgardism] meet in an original manner. He and Kafka are the two great exceptions, who require a specific approach'.[22] Only Brecht resolved the contradiction between classicism and avant-gardism 'in a genuine way, whereby going through expressionism was of enormous help to him'.[23] This striking turn by a supposed Lukácsian, defending Kafka and theorising Brecht, highlights Kofler's originality in the field of aesthetic theory, and earns particular regard – an originality that the already decidedly sparse secondary literature on Kofler has thus far not seen.[24]

Kofler's Theory of the Progressive Elite

The radical Brecht chapter of Kofler's *Theorie der modernen Literatur* goes directly back to the years 1957/58, Kofler developed his theory of the progressive elite using Brechtian aesthetics as an example. (This early theorisation of Brecht by Kofler has also, to my knowledge, never been appreciated or discussed in the compendious secondary literature on Brecht.) In November–December 1957 Kofler had published four small articles on Brecht in the left socialist weekly *Die Andere Zeitung*, which he afterwards assembled into a piece for the August 1958 issue of the left socialist monthly *Funken* under the title 'For

---

20 Kofler 1974, p. 106.
21 Kofler 1974, p. 107.
22 Kofler 1974, p. 19.
23 Kofler 1974, p. 24.
24 Recently Werner Jung (2001) has also wrongly attempted to reduce Kofler to a pure (and eclectic) Lukácsian.

an understanding of Bert Brecht', before this piece was then incorporated into *Zur Theorie der modernen Literatur*.

Starting from his assessment of the historical failure of social democracy and Stalinism, in 1957 Kofler posed the Hegelian question of who, then, practically embodied progress, if the forces responsible for it had failed. He therefore saw world history in a transitional stage, in which a new progressive/humanistic group/layer/movement had formed – he termed them the progressive elite (with elite not meant as an evaluative, but rather a sociological, description) – that was not to be distinguished by the old dividing lines of socialism and non-socialism, but instead was composed of progressive-minded people of socialist and non-socialist origin 'cutting across the traditional, social and ideological fronts'.[25] Dissident communists struggling against the half-measures of destalinisation; oppositionist social democrats and trade unionists struggling against bureaucratisation and integration; radical democratic citizens [*Bürger*] and socially engaged Christians – they are all united by their fundamental opposition to the dominant anti-humanism and nihilism in the late bourgeois society and formed 'an amorphous mass of a strongly fluctuating character', heterogeneous in their social and political composition, heterogeneous in their social and political views, heterogeneous in their appearance [*Habitus*].[26] 'Many "socialists" today, mostly without knowing it, stand where the tide of historical progress is being resisted; many who are sceptical about socialism, but who have preserved a liberal-progressive consciousness and struggle desperately against succumbing to the process of human deformation, wind up on the same side as socialism'. The progressive elite, according to Kofler, due to its transitional historical and sociological character, inevitably wavers between the justified and productive inclination towards ironic-utopian optimism, and counterproductive untenable utopianism shading into nihilism. It could progressively and humanistically renew the revolutionary movement, but it could also turn into the fig leaf of regressive tendencies, the embodiment of dominant nihilism, if one does not draw a clear line between nihilism and humanism. What directly connected this 'progressive elite' with Bert Brecht was 'the same movement into the ironic', 'the humanistic ideal, clearly or ambiguously shaped by the critical opposition against today's society', which, however, precisely because of the disappointment over the failure of progressive forces, appeared 'with features permeated with melancholy and desire' and 'in ironic brokenness'.[27]

---

25   Kofler 1960, p. 347.
26   Kofler 1960, p. 346.
27   Kofler 2000c, pp. 140–1.

Brecht's artistic work, per Kofler in *Zur Theorie der modernen Literatur*, was characterised entirely by the absence of a revolutionary workers' movement. Yet Brecht at least knew that this absence is also the cause of the apparent all-powerful conquest of mass consciousness by the day-to-day tendencies of alienation. He knew that it is the fault of the organised workers' movement if the population are missing the theoretical and practical means of resistance. 'Brecht belongs in this sense to the disappointed. But he is differently disappointed than the great current of the disappointed since Hitler's seizure of power; he fought on in his own way'.[28] On the one hand this led to Brecht's aesthetic also being a form of flight, as he circumvented the representation of the contemporary proletarian fate for lack of the original remnants of that pertinent milieu. On the other hand, he consistently adhered to his progressive and optimistic image of humanity. His realism transformed itself into what was, by and large, a symbolic realism, whose specific attribute was a certain form of irony. His consistent optimism connected itself in a specific manner with a 'philosophical' humour-filled scepticism, through which the optimism was both limited and strengthened at the same time.[29]

However, while such an ironically-broken optimism 'produces the connection between the powers of alienation and the striving for self-realisation, and elevates the contradiction resting therein into the problem', humour and irony in nihilistic art are absolutely dispassionate, because they are directed completely at the interior of the subject. Because the human as a grotesque no longer recognised the liberating smile, humour deteriorated [*verkomme*] into shallow comedy, into mere caricature.[30] Brecht's accomplishment was, in contrast, that he 'never let himself be misled to make concessions to the mood of desperation', and that with him the intellect was not crushed by emotion, but rather encouraged.[31]

Kofler's interpretation of Brecht makes him, as he writes in *Zur Theorie der modernen Literatur*, into a consummate poetic embodiment of his theory of the progressive elite. In this context, however, Kofler's 'Lukácsian' critique of avant-gardism acquires a markedly different accent. In these passages, the neo-classicist Lukács speaks far less than Henri Lefebvre, who called himself a neo-romantic, precisely to set himself apart from Lukács.[32] This is no coincidence, as it is precisely in his theory of the progressive elite that Kofler, like Lefebvre,

---

28   Kofler 1974, p. 208.
29   Kofler 1974, p. 216.
30   Kofler 1974, p. 103.
31   Kofler 2000c.
32   Lefebvre 1965, p. 9.

assumes a yet more indistinct world-historical phase of transition, which fed itself from the 'failure' of the old socialist forces, oriented to a 'third way', and, of central importance, was accordingly thrown back on irony as the methodology of knowledge acquisition. This approach is hardly compatible with Lukács's 'actually existing socialist' ['*realsozialistisch*'] approach.

In my opinion, Kofler is dealing here with an unresolved but revealing conceptual contradiction that he only insufficiently saw and, extensively concealing it by verbal loyalty to Lukács, drowned out. This contradiction between the political theory of the progressive elite – a theory that he never systematically developed – and Kofler's political aesthetic now unfolded on a seemingly peripheral, yet nevertheless conceptually essential question. How does one relate as a non-contemplative Marxist socialist, aiming to intervene, to a new contradictory period, whose central antagonisms, whose strengths and weaknesses, whose historical right is understood just as well as its historical illusions? How does one position oneself, what *attitude* does one have?

In terms of questions of political aesthetic, this means: Is avant-gardism (i.e. modernism) as historical form merely a phenomenon of political and intellectual decay, so that one can demand of individual artists that they appropriately rectify their thinking? Or does avant-gardism mirror that structurally transformed societal reality addressed by Kofler, which reality time and time again twists human thought with the entire power of societal objectivity, with the burden of late bourgeois everyday life?[33] A renewed form of realistic art is, in Marxist terms, dependent on there being – as at the beginning of the bourgeois epoch and as Fredric Jameson has argued – concrete historical forces of change, whose expression is precisely that realism.[34] What if, however, these 'forces responsible for progress in history' (Kofler) are just not up to their task and do not represent any concrete historical forces of emancipatory change? What if, along with the lack of such a concrete historical milieu, there is almost inevitably a want of realist artists? Can one, if late bourgeois alienation has ever more comprehensively buried itself in the individual (as Kofler himself determined), still rely on the *naïveté* of the artistic individual, as Kofler did? Can one, under the conditions of the absent revolution here, and the incomplete one over there, criticise art and artistic theory in the same manner as in a time when such a practically effective alternative to false bourgeois thought existed? A purely polemical and exposing critique of avant-gardism evidently misses the historical necessities here.

---

33   See Kofler 1960, Kofler 1964, and Kofler 1967.
34   Jameson 1974, p. 209.

Kofler's Intervention in the Adorno-Lukács Debate

Kofler therefore made it too easy for himself, in my opinion, when he defended Lukács against Adorno in the two essential questions under debate: the question of Lukács's attitude to Stalinism and Lukács's conception of realism. Against Adorno's accusation that Lukács dared only a timid, powerlessly crippled opposition to Stalinism, Kofler asserted Lukács's personal bravery and his anti-Stalinist attacks. In relation to Adorno's attack on aesthetic realism, he was indignant that Adorno degraded his old teacher Lukács and 'his subtle and ramified theory of realism' as a representative of a vulgar Marxist, bureaucratic concept of realism.[35]

The first answer is the weakest. Adorno had emphasised in 1958, i.e. immediately in the wake of the re-Stalinisation of the Communist world movement of 1957–8, in his review essay on Lukács's work *The Meaning of Contemporary Realism*, precisely the 'signs of a different attitude on the part of the seventy-five-year-old Lukacs', and even defended these.[36] 'Lukács's personal integrity is beyond question', Adorno writes in regards to the accusation cited by Kofler, that Lukács only 'ventures a timid opposition, crippled from the outset by a consciousness of his own impotence'.[37] Yet Lukács's book only offered 'something between the so-called thaw and a renewed freeze'.[38] 'To do justice to his book one must bear in mind that in countries where the crucial things cannot be called by name, the marks of official terror have been branded onto everything said in their place. But conversely, because of this even ideas that are weak and deflected, half-ideas, acquire a force in that constellation that their literal content does not have'.[39] Adorno above all refers here to Lukács's last chapter on critical realism in socialist society, and one can hardly dispute his view of things. What should one make of a thinker who, like Lukács, emphasises in the foreword to his work that he must finally 'no longer [speak] in *Aesopian* language' and then, in that last chapter, explains amongst others things, that it 'would be slanderous to assert that during the Stalinist period socialist democracy, or the socialist basis of economic construction, was totally destroyed. Yet the true face of socialism can only re-emerge if the forces working against it during past decades are eliminated [in the present and appro-

---

35 Kofler 1974, p. 96.
36 Adorno 1991, p. 217.
37 Ibid.
38 Adorno 1991, p. 218.
39 Adorno 1991, p. 237.

priately criticised in the past]'.⁴⁰ Is this not the old (*Aesopian*) attempt to render unto Caesar (here: the ruling bureaucracy) what is Caesar's, in order then to convince him all the more to listen to the wisdom of the loyal philosopher?

In this work Lukács once again hedges his perspective on historical Stalinism and the actually existing 'Stalinist' bureaucracy in convoluted language. Lukács also does not go beyond denunciations of 'sectarian, bureaucratic' 'narrowness' and 'distortion' [*Entstellung*], of 'mistakes, indeed crimes, of the Stalinist regime'.⁴¹ He conceals its role in his treatment of the historical conditions 'hardly favourable to the growth of critical realism'.⁴² In this work, Lukács also unreservedly promulgates the newest strategic turns of the ruling bureaucracy, when he declares the struggle for peace as central, and emphasises the necessity of national communist paths.⁴³ One may in part find Adorno's irony tipping over into cynicism problematic, but it surely does not miss its mark as the indictment culminates, diagnosing Lukács' claim that the overcoming of enduring societal antagonism has occurred in actually existing socialism (a 'barefaced lie', according to Adorno) as being founded in that 'spell that holds Lukács in its power and bars his longed-for return to the utopia of his youth', and 'reenacts the extorted reconciliation he himself detected in absolute idealism'.⁴⁴

Kofler is right to say that Adorno had underestimated the extent of Lukács's personal integrity and his personal resistance to the Stalinist bureaucracy. However, that changes nothing with regards to Adorno's fundamental evidence that Lukács's principal loyalty to actually existing socialism's rulers could not be shaken – even in his last, posthumously published and de facto anti-Stalinist work *Socialism and Democratisation* [*Sozialismus und Demokratisierung*] the apologia for historical Stalinism prevails.⁴⁵

---

40   Lukács 1969, pp. 9, 133. The English translations have been slightly modified based on the German originals and a missing clause added. The published English translation is based on revisions made by Lukács in 1962. (trans. note)
41   Lukács 1969, pp. 108, 111. The English translation lacks 'distortion' and changes 'of the Stalinist regime' to 'committed in the Stalinist period' (trans. note).
42   Lukács 1969, p. 91. The Kofler of the 1950s and 1960s (not of the 1940s and 1980s) consistently pointed out with polemical sharpness that experiences with historical Stalinism were and are also crucially responsible for the Western, industrially higher developed population not backing attempts at socialism in the West (see Chapter 3).
43   Lukács 1969, pp. 15, 109–10.
44   Adorno 1991, p. 240.
45   Lukács 1987. For a critical discussion of Lukács's book, see Christoph Jünke 2007b, Chapter 2 ('Georg Lukács' Probleme sozialistischer Demokratisierung').

More convincing, in contrast, is Kofler's defence of artistic realism. As pleasant as it is when Adorno fulminates against the glib use of 'the abusive term "decadent"' (to be 'stigmatized of decadent' covered 'all the atrocities of persecution and extermination, and not only in Russia'); as correct as it is to warn against a dialectical identity (unity) of art and science ('as though works of art merely anticipated something perspectivally which the social sciences then diligently confirmed'), it is, however, questionable to refer to '[c]onceptions like Beckett' (226) as 'objectively polemical' (226), because they 'become objectified through unqualified monadological immersion in their own formal laws, that is, aesthetically, and thereby mediated in their social basis as well' (230–1).[46] With Adorno and this line of argument, the shocking representation of senselessness becomes an emancipatory act. Kofler fittingly responds:

> Anyone who considers the depiction of the alienated and negative to be critique, merely because it is unreservedly and openly performed, errs. In this sense nihilism has always been 'critical'. It is an old truth that only the fundamental affirmer (the optimist) is critical, because he possesses a criterion, while the fundamental negator has still resigned and reconciled himself ... The shock that modern art allegedly transfers to the audience runs in the opposite direction: instead of liberation, shackling occurs.[47]

One can confidently ignore Kofler's polemically excessive phrase 'fundamental affirmer' here; the criticism remains unchanged. Avant-gardism as a 'force of negation' tends to remain stuck in that negativism, which is not infrequently crowned with an icing of cynicism. This latent nonconformist conformism – Kofler refers to it as naturalism – of avant-gardism can be disputed today as to its reach, but not in regards to its content.[48] The provocateur, this epitome of the avant-gardists, has not only extensively forfeited his subversiveness in this postmodern, neoliberal era, he has, in fact, mutated into one of the cultural and political henchman shouldering it. Under these conditions, Fredric Jameson pleaded as early as the late 1970s for a return to realism as the last subversion of the aesthetic conventions of modernism, for 'when modernism and its accompanying techniques of "estrangement" have become the dom-

---

46   Adorno 1991, pp. 231, 219, 226, 227, 230–1.
47   Kofler 1974, pp. 231 and 242.
48   Even an author as sympathetically-minded to the avant-gardists as Peter Bürger grounded his defence of the avant-garde at the beginning of the 1970s, interestingly enough, in its early form at the beginning of the twentieth century and explicitly detached the existing late form under discussion from his defence.

inant style whereby the consumer is reconciled with capitalism, the habit of fragmentation itself needs to be "estranged" and corrected by a more totalizing way of viewing phenomena'.[49]

With the same sensitivity that allows Adorno to perceive the embeddedness [*Eingebundenheit*] of Lukács's political and aesthetic positions in the actually existing socialist straitjacket, and its character of a normative 'educational dictatorship', Lukács conversely understood that Adorno's nonconformism carried along with it a notable conformist snag. Given that Kofler perceived the non-comformist conformity of an Adorno in the same manner as Lukács, and this entirely independently of him, Lukács's strengths were immediately apparent to him. Lukács's weaknesses, his character of a normative 'educational dictatorship', his embeddedness [*Einbettung*] in the ideological system of actually existing socialism, were, in contrast, misjudged as well as downplayed by Kofler, because he shared the ambivalences of Lukács's attitude, admittedly not to the same degree, but trending in the same direction. Kofler therefore could also not understand the strengths of Adorno's attack and sided – as he always did, if he saw Lukács attacked – with his revered teacher.

Kofler defending Lukács here beyond what is justifiable also has to do with him being far more sensitive than Adorno to opposition strategies of intellectuals under actually existing socialism, and hence knowing that an apologia for Stalinism did not necessarily make the apologist a Stalinist. On the other hand, Kofler also asserted his own limits in his attitude to 'actually existing socialism' precisely in his aesthetic writings when he understood modern aesthetics as merely consisting of three essential trends – first, the modern nihilistic avant-gardism; second, the moribund bourgeois critical realism; third, socialist realism à la Lukács.[50] The idea, self-evident in his own schematic and invoked in the same breath, of considering the 'Stalinist pseudo-realism' as a fourth distinct stream – for example, as worker-bureaucratic realism – did not occur to Kofler. For, like Lukács, he also proceeded from the illusory assumption that Stalinism along with its aesthetics were, ultimately, only a vestige of former times.

There remains a third reason for Kofler's partisanship. He considered the thinkers of the Frankfurt school as typical exponents of that progressive elite, wavering back and forth between humanism and nihilism, as the theoretical expression of precisely the nihilistic wing of a new Hegelian left that he had personally resolved to combat (see Chapter 6). In Kofler's confrontation with

---

49 Jameson 1979, p. 211.
50 Kofler 1974, p. 165.

Frankfurt critical theory, it was therefore obvious to defend Lukács, Frankfurt's main target, even to excess.

It is certainly correct to emphasise that Lukács's work '[is] a singular demonstration that he energetically fought the sensualistic and naturalistic version of reflection that is rampant in Stalinistically-misunderstood Marxism, especially by declaring the subjective moment, the personal character, and the particular fate of the individual poet and thinker to be a decisive co-determining factor in the formation of artistic and theoretical perspectives, that is to say, he left ample leeway for their subjective imagination'. Yet Adorno didn't claim that – at least not in that way. If Kofler accused Adorno of improperly attempting to blend classical realism and modern avant-gardism – an accusation moreover that indirectly confirms Adorno was not entirely so averse to realism as claimed – then Kofler had to remember that he himself indirectly called for such a new synthesis.

Why Choose?

Interestingly, then, it is precisely Henri Lefebvre who went down a differently accentuated path than Kofler in the question of aesthetics, which for him was the question of the aesthetic foundations of the 'new attitude'. In *Introduction to Modernity*, Lefebvre defends the modernist currents of surrealism and Dadaism, amongst others, against the Moscow party bureaucracy and Western Communists as a necessary contribution in the struggle for a left modernity. The Communist movement had turned away from this modernity, and tried 'to absorb the classical tradition and its art forms, which seemed quintessentially to belong to the bourgeoisie, within'.[51] Lefebvre formulates his principal reservation against that 'socialist realism' whose 'political excursions in this domain have left behind a blood-drenched wasteland', and as an imitative art, 'imitated – and goes on imitating – a social nature: that which has been established as real, order installed or restored, the real as conceived by political and military power'.[52]

The principles of socialist realism that he sides with, to consciously make oneself politically and socially useful and reflect new political possibilities, are not something that Lefebvre considers false, but rather as 'clear and coherent (overly coherent)':[53]

---

51 Lebebvre 1995, pp. 104. The quotations here have been at times modified to be closer to the German translation (trans. note).
52 Lefebvre 1995, pp. 249, 242.
53 Lefebvre 1995, p. 272.

Our principal reservation with regards to socialist realism, however, applies to its aspiration and tendency to change the partial into the total, the basic into the absolute, and means into ends. Furthermore it leads to works that, as soon as the interest aroused by the 'content' of these basic determinants has been exhausted, become boring ... In this dialogue of the deaf, there is no agreement about praxis and no agreement about theoretical concepts. One side talks about art (by which it means not necessarily just art for art's sake, but also beauty, which it believes in, or pretends to believe in, or no longer believes in, without really worrying too much about it) – and the other side talks about something else: polemics, ideological struggle, political directives. Why choose? In Stendhal's vision – and this is what gives it its value – choice is absurd and monstrous; it results in mutilation and one-sidedness. To choose, to want art as commitment [*Engagement*] and not art as beauty – that is, if beauty and art still mean anything – is to prefer the part to the whole. It is like defining love as reproduction. Why renounce fun, the game? Who has (and with what right) banished pleasure? Who has turned the romanticism of revolution into a moralising neoclassicism?[54]

Here, Henri Lefebvre does not take the side of artistic modernism any more than he takes the side of socialist realism. 'I would like to consider a supersession of romanticism and classicism which would also be a supersession of art, but would have the restitution of the romantic spirit as its fulcrum, while rejecting the consequences and degeneracies of the attitude which now bears its name; I would like to aim my sharpest criticisms at neoclassicism'.[55]

Lefebvre takes his insight, here, into the transitional character of his era (transition, possibility, third way, irony) in a more conceptually serious fashion than Kofler does. Due to that, he distinguishes himself from Kofler above all on the question of the analytical and political-theoretical *attitude* to take. In a fragmented, disjointed, and multiply differentiated world we must, according to Lefebvre, grasp the differences and unite that, 'if possible, what was divided ... We must never be reductive, we must never parenthesise, except provisionally'.[56] That Kofler lacks in contrast such a sovereignty has something to do with his biography and his character; more still and mainly with the specific development of the German left. Nevertheless, Kofler and Lefebvre are two pillars of

---

54   Lefebvre 1995, pp. 272–3.
55   Lefebvre 1995, pp. 362–3.
56   Lefebvre 1995, p. 43.

a third way in the age of transition, who have come nearer to aesthetics from two different ends.

For Kofler, aesthetics functions as a means of what he called from his first work, *Die Wissenschaft der Gesellschaft* (1944), the Marxist goal. In the same way that this was for him a normative imperative, so was aesthetics also a question of ethics. How must literature be created in order not to be an accomplice of dominant social conditions and powers? That was, for him, the decisive question of such a normative aesthetics. He could not satisfy himself thereby with the avant-gardist answer – that such an aesthetics must be entirely different, the strength of negation, for such an aesthetics, only able to find its immanent criterion in the overcoming of given conditions, but not in that to which this overcoming should lead, must sooner or later be disappointed and accommodate itself to the status quo.

Kofler saw in the aesthetic views of a part of the progressive elite – in my view, correctly – an indication of that elite's structurally-embedded nihilism, but he fought against it in a form that was not especially apt to pull over to his side those members of the elite who, according to his own analysis, were and are inevitably volatile.[57] However, the path from underestimation to ignorance of the strength of negation is not far. The more Koflerian aesthetics would find its purpose in the 1970s and 1980s to expand, with an epistemological critique, on the 'eternal', anthropological principles of beauty, the timeless rules of art, the more he threatened to lose sight of the question of whether and to what extent this can be a practical aesthetic contribution to liberation from late bourgeois conditions. Art as beauty here finally displaced art as commitment. Once more methodical generalisation of the principle of totality revealed its problematic nature, to the detriment of the practical political process of the historically concrete class struggle (in the widest sense of the word), completing itself through particularities. As Terry Eagleton rightly asks:

> Is Marxism ... just a matter of seeing reality steadily and seeing it whole? To parody Lukács's case a little: is revolution simply a question of making *connections*? And is not the social totality, for Marxism if not for Hegel,

---

57 As Kofler had already written in 1962 in *Zur Theorie der modernen Literatur*: 'Yet the ingenious and unscrupulous equation of anti-nihilist realism with kitsch that expresses itself in such attacks [of Adorno against Lukács] repudiates only the "modern" enthusiast himself and exposes his dialectically disguised nihilistic sting in the tail' (Kofler 1974, p. 95). The anticipatory strength and truth of this sentence ought to have made itself clear at the latest in the 1990s, as the fashion of a new cynical left intelligentsia to fulminate against other leftists as 'do-gooders' passed over into the cultural mainstream of the entire society.

'skewed' and asymmetrical, twisted out of true by the preponderance within it of economic determinants?[58]

Kofler's aesthetic conservatism lies less therefore, in my view, in the anthropological theorisation of classical realism, as it were, than in its political utility, in the methodical importance that Kofler also assigned to aesthetics. Kofler, and he shares this with Lukács as well as with Adorno (not, however, with Lefebvre), stands in the tradition of a Marxist cultural critique that tends to dissolve politics into culture, conceiving of emancipatory processes that can only take place politically as essentially cultural.[59] For Lefebvre, on the other hand, socialism, that is, the socialist movement, is not only a programme to be realised, but also a lifestyle. In the face of a world-historical transition, in the face of an almost completely alienated and reified everyday life, it is necessary 'to produce everyday life, consciously to create it'.[60] Socialism, i.e., the socialist movement, had however not yet found the necessary lifestyle for it. 'Socialism cannot work magic … Socialism has to find its own style too'.[61]

Those who seek productive dialogue between long hostile positions and currents can take up such an insight. A fundamentally renewed socialist movement – ever less in view, but also more necessary than ever – must bind anew the dialectical threads of goals and means, of totality and contradiction, of theory and practice. Just as such a movement distinguishes itself through its criticism as a force of negation, it cannot limit itself in its criticism to negation. It requires a critical criterion from the beginning that is nourished, essentially, by an anthropological and utopian image of man as by the search for a sociologically valid political path to its realisation. To read Lukács anew without his latent embeddedness in an educational dictatorship is as exciting as a new reading of Adorno without his latent embeddedness in a nihilistic pessimism.

And art? It will be in this process what it once was: the expression of new movements and requirements, not their historical and philosophical replacement.

58 Eagleton 1991, p. 100.
59 See the powerful critique in Mulhern 2000 and Mulhern 2002.
60 Lefebvre 1995, p. 124.
61 Ibid.

CHAPTER 6

Pseudo-Nature and Pseudo-Critique: Krahl, Kofler, and the Critique of the Frankfurt School Intended for Practice

> Alienation is never the entire person, even in situations of general alienation.
>
> LEO KOFLER, 1962

∴

Hans-Jürgen Krahl's Critique

On the occasion of the death of Theodor W. Adorno at the beginning of August 1969, one of his most talented students and a leading activist of the Socialist German Student League [*Sozialistischer Deutscher Studentenbund*, SDS], Hans-Jürgen Krahl, wrote a notable obituary in the *Frankfurter Rundschau*. This was not only because he was trying to formulate what was specific to Adorno's work within those confines. He also drew a line to the political debates of the period around 1968 in general and more specifically to the political debates between the Frankfurt SDS and Adorno, which had recently caused a commotion across West Germany.

Krahl begins his obituary with the assessment that Adorno's intellectual biography '[is] marked even unto its aesthetic abstractions by the experience of fascism'.[1] Adorno himself came up with the famous image of the 'damaged life' for this. Without much of a detour, Krahl comes to speak of what, in his opinion, this damaged life represents in Adorno. He was not able, writes Krahl, 'to transform this private passion in light of the suffering of the damned of the earth ... into an organised partisanship of theory for the liberation of the oppressed'. He continues:

> Adorno's social theoretical insight, which accordingly sees 'the afterlife of National Socialism in democracy as potentially more threatening than the

---

1 Krahl 1971a.

afterlife of fascist tendencies against democracy', allowed his progressive fear [*Furcht*] of a fascist stabilisation of restored monopoly capitalism to turn into a regressive anxiety [*Angst*] towards the forms of practical resistance against this tendency of the system.

The linchpin of Krahl's Adorno critique thus deals with the famous problem of theory and praxis. Adorno, according to Krahl, shares 'the ambivalence of political consciousness of many critical intellectuals in Germany', who denounce 'every [act of] praxis *a priori* as blindly actionistic' and do not know how to distinguish between 'an in principle correct pre-revolutionary praxis and its manifestations as an infantile disorder in emerging revolutionary movements'. Like no other, Adorno had communicated the 'authority-unveiling emancipatory categories', yet Adorno's own negation of late capitalist society remained abstract and had, as Krahl says, 'closed off the requirement of the determinacy of the determinate negation'. This still abstract critique of the student protest movement had driven Adorno into a 'complicity with the ruling forces that he himself barely perceived'.

A few months later, at the end of 1969, Krahl came back around to the topic of the immanent contradictions of critical theory. The achievement of critical theory is, for Krahl, the theoretical recognition of society as pseudo-nature, secondary nature, the recognition of reification and fetishisation. In this way, the whole of society is made apparent as a totality of dominance. Critical theory, according to Krahl, thus shares with the bourgeois tradition of German idealism the insight into the meaning of the concept of totality. On the other hand, it shares with the proletarian tradition the materialisation of this concept of totality, its expansion of content with regard to commodity production and circulation of exchange. However, as Krahl writes concerning what is missing here, 'the practical class standpoint, to say it for once in such a reified way, did not go into the theory in a theoretically constitutive way'.[2]

Krahl here recognises a bogging down in bourgeois individualism that also demonstrates itself in the uncritical adoption of psychoanalysis, which fundamentally remains fixated on bourgeois individuality. Ignored thereby are the individuation processes in the proletarian milieu, which are fundamentally mediated by class organisations. Political organisation is an object-constitutive practice as well, and this level was not seen by Adorno and the other members of the Frankfurt School – a practice therefore, which first unfolds as the practical object of politics. It is, however, still enforced by the irrationality of

---

2 Krahl 1971b.

abstract work, but already contained within it the overcomings [*Aufhebungen*] of the same, a type of solidaristic association, and in this way leads to another unity of the world of perception and concept.

Hans-Jürgen Krahl alludes to the fact that parts of the academic intelligentsia, whom he – in Marxist terms – includes in the conception of the modern worker as a whole [*Gesamtarbeiter*], can also organise outside of the traditional labour movement, and through the means of their organisation, are in a position to set societal-wide emancipatory processes in motion, which can take on a revolutionary character. Meant here are naturally the SDS and comparable organisational forms that Krahl sees as revolutionary subjects, which are in the position to develop political consciousness and political object-constitutive practice and, in this way, to break out of the cage of the administered world [*verwalteten Welt*].

This is an interesting thesis that would reward examination. However, that is not what concerns me in the following section. My point of departure is also not that one of the most talented Marxists of German post-war history – a student of Adorno and at the same time a central leading figure of the Frankfurt as well as the West German SDS – made a critique at the height of the '68 revolts, and from within the tradition of the Frankfurt School itself, that has not lost its sharpness and currency. What I am above all concerned with is that in 1969 such a critique was not at all as new as it appeared.

Horkheimer, Adorno, and their pupils influenced the West German left as early as the 1950s and early 1960s. At that time they were already correspondingly respected by and challenged from the left. One can read some of that in Alex Demirović's important work on the Frankfurt School.[3] Demirović, however, limits himself in his account to the critique of Horkheimer/Adorno coming from the ranks of the SDS. In 1957, he cites the critique of the student Tworeck from that year as an initial typical example: criticising Horkheimer/Adorno as having retreated into the ivory tower and shunning politics as they would fire. In more explicitly political milieus they encountered reservations that were just as strong. This criticism, however, was never formulated or theorised. For example, Theo Pirker, who as an associate of Victor Agartz in the 1950s was one of the central figures in the left socialist wing of the trade union movement, made his not atypical disapproval of the Frankfurt sociologists clear in his memoirs.[4] A further example is Wolfgang Abendroth, who, however, first revealed his likewise firm critique of the Frankfurters after 1968.

---

3   Demirović 1999a, Chapter 7.
4   Jander 1988, p. 56.

The historical credit of being the first to criticise, theoretically and fundamentally, the social philosophy of the Frankfurt school, belongs however to the German-Austrian sociologist and philosopher Leo Kofler. From the beginning of the 1960s a comprehensive critique of what he later came to call 'Marxo-Nihilism' pervades Kofler's wide body of work. His ambitious attempt to formulate an alternative social philosophy to that of the Frankfurt School was completely pushed aside at the time and is largely forgotten today.

Leo Kofler's Critique

Leo Kofler, who had been living in West Germany since the end of 1950, had already come to know Max Horkheimer, Theodor W. Adorno, and Friedrich Pollock at the beginning of the 1950s, immediately after his relocation from Halle to Cologne. He even hoped at the beginning to be able to work at the Frankfurt Institute for Social Research. Even after this had foundered, he maintained good connections with Frankfurt and approvingly cited Adorno in particular in his writings. In his private letters, however, he gave free rein to his discontent by the end of the 1950s. Thus, for example, his complaining to the young Frankfurt SDS comrade Oskar Negt that 'Adornoian prepotency (in order to not use a sharper expression) has gripped individuals of their group and has not let them out of their clutches'. Here, in this early document of rupture, it becomes clear that Kofler's critique of Adorno and critical theory was not insignificantly fed by his practical experiences with his students, whom he knew well – for Kofler was one of the most requested speakers in the Frankfurt SDS in the 1950s, especially in the latter half of that decade.[5] Kofler's Adorno critique is, from the beginning onwards, less a critique of a specific thinker and more a critique of the *Frankfurt School* establishing itself at that time. Adorno is 'only' important insofar as he lay the groundwork for those who became known as the second generation of the Frankfurt School in the 1960s.

Kofler first criticised Adorno openly in his 1962 work *Zur Theorie der modernen Literatur: Der Avantgardismus in soziologischer Sicht*. Following – quite independently – Georg Lukács's aesthetic writings, he criticises the modern artistic avant-garde. At the end of the 1950s, the publication of Lukács's *Wider den missverstandenen Realismus* had brought forth manifold criticisms from Western literary specialists and reviewers, including Adorno.[6] Kofler now defended Lukács' vindication of a non-Stalinist understanding of socialist realism

---

5 See Demirović 1999b and Jünke 2007a, Chapter 5.
6 Published in English in 1963 as *The Meaning of Contemporary Realism*. (trans. note)

and accused Adorno of misunderstanding Lukacs's approach as half-Stalinist and of wanting to illicitly associate realism and avant-gardism. With Adorno, the shocking depiction of senselessness became an emancipatory act, according to Kofler. Yet it is exactly the artistic avant-garde that he considers a modern pseudo-oppositional nihilism, from which one must theoretically distance oneself as a Marxist socialist:

> He who believes the depiction of the alienated and negative to be criticism, only because it is ruthlessly and openly performed, errs. In this sense nihilism was always 'critical'. It is an old truth that only the fundamental affirmer (the optimist) is critical, because he possesses a benchmark, while the fundamental negator has always resigned and reconciled himself.[7]

Kofler expanded this criticism, at first confined to questions of aesthetics, in 1964. Initially, in an essay dedicated to Marxist aesthetics in a student periodical he spoke of the ontologisation of alienation by Adorno.[8] In his work *Der proletarische Bürger*, he accuses the Frankfurt School of sociologists of a positivist narrowing of thought. On the one hand being critical and left-wing, on the other hand reconciling oneself with alienated reality. Adorno was subject – not least because of 'justified aversion to the Eastern terror' – to the ideological and moral pressure of the West and had cleansed the dialectic 'of all its intrinsically appertaining objectives of the "realisation of philosophy"'.[9] Once again, Kofler refers to Adorno's defence of absurdist novels and theatre, which overlooks 'that the naked depiction of horror misleads the viewer or reader into desperate compensation' when it does not establish the connection to that overall social process 'in which the opposing tendencies are equally potent, the tendencies of the future': 'Following the intended approach, on their part for the first "left" criticism of alienation (whose meaning in parts should in no way be limited), turns into unintended accommodation to the alienated culture of the bourgeoisie. The positivism thrown out before has crept in again from behind'.[10]

Here yet again, it is above all Adorno's student Habermas who brings the 'theoretical de-revolutionising' to a head. His concept of a 'contingent dialectic' limits itself to the mere immanent rational criticism of what is existent and accommodates itself to bourgeois capitalist relations. In a noteworthy anticip-

---

7   Kofler 1974, p. 231; see Chapter 5.
8   Kofler 1987.
9   Kofler 1964, p. 105.
10   Kofler 1964, pp. 107–8.

ation of the Habermas controversy of 1968, Kofler already predicts here in 1964 the consequence of Habermas's thought:

> This means however that change is left to others. Should, however, a few Adorno students come up with the idea to draw the conclusion from that torso-like criticism of alienation that things must be changed in a certain direction, that wouldn't work, because that would be 'realisation of philosophy' and deployment for an eschatological classlessness – entirely according to the concept of the bourgeois positivists.[11]

In the middle of 1965, in a student newspaper from Tübingen, Kofler already speaks of the 'pseudo-dialectical roundabout reactionaries [*Hintenherumreaktionäre*]' of the Frankfurt tendency and announces a thorough engagement with them. This is followed in the beginning of 1966 in an essay in the periodical *Kürbiskern*, which was later – lightly modified – included in Kofler's work *Der asketische Eros* (1967). The essay 'The Three Main Stages of Dialectical Social Theory' marks the high point of Kofler's critique, for here he criticises Frankfurt social philosophy not only with great sharpness, but above all historicises it. For Kofler, Frankfurt critical theory is a historical hybrid form – ideological expression of a new historical transitional period. In the history of ideas it marks a new historical stage, the third stage of dialectical social theory after Hegel and Marx, which however is also distinguished by regressing from Marx, i.e., to a relation of theory and practice that bears more resemblance to Hegel than Marx.

Critical theory is not at all the only contemporary regression into pre-Marxist social philosophy for Kofler. Besides Frankfurt's 'Hegelian World Spirit idealism' ('If for Hegel the world spirit is identical with reason, for Adorno it is identical with unreason') there also exists on the left a step backwards into the mechanical materialism of Stalinist thought, which Kofler had criticised at length in other places.[12] The Frankfurt tendency of thought by contrast is a typical exponent of what he calls the progressive elite, part of a new Hegelian left, as he occasionally writes. This progressive elite is critical and nonconformist: using an emancipatory perspective it puts new phenomena of modern society under a critical light. It attacks late capitalist reification and fetishisation, thereby contributing to general enlightenment. It however elevates these

---

11   Kofler 1964, p. 106.
12   Kofler 1964, p. 173. For critique of Stalinist mechanical materialism, see Chapter 3 of this work.

tendencies 'in a quasi-philosophical manner to the general, or, expressed sociologically, to the negative fate of inescapable violence', and thereby partially lapses into the ideological myths of late bourgeois thought.[13] As Kofler wrote in 1967:

> To all appearances, the completion of the critical path is reached when it is recognised that without exception all phenomena are so totally reified that with the exception of the purely theoretical position of dialectical criticism, there is no point at which there can be an escape. There arises then an image of a restlessly reified 'second nature' and thereby ... an in many ways false image of today's society.[14]

As he writes here, directed against Marcuse and Adorno: one who cannot see any possibilities of escape from this dominance of reification that has become a second nature, aside from a purely theoretical position of dialectical critique – such a person's theory condenses itself 'into a type of nihilistic perspective that does not remain without an effect on one's actions, even if it is only to refrain from critique of responsible institutionalised power'.[15]

Frankfurt critical theory therefore fluctuates between the critical Marxist tradition, from which it comes, and those bourgeois cultural influences that the critical theorists are exposed to from both their origin and their dependence on university life. For this reason, Kofler calls them a term coined by Georg Lukács, nonconformist conformists; speaks of a conformism disguised by nonconformism; and also sees differences within this 'Adorno current'. If Adorno 'is an extreme pessimist with a nihilistic sting in the tail [*nihilistischen Pferdefuß*]', Marcuse's pessimism avoids any nihilism.[16] However Adorno and Marcuse's fluctuation first turns into a new anti-Marxist conformism with their 'successor' Jürgen Habermas, who in the 1967 revised version becomes the actual addressee of Kofler's criticism, 'for [Habermas] draws the conclusions that are inherent in the entire tendency':

> Under the deftly feigned appearance of a total criticism of all that exists – 'critical theory' that is at the same time 'contingent' – and refraining from any political engagement, the position occupied as a neutral observer becomes a form of acceptance of all that exists and of making ends meet

---

13 'The Three Main Stages of Dialectical Social Philosophy' in this volume, p. 213.
14 Kofler 1967, p. 137.
15 Kofler 1967, p. 137.
16 'The Three Main Stages of Dialectical Social Philosophy' in this volume, p. 213.

for Habermas, and is rewarded through a distanced well-meaning kid glove treatment on the part of bourgeois institutions (amongst others, the universities, press, radio, television, and sociological and philosophical congresses). With this, the requirement to be a third force beyond Stalinism and bourgeois decadence, and to found a critical neo-Hegelianism as a secure methodological foundation, has lost in favour to that tendency. This third force would at the same time exert itself for a rigorous critical demarcation from bourgeois and Stalinist degenerative phenomena while not shying away from openly Marxist political engagement.[17]

With that 'third force' Kofler above all means himself – in the essay from 1964 he had already interpreted the theoretical and political dispute between Adorno and Lukács as a 'dispute amongst competitors for leadership within the neo-Hegelian left'.[18] Kofler sees the materialist cause symbolised by the theoretical regression in the Frankfurt School as itself rooted in contemporary relations – the reification and fetishisation processes of 'late bourgeois' society of the second half of the century that has hardened into a 'second nature'. Both aspects refer to that historical and theoretical context without which Kofler's critique of critical theory remains incomprehensible – and thus, from which Kofler's analysis of late bourgeois society and his conception of a progressive elite is deduced.

Progressive Elite in the Late Bourgeois Period

In the second half of the 1950s Kofler had taken up his old studies of bourgeois society again, in order to apply them to the neo-capitalist period. He bundled this analysis into his work *State, Society, and Elite between Humanism and Nihilism* [*Staat, Gesellschaft und Elite zwischen Humanismus und Nihilismus*], published in 1960, in which he showed to what extent postwar capitalism remained an antagonistic society marked by exploitation, injustice, and domination, where some have what others are lacking. Lord and serf, bourgeois elite and proletariat, continued to exist. Even if the latter had become materially better situated in the meantime, so too had economic dependence and insecurity remained, along with the knowledge of social inferiority, the consciousness of

---

17   Kofler 1967, p. 310.
18   Kofler 1987c, p. 139.

a gap between the top and the bottom. For Kofler this society's mechanisms of domination had deeply changed: repression increasingly internalised itself, dominance 'spiritualised' [*vergeistige*] itself. The ideological overlaid the social as the means of societal integration and the bourgeoisie had finally repressed its radical democratic and humanist demands from the early bourgeois period, and had become 'nihilist', i.e., anti-humanist. Freedom came to be conceived only in the negative sense, as *freedom from*, no longer in the positive sense of *freedom to*. If anything remained of the latter, it was the freedom to consume – insomuch as one can afford it.

For Kofler, this process of late capitalist reification – different from Herbert Marcuse, of whose work Kofler's analysis is, not coincidentally, reminiscent, given that he had already attentively studied him in the 1950s and attempted to make him known in West Germany – is not at all one-dimensional, or seemingly unavoidable. The ongoing class struggle, on the contrary, is reflected in the consciousness of the simple, not completely acclimatised worker and can, when appropriately and consistently addressed, even be politicised. Kofler did not hold with a thesis of a supposed hopelessly integrated workforce [*Arbeiterschaft*]. Although just as much a homeless leftist beyond social democracy and Stalinism as the members of the Frankfurt School, Kofler held fast to the workers' movement and class struggle. The repressive order was, he insisted repeatedly and with emphasis, not able to manipulate 'concrete conditions in their manifold contradictoriness and unforeseen variation'.[19] Critical consciousness is contained, even within that which is reified, and with that the possibility of humanist enlightenment. With provocative voluntarism, he wrote, for example, in 1967: 'Class consciousness today is what one can make out of it, if one wants to!'[20]

That such a will was not truly present any longer with the Social Democrats and the Moscow-oriented Communists was also something of which Kofler was convinced. For him, both currents were an expression of an encompassing bureaucratisation of the workers' movement that hindered general human emancipation and which had to be broken up, with the aid of a new type of vanguard. What was specific to this pariah-like, fence-sitting progressive elite was their rebellion against all that exists, their taking seriously the old humanist ideas and promises and, derived from that, their rejection of the soulless, anti-emancipatory status quo – whether in the West or the East. Even as this progressive, humanist elite could not replace the historically destined worker's

---

19   Kofler 1987c, p. 156.
20   Kofler 1987c, p. 320.

movement and therefore remained a mere transitory substitute for that sclerotic workers' movement, nevertheless they were 'an *indispensable* fermenting agent ... who preserved society from rigor mortis'.[21]

On the other hand, such an indispensable fermenting agent also exhibited a regressive drawback. For because they were not socially, politically, and culturally entrenched, these humanist individuals were inclined to rebellion against all that exists just as they were to the risk of succumbing to the coercion of the ruling alienation, thereupon adapting themselves to temporising passivity, to contemplation at times desperate and at times cynical. In this way, the move towards the positively utopian, directed against the prevailing integrated practice and alienation, continuously threatened to turn into an adrift utopianism, out of touch with everyday life.

Kofler's perspective on the regressive tendencies within this progressive elite is only decisive insofar – and here I come back to critical theory – as he held the 'Adorno current' to be a embodiment of these tendencies. The critical theory of the Frankfurt School saw no true escape from the administered world of postfascism. While Marcuse still oriented himself to socially marginalised groups, hopelessness was almost a programme for Adorno. The inscription in front of Dante's hell, 'Abandon all hope, ye who enter here', might well have been echoed by Adorno, granted with the undertone of understanding this as the last moral means of revolt against the false rulers. Precisely this attitude was opposed by Kofler. Similar to Ernst Bloch, Kofler is also a philosopher of hope: 'In all human activity is hope, for all activity is directed at goals that wish to realise the unrealised'.[22] The self-realisation of man appears principally possible to him because 'the quiescent possibilities in human facilities' all-rounded and "infinite" unfolding in the historical sphere' is foreseeable.[23] Consciousness as well as work, conceived as human activity, are for him guarantees of the malleability of the ruling status quo. As he wrote in 1966:

> All the more are we obliged to help prepare the future with the help of a *daring* critical theory and to reject all Marxo-nihilism; we have no right to make pessimistic preliminary decisions, but as humanists we are bound, in the face of the possibilities opening up ..., to do our duty, each in his own way and in his own place.[24]

---

21 Kofler 1960, pp. 346, 348. Emphasis added.
22 Kofler 1960, p. 314.
23 Kofler 1960, p. 379.
24 'The Three Main Stages of Dialectical Social Philosophy' in this volume, p. 223.

Kofler's image of a 'daring theory' highlights his agreement with the Frankfurt School very well, as well as his criticism. This, however, would not be understood by the 1960s New Left. The sharp critic of Adorno was confronted with sustained silence, which in turn drove him to a degree of embitterment and rigidification. In any case, the theory of the progressive elite that he had developed in the 1950s, which ran right through his entire writing into the 1980s, found no reception amongst the young rebels at all. His closeness to the New Left remained unreciprocated; his ambitious attempt to work out an alternative social theory to that of 'Frankfurt' had no chance with the young generation of intellectuals. Their fierce debate over Adorno's role in 1968 would not change that, nor student disappointment with Jürgen Habermas, who – as Kofler had predicted – eventually accused the SDS of left fascism. *The Left Answers Jürgen Habermas* [*Die Linke antwortet Jürgen Habermas*] was the title of a much-discussed book that appeared in 1968; Leo Kofler does not even appear in it as a footnote. He himself had long been pushed out of German discussion. Living in Cologne, his articles and books appeared at that time primarily in Austria and Switzerland. The eventful year of 1968 also saw Kofler not present in public life beyond his book *Perspektiven des revolutionären Humanismus*. Even the original attempt recorded there to bring the thought of the seeming antipodes of Lukács and Marcuse together for the New Left was not appreciated by his target audience. Not even by Hans-Jürgen Krahl, who betrayed no awareness of Kofler in any of his texts before his untimely death in 1970. If one compares both of their approaches, this non-awareness is all the more peculiar, since both thinkers' criticisms of the Frankfurt School are uncannily similar.

Theory and Practice in Western Marxism

For this purpose, we have to return once more to Hans-Jürgen Krahl's criticism of critical theory in 1969. What does he criticise in essence? He first credits Adorno and others for having revealed and attacked the social processes of modern pseudo-nature. He notes that the experience of fascism has entered critical theory as a constituent element. At the same time, he makes clear that this fixation on the fascist experience has led to getting bogged down in bourgeois individualism. This and the non-understanding of proletarian socialist class struggle have limited their criticism of capitalism, allowing its negation to become abstract. The practical class standpoint or, phrased differently, the question of political organisation, has not gone into their theoretical work. All of this made them, in the heightened situation of 1968–9, into enemies of the student left and drove them to complicity with the 'ruling forces' [*herrschenden*

Gewalten]. Complicity with the 'ruling forces', in my eyes, does not here mean complicity with 'the rulers' [*den Herrschenden*], but rather with the ruling order as such.

Let us now consider Kofler's criticism of critical theory, introduced publicly at the beginning of the 1960s and fully formulated in 1966, three years earlier than Krahl's criticism.[25] We can determine substantial points of agreement. For Kofler too, the chief merit of the Frankfurt School is their specific criticism of societal pseudo-nature. Comparable to Krahl is Kofler's central criticism that the Frankfurt School has partially succumbed to the ideological myths of late bourgeois thought. What Krahl gently pointed out as complicity with the ruling forces is, in Kofler – going a step further – the criticism of Frankfurt pseudo-opposition: their classification as 'nonconformist conformism'. For Kofler, just like Krahl, the Marxist concept of totality is at the centre of the dispute. Equally central is the concept of contingency, which Kofler assesses as absolutely negative and whose relevance Krahl prefers to leave open. For Kofler as with Krahl, the criticism of critical theory amounts to a criticism of the missing theory-practice relationship and to Adorno's – speaking in terms of reification – missing class standpoint. There are further structural similarities: the criticism of the adoption of individualist psychological theorems, and the centrality of Jürgen Habermas as a focus of their criticism. And both hold Adorno's contradictions responsible for Habermas's revisionism.

A great difference between Krahl and Kofler's criticism is that with Kofler the 'experience of fascism' is – theoretically, not biographically – significantly blanked out, not only in his criticism of the Frankfurt School, but also in his own work (once one turns away from his indirect processing of the world-historical defeat of the revolutionary workers' movement in the form of the theory of the progressive elite).[26] Likewise, a criticism of Kofler is to say that he did not grapple with Adorno or Habermas's theory in concrete detail. This led to a certain distortion or abbreviation of the criticism, because by its nature it emphasised the negative elements, and the positive elements tended to be neglected. However, it must be mentioned that the positive elements are also clearly named by Kofler, and that he at least engaged with Adorno, Marcuse, and others repeatedly, while he in turn only earned angry silence from them.

Therefore it appears to me more sensible to criticise another connected aspect in Kofler. I have outlined his theory of the progressive elite, outlined that

---

25   In later writings – above all in Kofler 1971 – this criticism undergoes an additional radicalisation.
26   On Kofler's analysis of antisemitism, see Jünke 2007a, pp. 524–5.

for him this progressive elite is a heterogeneous historical transitional formation, which partially dissolves the old dividing lines between socialism and non-socialism and, despite its partially problematic tendencies, is judged as a whole positively and as historically positive. Kofler unambiguously counts the representatives of Frankfurt critical theory amongst this progressive elite, despite his criticism. When, however, the progressive elite and critical theory, as part of the same tendency, are historically justified, although politically they are only fracturedly humanist, one can barely criticise this fracturedness from a revolutionary humanist vantage point in the same manner as one earlier debated between socialism and non-socialism. A purely polemical and unmasking criticism obviously disregards the historical necessities. Yet Kofler's criticism often has somewhat too much of this mere unmasking criticism and too little of a 'sublating criticism' [*aufhebenden Kritik*].

So much for the points of agreement and differences in Kofler and Krahl's criticism of the Frankfurt School. In one aspect Kofler certainly qualitatively exceeds Krahl – and precisely here I see the particular currency of Koflerian criticism. Kofler releases his criticism from tiresome reference to the personalities involved and formulates a sociology of the Frankfurt School that can contribute to its historicisation. He interprets critical theory so described as a historical third stage of dialectical social theory after Hegel and Marx. This third stage distinguishes itself in that it falls behind Marx into a kind of Hegelian world spirit idealism, into a quasi-philosophical system of thought that once again divides theory and practice and that partly falls into the reification and fetishisation tendencies of the late bourgeois age, preaching an ultimately conformist nonconformism – one that is constitutionally enlisted into late bourgeois society as half-oppositional thought.

With this, a final revealing parallel is broached. In the middle of the 1970s the British Marxist and historian Perry Anderson undertook a much-noticed attempt to historically and comparatively classify so-called Western Marxism as an overarching tradition in the twentieth century.[27] Be it Horkheimer, Adorno, Marcuse or Henri Lefebvre, Jean-Paul Sartre and Lucien Goldmann, be it Georg Lukács, Karl Korsch or Lucio Colletti – they all, according to Anderson then, signified an at times more, at times less sustainable division of Marxist theory and socialist practice. They all reacted thus to the disappointment of both the Stalinist deformation of Soviet society and Marxism, as well as to the social-democratic workers' movement's capitulation without a fight in the face of European fascism. If there was still an adequate approach to political prac-

---

27 Anderson 1979.

tice, it lay rather in the Communist movement, if likewise in broken form. With disengagement from one's political associations, however, one isolated oneself from the proletarian milieu, academicised and was often made to be an isolated lone combatant. One barely engaged with economy and politics, rather with philosophy and culture. One discovered the early Marx, drew on pre-Marxist traditions of thought, above all that of idealism and Hegel, and also integrated contemporary, non-Marxist systems of thought, such as Freudian psychoanalysis. In the foreground of theoretical interest would be first and foremost problems of epistemology and questions of Marxist methodology, applied to hereto neglected areas such as aesthetics and questions of societal superstucture, of culture and ideology.

Anderson also spoke – without taking notice of Kofler – of how Western Marxism 'as a whole thus paradoxically inverted the trajectory of Marx's own development itself', and that behind this esoteric language hid a sociological problem.[28] The relationship of theory and practice lay at the centre of investigation for him as well. Additionally, for Anderson, the Frankfurt School was the paradigm of Western Marxism. With the relocation from the USA to West Germany, he wrote, the Institute for Social Research moved

> steadily towards adaptation to the local bourgeois order, censoring its own past and present work to suit local academic or corporate susceptibilities, and conducting sociological surveys of a conventionally positive character. To camouflage itself in its new habitat, a virtually complete retreat from politics was executed.[29]

Anderson also deemed that Marcuse, as a so-to-speak left wingman, maintained a revolutionary position, yet his thesis of the integration of the working class was derived from the context of specifically Western Marxism and less from historical reality.

Against this background, Kofler's historical classification of the Frankfurt School reads like a formulated ideology critique of this Western Marxism. Kofler's theory allows us thus to understand the historically unique impact of Frankfurt critical theory in contemporary struggles in the history of ideas and to read it historically as a specific expression of the late bourgeois period. That critical theory in today's conflict of the faculties must serve for both – as a model of the greatest possible intellectual opposition as well as an expres-

---

28   Anderson 1979, p. 52.
29   Anderson 1979, p. 33.

sion of the intellectual refoundation of the Federal Republic of Germany – this seeming paradox allowing itself to be solved with, following Kofler, a vigorous 'Both-And!'[30]

Nevertheless, if Leo Kofler delivers both the earliest and most systematic ideological criticism of the Frankfurt School and Western Marxism, there is also a paradox hidden in himself. For Kofler is himself, admittedly not in all aspects, but in the essential ones, a representative of Western Marxism, as I have laid out in other places.[31] What Perry Anderson explains about the central problem of Western Marxist understanding of theory and practice – which Kofler registered so sensitively as well as early – hits on, if not the form, then accordingly, the structure of Kofler's respective self-understanding: Western Marxism is distinguished by a 'defiant theoreticism', by 'effectively suppressing the whole material problem of the unity of theory and practice as a dynamic bond between Marxism and mass revolutionary struggle', as it claims from the start that both concepts are identical. According to Anderson, this is the motto of 'Western Marxism in the epoch after the Second World War. They indicate the underlying ground shared by the most disparate intellectual positions within it'.[32]

Defiant theoreticism covering up the practical problem of mediation [*Vermittlung*] could also stand as the motto of Kofler's work. He also, throughout his life, reduced social practice to educational work, in the widest sense of the word, and, in theoretical work, saw the essential lever of a renewed socialist practice. Kofler's own notion of practice was accordingly reduced. He essentially restricted himself to education [*Aufklärung*] and did not ask, as Krahl would say, the organisational question. Considered from this point of view we can regard the Frankfurt School and Leo Kofler as two opposite poles of Western Marxism, the poles of pessimism and the optimism, respectively. While Horkheimer and Adorno's sociopolitical position was that university milieu which formed the student New Left in the 1960s, with Kofler it was education work in the adult education centres and trade union circles. Kofler's 'politics of truth' [*Wahrheitspolitik*], to use a central term from Demirović, was not – or not primarily – that recruitment and stablisation of intellectual elites, those Adorno and Horkheimer had in front of their faces, theoretically and politically. Kofler aimed far more at those people who, in political and apolitical associations, in educational establishments and cultural associations, were the potential support of a renewed layer of progressive socialist 'tribunes of the

---

30 Demirović 1999a and Albrecht et al. 1999.
31 Jünke 2007a, pp. 169–70.
32 Anderson 1979, p. 73.

people'. That these two milieus did not really come together in the years before and after 1968 mirrors itself in the theoretical and political struggle over hegemony between Kofler and Frankfurt. Yet despite all the lasting differences and despite the fact that Kofler's production of theory at least made an effort regarding the unity of theory and practice, he was 'only' capable of expressing that *theoretically* – in practice, Adorno, as well as Kofler, similarly accomplished 'only' educational work. Ultimately even Leo Kofler could only partially disengage himself from the historical context of Western Marxism.

Timetable of the Life and Work of Leo Kofler

1907 On 26 April Leo Kofler is born as the first of two children of the Jewish tenant Markus Kofler and his wife Mindel in Austro-Hungarian East Galicia.

1915 The family flees to Vienna due to war.

Until 1927 Attends elementary, secondary, and commercial school.

1927 Kofler works as an employee until the world economic crisis of 1929 and then becomes unemployed. Joins the Socialist Young Employees [*Sozialistische Angestelltenjugend*] in 1927 and soon becomes a speaker for the socialist Vienna Education Centre [*Wiener Bildungszentrale*].

1930s In the early 1930s, he becomes involved in the Social Democratic Workers' Party (SDAP) on its left wing and, after the destruction of Austrian democracy in 1933–4, withdraws to academic studies with Max Adler.

1938 After the annexation of Austria by fascist Germany, Kofler flees to neutral Switzerland in July 1938. As a Jewish refugee, he is interned there in an emigrant camp in Basel and continues his theoretical studies of Marxist dialectics begun in Vienna under the lasting influence of the writings of Georg Lukács.

1940–4 Involvement in labour service, and completion of the book *Die Wissenschaft von der Gesellschaft: Zur Methodenlehre einer dialektischen Soziologie*, published in 1944 under the pseudonym Stanislaw Warynski. A large part of his family dies in the Holocaust. His parents are shot near Minsk in 1942.

1944–7 After release from the labour service, he works on *Zur Geschichte der bürgerlichen Gesellschaft: Versuch einer verstehenden Deutung der Neuzeit*, which will be published in East Germany in 1948.

September 1947 Moves to the 'Soviet Occupation Zone' of Germany, later the German Democratic Republic (GDR), and joins the ruling Socialist Unity Party of Germany (SED). Begins teaching at the University of Halle, with additional extensive lecturing activity in other educational institutions for adult education. Receives his qualification for a professorship [*Habilitation*] and becomes a professor of medieval and modern history.

1949 In the course of the Stalinisation of the SED and GDR, Kofler's antibureaucratic understanding of Marxism gets caught in the crossfire of the party authorities. Following public criticism, he demonstratively leaves the SED at the end of January 1950, is granted leave of absence and declared an 'ideological pest' and anti-state 'Trotskyite'. Work on *Geschichte und Dialektik: Zur Methodenlehre der dialektischen Geschichtsbetrachtung*, a theoretical critique of the bureaucratic and mechanistic understanding of Marxism, which will be published in West Germany in 1955.

Autumn 1950 After being banned from his profession and threatened with arrest, he flees with his future wife Ursula Wieck via West Berlin and Hamburg to Cologne.

From 1951 Works as an academic author and adult education lecturer, as well as in trade union education work, and from 1953 onwards, also as a lecturer at the (trade union) Social Academy in Dortmund. Lecture tours to local groups of the Socialist German Student Union (SDS) and the Young Friends of Nature [*Naturfreunde-Jugend*]. He writes mainly in the left socialist press.

1951–2 Several writings on the Marxist critique of Stalinism (above all, *Marxistischer oder stalinistischer Marxismus* and *Das Wesen und die Rolle der stalinistischen Bürokratie*) appear, some under the pseudonym Jules Dévérité.

1953–5 As a result of trade union and socialist educational work, a series of educational booklets on the history of bourgeois society and Kofler's conception of socialist humanism is published. Criticism of bourgeois tendencies in West German social democracy, including *Marxistischer oder ethischer Sozialismus* [Marxist or Ethical Socialism] (1955).

Second half of the 1950s Long-term collaboration with the Hamburg-based *Andere Zeitung* (*AZ*), and cooperation with the influential trade union leftist Viktor Agartz, including collaboration on his magazine *WISO: Korrespondenz für Wirtschafts- und Sozialwissenschaften*. He intensifies his lecturing activities at the Frankfurt SDS and in the milieu of the 'homeless' left, at the *International Society for Socialist Studies* among others, which publishes his writings on Marxism and socialist humanism.

1960 Sociological analysis of late bourgeois class society in *Staat, Gesellschaft und Elite zwischen Humanismus und Nihilismus*.

1960s Expansion of his topical engagement to include questions of literary theory (*Zur Theorie der modernen Literatur*, 1962), increasing criticism of the 'Marxo-Nihilism' of the Frankfurt School around Theodor W. Adorno and Jürgen Habermas, as well as consolidated expositions of his sociological critique of the supposedly levelled middle-class society (*Der proletarische Bürger*, 1964), his socio-philosophical critique of late bourgeois ruling ideology (*Der asketische Eros*, 1967) and his political visions (*Perspektiven des revolutionären Humanismus* [Perspectives of Revolutionary Humanism], 1968). In 1966 the new revised edition of *Zur Geschichte der bürgerlichen Gesellschaft* was published by Luchterhand-Verlag, with numerous new editions reprinted up to the 1980s.

After 1968 Lecturer at the Cologne Art Academy. Rediscovery of Kofler's early writings in the form of pirate editions by the student movement. Continuation of analyses in literary theory in *Abstrakte Kunst und absurde Literatur* [Abstract Act and Absurd Literature] (1970), as well as criticism of late bourgeois ruling ideology in *Technologische Rationalität im Spätkapitalismus* [Technological Rationality in Late Capitalism] (1971).

1972 Begins teaching at the Ruhr University Bochum, which continues until 1991. On his sixy-fifth birthday, Kofler is awarded the Golden Badge of Honour [*Goldene Ehrenzeichen*] of the City of Vienna, a kind of honorary citizenship, in recognition of his literary merits. The collection of essays *Zur Dialektik der Kultur* is also published.

1973 In *Aggression und Gewissen: Grundlegung einer anthropologischen Erkenntnistheorie* [Aggression and Conscience: Groundwork of an Anthropological Epistemology], he develops his attempt to combine Marxism and (philosophical) anthropology.

Second half of the 1970s *Soziologie des Ideologischen* [Sociology of the Ideological] appears in 1975, and an examination of Herbert Marcuse's aesthetics, *Haut den Lukács: Realismus und Subjektivismus* [Hit Lukács: Realism and Subjectivism, the title refers to a test-of-strength attraction at fairs], in 1977. 1980 sees the publication of the Festschrift for Kofler, *Marxismus und Anthropologie* [Marxism and Anthropology], edited by Ernst Bloch and others, in which Helmut Fleischer, Wolfgang Fritz Haug, Agnes Heller, Ernest Mandel, György Márkus, Adam Schaff and others examine aspects of Kofler's work.

First half of the 1980s In 1981 the essay volume *Geistiger Verfall und progressive Elite: Sozialphilosophische Studien* [Mental Decay and Progressive Elite: Socio-Philosophical Studies] is published. Small occasional publications on anthropological questions (*Der Alltag zwischen Eros und Entfremdung: Perspektiven zu einer Wissenschaft vom Alltag* [Everyday Life Between Eros and Alienation: Perspectives on a Science of Everyday Life], as well as *Eros, Ästhetik und Politik: Thesen zum Menschenbild bei Marx* [Eros, Aesthetics and Politics: Theses on the Concept of Man in Marx]), on the critique of the Green Alternatives (*Kritik der Alternativen*) and on neo-conservatism *Der Konservatismus zwischen Dekadenz und Reaktion* [Conservatism between Decadence and Reaction].

Second half of the 1980s Critique of the emerging neoliberal (he still calls it Manchester Liberal) social Darwinism as Kofler increasingly takes the side of the Soviet Union in the competition between the systems. He sees in Gorbachev the great hope for a new beginning of the socialist movement (*Aufbruch in der Sowjetunion?*, 1986). In 1987 a volume of autobiographical conversations, *'Die Kritik ist der Kopf der Leidenschaft': Aus dem Leben eines marxistischen Grenzgängers* ['Criticism is the Head of Passion': From the Life of a Marxist Border Crosser], is published. In 1991 the Festschrift *Die versteinerten Verhältnisse zum Tanzen bringen* [Bringing the Petrified Relations to Dance] is published, in which, among others, Ursula Beer, Detlev Claussen, Diedrich Diederichsen, Frank Deppe, Frigga and Wolfgang Fritz Haug, Joachim Hirsch, Reinhard Kühnl, Ernest Mandel, Oskar Negt and Ursula Schmiederer publish articles on contemporary Marxist theory.

1990 On a guest lecture tour in the still existent GDR, he renews his criticism of the predatory ideology of Western capitalism in Halle, Leipzig, and Berlin.

Spring 1991 Kofler suffers several strokes from which he never recovers. In 1992, the first complete new edition of *Zur Geschichte der bürgerlichen Gesellschaft* is published.

29 July 1995 Leo Kofler dies after a long illness, and is buried in Cologne.

1996 Founding of the Leo Kofler-Gesellschaft in Bochum (www.leo-kofler.de).

Illustrations

ILL. 1　　Leo Kofler (m.) in the early 1940s performing work duties in a Swiss refugee camp
WITH KIND PERMISSION OF THE LEO KOFLER-GESELLSCHAFT E.V.

ILL. 2　　Leo Kofler with his wife Ursula in their new hometown, Cologne, 1950s
WITH KIND PERMISSION OF THE LEO KOFLER-GESELLSCHAFT E.V.

ILL. 3   Leo Kofler working at his desk in the late 1960s
WITH KIND PERMISSION OF THE LEO KOFLER-GESELLSCHAFT E.V.

ILL. 4   Leo Kofler teaching at the Cologne Academy of Art, 1971
WITH KIND PERMISSION OF THE LEO KOFLER-GESELLSCHAFT E.V.

Appendix: Six Essays by Leo Kofler

On Freedom [1951]

We shouldn't fool ourselves: There is no social freedom without freedom for the individual, who strives for self-determination and independence, and who, as long as there is human history, has understood, understands, and will understand by freedom the greatest possible freedom from all barriers and bonds.* In comparison to previous social epochs, bourgeois society represents the last and highest form of freedom within class history. But it is an error of bourgeois ideology to equate this form of freedom with absolute freedom. For bourgeois freedom, which grants the individual freedom of movement to a large extent, is at the same time a form which only feigns such freedom by not merely permitting but presupposing the continued existence of strong bonds restricting freedom, i.e., essential elements of unfreedom, under the appearance of freedom. The contradictory character of bourgeois freedom is an expression of the contradictory character of bourgeois class society in general. It is based on the fact that *on the one hand* the individual – *each* individual – appears in bourgeois society as a completely autonomous and equal owner of commodities (owner of shoes, of intellectual products, or labour power) and thus as a completely autonomous and equal contractual partner, but *on the other hand*, the one-sided ownership of the means of production, that is, excluding whole classes, simultaneously abolishes this autonomy and legal equality of individuals. The contradiction expressed by this fact is the contradiction between the merely de jure (formal) and the de facto (social) state in bourgeois society, which is based on the distribution of property.

It could be shown (which is not the intention of this essay, which tries to give only the most important conceptual definitions) that this phenomenon, which is known in Marxist theory as *alienation* and *reification*, necessarily results from the aforementioned contradictory character of bourgeois existence. The importance of such an investigation would then lie in proving that, even for the bourgeois class in possession of the means of production, the contradiction between formal and social freedom has its effect, albeit a particular yet very concrete and profound one, on the freedom of the bourgeois individual; the bourgeois individual too sees themselves inescapably entangled in the contradiction between formality and factuality, the condition itself working its way deep into bourgeois thinking.

---

* [Originally published as "Über die Freiheit" in: *Pro und contra: Diskussionsblätter für demokratischen Sozialismus*, May 1951, pp. 74–5.]

The abolition of the contradiction between formal freedom and social unfreedom means the abolition of bourgeois society in general; it is not possible *within* this society. If we recognised at the beginning that *one* essential definition of freedom is that it gives the individual the greatest possible independence and self-determination, then there is no doubt that socialism, which must be the necessary consequence of the abolition of the above contradiction – and we mean, of course, the completed socialism which no longer needs transitional measures – is the historical incarnation of freedom. At this level of historical development, whose historical possibility can only be denied by reactionaries and ignorant people, the freedom of the individual is fully established both from the legal point of view (as opposed to the feudalistic bond that occurs in legal *form*, for example) and from the economic point of view (as opposed to any class society).

But it would be disastrous, especially for socialists, to believe that with this determination of freedom as the freedom of the individual from bonds through which they see themselves economically or legally subject to other individuals or objective powers, the final determination of the concept of freedom would also have been won.

As much as it is true and understandable that in all class society the longing to shake off such bonds dominates people, i.e., that the simple non-existence of these bonds, which is something merely negative, is equated with freedom par excellence, it is equally justified to meet such a merely *negative concept of freedom* with suspicion. This mistrust has nothing to do with the reactionary slander of man, according to which individuals who have been fully liberated will only give themselves over to laziness, gluttony and carnal lust and fall prey to degeneracy. Not only is labour a natural urge and need, and when it is freed from all inhuman constraints can become a *pleasure*, like many other activities which man today already undertakes voluntarily and again out of a deep need, but, in addition, under the supervision and education of an organisation of society placed exclusively at the service of man, man can be taught to make fruitful use of his strength and talents without restriction of individual freedom. But this is only in passing.

Our mistrust of the merely negative concept of freedom results precisely from our conviction of the infinite possibilities for the unfolding and development of the human personality, a conviction which we share in principle with the great bourgeois humanists of the period of bourgeois ascendance, if the essential differences in opinion resulting from the insights of scientific socialism are accounted for. The fact that we are in agreement with Marx in this respect is demonstrated here by only one example. According to Schiller, the division of labour is to blame for the deformation of man, who is subject to 'culture' and has become alienated from the state of 'nature', like the one he found as a beautiful perfection in Greek antiquity; with this the *whole* man has been lost; the most essential characteristic in the behaviour of the man who is still capable of his totality is the 'ludic drive'. Marx and Engels likewise criticise the personality dividing effect of the division of labour and demand the restoration of the *whole* man – as Schiller very aptly describes the free disposal of the individual over the variety and potency of his powers and dispositions in the form of their constant activity and exercise as the ludic drive, so too does Marx, who in his main work, *Capital,* expresses himself in a similar way at least twice, for example, when he speaks of the 'free play of mental and bodily powers'. It is highly indicative of the narrowing of socialism to a naive 'happiness' and sausage-end socialism in both reformism and Stalinism – oh, what wonderful harmony between the enemy brothers results from the theoretical ignorance and dogmatisation of Marxism! – that this important passage in Marx was hardly noticed and even less recognised for its theoretical significance.

The attentive reader will already have understood from the above what *further definition of the concept of freedom* we consider indispensable from the socialist perspective. In addition to the two negative definitions of personal or formal, and economic or social freedom, negative because they are aimed merely at overcoming the social bonds and barriers which have arisen historically, there is the *third positive definition*: this is the fact that man can enjoy freedom fully and become a free being in the true sense of the word only when he has reached that level of social development at which the *free development of his personality into totality and harmony* has become a practical possibility. This fact can be expressed in the form of an abbreviated definition: *freedom is personality*! A man who is not aware of his powers, who preserves his talents in a state of slumber and does not use them productively, is never free, even if the desire awakened under the inhuman conditions of capitalism for the creation of those freedoms which we have called negative ones appears to him as the incarnation of freedom in general.

In this context, there is still the question of the relationship between the two negative definitions of freedom and the positive definition. The answer is to be found in the *relationship of the preconditions for the realisation of freedom*. At the same time, these preconditions are only preconditions with regard to the final goal of socialist freedom, goals to be realised, in turn, in the historical process itself, and therefore, *for their part, stages of the realisation of freedom.*

To have not recognised or insufficiently considered this dialectical relationality and contradiction in the historical and concrete concept of freedom is a common (epistemological) deficiency of numerous otherwise completely different views on freedom, from the bourgeois humanists of the eighteenth century to the vulgarisers of Marxism, who explain freedom as the absence of unfreedom, similar to some economists who, according to a saying of Marx, have explained *Armut* (poverty) with the use of *poverté*.

At a time before the Russian revolution, such an equation of freedom with the possibility of the development of personality might still have appeared as a completely abstract, meaningless 'idealist' construction that in no way affects political practice. While in some countries, with great difficulty, individual freedom with all the consequences of freedom of conscience, freedom of the press, freedom of assembly and freedom of organisation had already been secured to a certain extent, in view of the impoverished masses living under inhuman conditions and exploited beyond measure by capitalism, one could truly think of nothing else but the fight for social freedom, i.e., freedom from misery, economic pressure and exploitation, by means of the destruction of bourgeois class rule. Although the future development of the human personality has always been the subject of lively discussion in small circles and in a utopian manner, even in those circles it was not always taken entirely seriously. The obvious problem, which directly confronted all socialists, was the *economic* betterment of the masses.

However, the deficiency of such a one-sided view became apparent as soon as the first socialist state in the world attempted to realise the socialist ideals. At first, objective circumstances such as the economic ruin resulting from war and civil war, Russia's economic backwardness, and the need to rearm in the face of external threats made the solution of even the purely economic problem of freedom difficult. Yet it was not only the objective difficulties that were to blame for the spread of a shallow economism which disregarded man and his individuality, and the longer it lasted the more an anti-humanistic touch was imposed on all economic and especially political practice; no less to blame for this was *the narrowing of the socialist problematic to a one-sided economic view*, stemming still from the capitalist structure of reification that continued to have an effect in "socialist" economism, wherein it was precisely this *stagnation in the idea of the economic liberation of man* that was partly to blame for the mechanisation of political and theoretical thought, which constitutes an essential characteristic of the ideology of the Soviet bureaucracy.

Anyone who has studied the peculiar phenomenon of the bureaucratisation of socialist theory in the Soviet Union and has had the opportunity to study it in detail will not be able to avoid the economisation and the closely-related dehumanisation of thought and practice. One of the most interesting, but also saddest phenomena in the process of the degeneration of bureaucratic ideology is the negation of the necessity of maintaining individual freedom, which is merely *formal* under capitalism, but has reached a *higher* level of realisation under the socialist economy, which, as long as it cannot be completely denied as a necessity in the eyes of the working and socialist-thinking masses, is only granted a certain leeway in an illusory way (partly even using the usual deception, as can be observed especially in the Eastern Zone).[1] The decisive point here, however, is that precisely because of this deficient view of the fundamental role of individual freedom in the socialist state (which can certainly be reconciled with vigilance against the class enemy), the question of the development of the human personality in the sense described above is also completely overlooked, the relationship between negative freedom as a precondition and positive freedom as realisation remains unrecognised, and thus *the humanist standard for socialist action, i.e., the indispensable corrective in all socialist treatment of man, economy, politics and science, is simply missing*. The disastrous consequence is the degradation of the working man to a passive tool of an economic goal, his elimination as a truly democratic and formative force (see Yugoslavia, where a real democratisation of social life has recently been successfully carried out), the destruction of free discussion in the pursuit of knowledge with all the consequences of the dogmatisation of Marxist theory, its degeneration into a vulgar economism and the childishly naive equation of bureaucratic thinking with Marxist creativity, etc.

However, even if in their revolutionary ascent the great ideologues of the bourgeoisie always understood by freedom the possibility of the unending development and restoration of the totality of the personality, which unfolds on the basis of laissez-faire and the social harmony that arises from it, there is nothing left of this former humanistic ideal in today's bourgeoisie. All that remains is an empty competitive individualism, saturated with a pessimistically decadent view of man, again coming close to the idea of a Hobbes, according to which man is by nature nothing more than a predator pursuing its own interests. In the two apparently fundamentally opposed forms of *capitalist individualism, liberalism* (now represented by Röpke and Hayek) *and monopolism, which in reality have the same roots*, the old humanistic ideal of the bourgeoisie has equally lost its right to a home. This ideal has been replaced – whether conceded or not is irrelevant – by the idea of the right of the strongest, and that is the right of the property owner.

By what right fingers are being pointed at the Soviet Union from such a position is completely unfathomable. Reactionaries are in the habit of referring to

---

1 Kofler is referring to the Soviet Occupation Zone of Germany in the immediate postwar period and presumably also to the German Democratic Republic (East Germany), unrecognised at this point by the Federal Republic of Germany (FRG) (trans. note).

their democracy. Yes, it is indeed *their* democracy that we have in mind. How many socialist or even Marxist professors are allowed to teach at universities on the basis of the good old democratic right of equal freedom of expression? Not worth mentioning! Bourgeois democracy is only a *form*, behind whose golden-yellow robes the *dictatorship of the bourgeoisie* hides, ready to burst forth at any time a serious step is to be taken from merely formal to social freedom, that is, a step which threatens to shake the bourgeois anti-freedom monopoly on the means of production.

The critics who mock the dictatorship in the Soviet Union forget that the bourgeoisie also used the dictatorship to come to power. Should we remind them of such striking examples as the Jacobin dictatorship, the Cromwell dictatorship and Calvin's dictatorship in Geneva? That will not be necessary, because they are too educated not to know that. But their education does not go so far as to know that their own democracy, *'their'* democracy, of which they are so infinitely proud, was not the work of the bourgeoisie at all, but the work of the restless inferior classes. We want to 'remind' them of this with a few brief historical references.

The whole history of the emergence of bourgeois democracy is burdened by the contradiction that, on the one hand, the idea of popular sovereignty is written on the banners of the revolutionary bourgeoisie, but, on the other hand, the same bourgeoisie constantly declares that *popular sovereignty* is not to be understood as the sovereignty of the *whole* people, but only as the *sovereignty of the propertied*. In the *Communist Manifesto*, Marx expresses this, stating that for the bourgeoisie 'the person is the owner of property'. According to the view underpinning this equation of bourgeois consciousness, the person without property is ultimately not a person, and therefore not a fully-fledged legal subject and not capable of making full use of the rights of liberty. John Locke, for example, in his 'Two Treatises', in the course of a meditation on slavery, expressly states that the propertyless are to be regarded as not belonging to society. Similarly, Cromwell argues in his discussion with the soldiers' councils that the dispossessed cannot be granted the right to vote because they have no interest in the state. In the first National Assembly of the great French Revolution, a physiocratic supporter, that is, a consistent representative of the bourgeois conception of society, made a similar argument by proposing that the dispossessed should not be granted the right to vote because they do not belong to society (!). Even in the second, more radical version of 'An Agreement of the People' by John Lilburne (leader of the Levellers in the great English Revolution), in which for the first time a complete programme of bourgeois democracy was established, the right to vote is withdrawn from the dispossessed. Up to Kant, Schön and beyond, this position of non-admission of the dispossessed to the full enjoyment of civil liberties is maintained by bourgeois ideologues.

The picture is precisely the reverse of today. Whereas in earlier centuries the humanistic belief in the future development of society towards a harmonious state and the associated development of the human personality of *all* members of society was accompanied by a deep mistrust of the dispossessed (John Milton, for instance, who also wanted to see the right to vote restricted), in the big tent of stabilised democratic dictatorships of the bourgeoisie, a deep inhuman pessimism goes hand in hand with the knowledge, based on experience, that the bourgeois 'democratic' method of rule is fully sufficient to break the revolutionary thrust of enfranchisement to the popular masses, thus hand in hand with a reactionary trust in the dispossessed.

Attempts have been made to explain the ruptures in the idea of popular sovereignty, that is, the basic programmatic idea of bourgeois democracy, by the old revolutionary pioneers of bourgeois democracy out of the fear that the ignorant journeymen, servants and workers, many of whom were in the service of the feudal nobility, would give their masters the vote (Vorländer, Max Adler, Bernstein, Meusel and others). But there are three things that speak against this view, which is a commonplace credulity towards the arguments and excuses of the ideologues of the past themselves.

First, this argument is by no means always used, not even in the majority of cases. Rather, the inability of the dispossessed to subject his interest to society is often openly and far more convincingly emphasised – *which is always understood as a society of the possessing* (very explicitly in Locke's case).

Second, it is striking that one never thinks about depriving the right to vote from those whom one fights in open field battles and sends to the scaffold by the hundreds – the nobility. We have here a proof that *the possessor* is always judged to be capable of using the rights of freedom, provided that they do not oppose these rights of freedom themselves. The nobleman, then, who submits himself to bourgeois society and its laws, is a property owner, a person, a citizen as well as a bourgeois; *he who possesses property* is therefore capable of using the right to vote from the outset.

Third, even at a time when it had long since been proven that the popular masses were anti-feudal and, later, when the feudal reaction was no longer a serious danger, the bourgeoisie refused to allow the dispossessed to vote. In 1793, it was the popular masses under the leadership of proletarian elements that had forced the democratic constitution of that year, which gave *everyone* without exception the right to vote. It was clear from that moment on that the people were as anti-feudal as the bourgeoisie. But in 1794, after the fall of Robespierre, it was the same bourgeoisie that again disenfranchised the dispossessed. On the other hand, they tend to invoke England and its 'liberal' electoral reforms. It is, they say, the England of old liberal traditions, of the time-honoured parliamentary form of government and of habeas corpus. But it is also the England under whose 'parliamentary' forms of government the greatest peasant clearance in modern history took place, even outshining the Prussian (the Enclosures of the eighteenth century, which Marx calls a *parliamentary* plunder'). Moreover, the English 'parliaments' were consistently more feudal than the French *états généreaux* at the same time, in which the bourgeoisie consulted for itself, while in England the knightly nobility was associated with the bourgeoisie who, as all honest historians from [Julius] Hatschek to Trevelyan readily admit, always knew how to assert its feudal (!) interests. We cannot prove in this context that it was the same with the other 'liberal' institutions and documents. Only the act of habeas corpus will be mentioned, because its fate proves how little one was inclined to take seriously the little shred of popular democratic sovereignty realised in this document, at a time when the bourgeoisie already had quite some say.

Already between 1688 and 1723 the act of habeas corpus had been repealed no less than seven times; that was still a 'medieval' period. Yet even when English society was sufficiently developed to take the first steps towards *bourgeois democracy*, Pitt the younger, who certainly cannot be regarded as a representative of feudalism, suspended it in 1794, a state which lasted until 1802. A further suspension took place from 1817 to 1818, followed by the notorious 'Six Acts' of 1819.

Finally, the famous 'liberal' electoral reforms of England in the nineteenth century. In short, even when they took an extremely moderate form, that is to say, one undemocratically directed *against the people*, the popular movement had to provide a great deal of aid, for the liberal bourgeoisie was utterly afraid of too great an expansion of the electorate. In 1794, 1815 and in the movement of Chartism, which reached its most radical stage in the 1820s, we have highlights of the struggle for universal and equal suffrage. Here, proletarian and petty-bourgeois elements always lead, not 'liberal' bourgeois elements. When, as a result of the July Revolution in France and the Belgian Revolution of 1830, the reactionary Wellington ministry is overthrown, the bourgeoisie, in its own interest (!), condescends to an electoral reform that is a slap in the face to the concept of popular sovereignty. The electoral reform of 1832 is a reform that completely excludes the dispossessed. It is again these dispossessed who, through a movement on the streets (especially in Bristol and Manchester), break the resistance of the House of Lords. The second electoral reform of 1867, proposed in a very modest form by the *liberal* leader Gladstone, was *rejected by the liberal majority*, but as a result of the reactionary anxiety of the liberals, cleverly taken out of their hands and carried out by the *conservative* Disraeli. But even so, although Disraeli goes far beyond Gladstone's proposals, it too is still an essentially undemocratic reform. From then on (1884) electoral reform proceeds apace, *for the proletariat shows all signs of the loss of faith in its own strength and with it of turning to bourgeois liberalism.* In 1864, Marx speaks in the *Inaugural Address* of the degeneration of the English working class. In 1868 the election ends with the complete defeat of the workers' candidates. The bourgeoisie recognises that it is possible, wiser, and easier to hold on to power with the help of the popular masses than against them. The bourgeoisie learns that a relative monopolisation of public institutions for the shaping of opinion is a far more reliable means of rule than mere violence.

Yet in spite of the contradictions which have been pointed out, and which permeate the ideology and practice of revolutionary bourgeois humanism, the historian, faced with the complete decadence of today's bourgeois ideology, cannot avoid speaking with respect of that great ideal of humanity which, in spite of all its inhibitions, the old bourgeois humanist thought had in mind. What is more: insofar as the ideals of the great bourgeois ideologues were ideals of freedom, they form an important component of a higher and scientifically-founded basis, which socialism can build on, albeit not uncritically.

Overlooking the positive element in the bourgeois progressive idea of freedom implies the danger of economising and vulgarising the socialist concept of freedom. To counter this danger must be one of the main tasks of socialist theoretical work. Only when we succeed in proving that socialism makes possible the realisation of all the great ideals of humanity, can we then hope to awaken that faith in it which the people will need in their struggle for freedom.

Liberalism and Democracy [1959/1972]

The tragic contradiction in the essence of the liberal bourgeoisie, verifiable in the historical material, had enabled conservatism, which was still semi-feudal in the nineteenth century, and was at any rate aristocratic and feudal-Christian in character, to gain several advantages for itself by skilfully exploiting liberal weaknesses.* Thus the Conservative Party in Britain under the leadership of Disraeli was able to achieve considerable successes for itself precisely at a time when the Liberals, following external pressure, began to reluctantly implement weak electoral reforms. Let us remember once again that it was the Liberal majority who, in protest of their own leader, Gladstone, rejected his moderate electoral bill, while Disraeli pushed through an improved version and won the following elections. If one draws a comparison with the modern and consistently Christianity-professing conservatives, the path leads via Bismarck as a transitional phenomenon to various political leaders of European countries. All in all, this movement, connected to its existing tradition and in accordance with its own intentions, may be summarised under the characterisation of 'social conservatism' (*Sozialkonservatismus*). The difference to earlier times, particularly in the period of Disraeli, is to be found in the fact that this social conservatism no longer exists in its original purity, but has instead mixed itself strongly with liberalism, which could happen because the once monarchic and medieval estates-based (thus also romantically oriented) conservatism played out its historical role and liberalism became conservative. Only certain remnants of an equally conservative, albeit somewhat firmer liberalism have converged into their own, mostly smaller movements, yet they have also lost the once fundamental humanist disposition, not, indeed, without carrying forward that which was already developed in the contradictions of the old bourgeois liberalism, as we could demonstrate.

Before we turn our attention to this liberalism more closely, we must first state several remarks in advance on the still considerable social conservatism that has swallowed up the mainstream of liberalism and which, if we look closely at matters of economy, state, and politics, has itself been in the liberal bailiwick for a long time.

It is interesting to see how social conservatism has changed. In the previous century, most typically in Britain, it still had a genuine streak of social criti-

---

* [Originally published as "Liberalismus und Demokratie" in: *Zeitschrift für Politik* Heft 2/1959, p. 113 onwards. Reprinted (in this extended version) in Kofler 1972, page 141 onwards.]

cism in the face of the disintegration of the feudal world and the spreading mass industrial misery, most notably in its leading representatives, Carlyle and Disraeli. With one eye squinting at the Middle Ages, to which it attached an undeserved halo, it looked across with the other towards an order in which, under the leadership of the monarchy and its affiliated powers, the working masses were to be aided against the harsh seizure of the capitalist enterprise. Social conservatism dreamt of an alliance between people and monarchy, the latter intended to bestow endurance against the claims of liberalism and its whispers of progress. Lassalle, as is well known, took advantage of this circumstance to draw Bismarck's attention in personal conversations to the possibility of strengthening the monarchy and weakening liberal capitalism by means of granting the elective franchise. Bismarck recalled this when it was far too late for him and he saw himself forced to enact the elective franchise at the same time as laws against the 'radical horde'. However, under more pristine conditions, Disraeli was able to carry out, for this period and above all in comparison to the liberal ones planned by Gladstone, radical reform of the elective franchise, even though the liberals and not the conservatives would have been the ones called to do this, according to the principle of popular sovereignty that had pitted the bourgeoisie against feudalism for centuries. British social conservatism at that time still had, despite its misjudgement of the true historical tendencies and despite its conservative utopianism, a genuinely popular orientation. Its transformation in the course of further development, its moulting into the capitalist form, the distinction that takes shape between Disraeli and Churchill, is precisely the difference that exists between the old and the modern social conservatism in general, assuming the latter still deserves this attribute, endeavouring in certain utterances to propagandistically bestow on itself the semblance of the 'social'. It is the difference that characterises itself through an oppositional ressentiment against the bourgeois capitalist world, born out of a romantic anti-capitalism, against both its narrowly profit-minded exploitation as well as its miscellaneous petty bourgeois narrow-mindedness in the intellectual and cultural domain, against its individual and social immorality, a ressentiment that is lost and transforms itself into a tactical readiness to remedy some defects in society. Modern social conservatism has fully reconciled itself with capitalism, has itself become 'liberal', except for a few Thomistic and estates-based idioms that still recall its origin. One reads the novels of Disraeli or Carlyle's famous work *Past and Present*, in which, just like Balzac, he wistfully attacks the degenerated nobility in order to unmask their responsibility along with the bourgeoisie for the suffering of the people, and one clearly recognises the contrast to today.

In between lies Bismarck, at the halfway mark, as it were. If for Disraeli, beyond his tactical intent to bond the representatives of the middle class and working masses to himself through an improvement of the elective franchise and thus to beat the Liberals in Parliament, the elective franchise was a very serious concern by virtue of being born from a premonition of future democratic developments, it was utterly different for Bismarck. As a true Junker, he also hated the shopkeeper spirit of the rising bourgeoisie, though he recognised their inevitable historical function as little as Disraeli did. Yet recognising well the new power of the working class successfully organising before his eyes, he could not and did not wish to ally with either the bourgeoisie (which he later did as a result of the ingratiation of the National Liberal Party of the Grand Burghers) or the socialist working class. Thus he considered the elective franchise and concessions of petty social legislation as necessary tactical means of self-assertion, which is already discernible from the fact he did not shy from hard repressive measures against the working class. Just how little he took the democratic elective franchise seriously – and he remembered very well that none other than Lassalle had persuaded him to do so – is demonstrated by the fact that he blunted its edge with blatant manipulation of the Reichstag and the Bundesrat. In any case, it is certain that Bismarck considered every social and democratic concession a tactical means with which he could deceive history, as it were. However, this tactic itself was essentially anti-capitalist in its intention, that is, buoyed by the hope that bourgeois progress was pushed through by the kicks that he delivered to the nation, and that this nation, with corresponding political energy against social democracy, would become a reliable pillar of the Prussian monarchy. That Bismarck did not recognise the positive side of the anti-feudal development of capitalism was his tragedy, as was the tragedy of all or half of social conservatism in general. The factory owners and merchants were repugnant to him and he did not see the complicated connection between them and Lessing or Goethe.

Modern 'social' conservatism has entirely reconciled itself with capitalism, which came easily to it, because the contrast between feudalism and bourgeois order has become irrelevant even in those remnants that played a role at the time of Bismarck. It can be discerned ideologically and distinguished from liberalism through its constant opinion that the midwife of modern society, the French Revolution, was a dangerous historical error. Today's conservatism, still not relinquishing its social styling, no longer has any real concessions to allocate to the people, because the concessions that capitalism can allocate have already been wrested from it in hard struggles, and what remains belong to the programme of the trade unions, since these, in their present-day 'integrated' form, must also have something to justify their existence. Modern social conservatism is thus vastly more capitalist and conservative than social. The social is a mere tactic here, a magic hood of disguise, no longer, as with Bismarck, to hinder capitalist development, but rather to promote it, to secure its rule. 'Social' conservatism has become bourgeois, or what in the final effect means the same thing; it has ceased to exist, except in the phrase, in the jingling of bells, that it attaches to itself and the bourgeoisie occasionally uses to give itself a milder appearance than its bourgeois egoist one. What truly exists is the bourgeoisie in its pure form. Illuminating its essence is the task of the following investigation.

In 'On the Jewish Question', Marx brilliantly analysed 'the decomposition of man into the public citizen and the private citizen', the *citoyen* and the *bourgeois*, which arises from the 'conflict between the general interest and private interest'. Marx shows how public interest produces the citizen [*Bürger*] interested in public welfare, the *citoyen*, and, at the same time and in the same person, private interest produces the egoistic private citizen, the bourgeois. However, the dialectical tension between the *citoyen* and the bourgeois in the breast of the modern citizen results, as the most recent experiences teach, in various modes of behaviour, each according to the concrete historical and social situations, which must constantly be analysed anew. If already in the period of the ascent of the bourgeoisie (*Bürgertums*) the *citoyen* prevailed just as often over the bourgeois, e.g., in his humanist perspective, as the bourgeois over the *citoyen*, e.g., in the denial of the elective franchise, there has been many a change since the victory of the bourgeoisie.

Despite the inextricable internal contradiction in the nature of the citizen, which is dissoluble because it is based on the class divide in society, Marx discerns the historical progress that is associated with bourgeois society. Thus he can say: 'Political emancipation [i.e., the purely political and formal liberation of man] is, of course, a big step forward. True, it is not the final form of human emancipation in general, but it is the final form of human emancipation within the hitherto existing world order', namely that divided by class.

However, with the completion of this political, that is, formal democratic emancipation, thereby reaching the stage in which the first indications appear that it must give way to another, higher one, i.e., a social emancipation transcending the formal one, the bourgeoisie loses interest altogether in human emancipation. In the time of bourgeois ascent and struggle, the guiding ideal of an economic order based on freedom always remained, in which not only would everyone attain sufficient property, but also have occasion to develop their powers, facilities and talents to the height of truly human existence which results from a harmonious personality in the uniform use of their mental and spiritual powers. This goal has been set in the present day by socialism, which recognises that it is only (relatively) realisable in classless society, because in class society the humanisation of man must intrinsically remain an eternal contradiction.

The best evidence for the correctness of this view is the behaviour of the bourgeoisie itself. By resignedly dropping its original ideals, throwing itself into the arms of pessimism and hostility to progress, it unintentionally admits that the realisation of humanist goals is impossible within the bourgeois order. The 'modest' relinquishment unmasks the frantic and demanding conduct. The world only remains 'useful' for the bourgeoisie, endurable for profit, otherwise it has become meaningless and empty. The remaining 'freedom' is no longer the freedom to realise ideals and to elevate man – someone who still wants this becomes suspicious! – but rather the freedom of competition, of the jungle. Effectively everything has been achieved, there was history, but in the future there won't be anymore. The problem of public welfare that was before the eyes of the *citoyen* becomes purified of all humanist and optimistic implications: it becomes a purely technical problem that must also be 'solved' on behalf of 'order', as one solves the problem of sewage, for example. The 'solution' ultimately means the defusing and 'integration' [*Einordnung*], i.e., the subjugation, of man. The desires of the old liberalism are ridiculed as vulgar (Röpke, Weinstock, etc.) and freedom is left to those who are capable of it (existentialism). However, those who are capable of it in this society are only the strong – like in the jungle. If one asks for what purpose and for whom this freedom is supposed to be good, it is philosophically and shamefacedly admitted: for the ego of the strong. Thereby all democracy is openly betrayed, for democracy is, according to its political intention, always the advancing possibility of freedom for all.

Thus, within the contradiction between the *citoyen* and the bourgeois, the latter prevails over the former. The contempt that the strong bourgeois bestows on the starry-eyed *citoyen* finds itself strengthened in the latest development, in which the once bourgeois democratic *citoyen* is found again as the trade unionist and 'socialist'. Thereby the deep abyss that opened between the *citoyen* and the bourgeois in this century does not remain without effect on both. I have extensively described elsewhere both the positive effect, because humanist, as well as the negative effect, because it leads to the representatives of the *citoyen*-esque consciousness in the trade union and socialist movement having that consciousness diluted with bourgeois illusions. The effect on the bourgeois is still to be investigated. Here it is primarily about that type of bourgeois that Marx in his time only partially and only marginally had in mind, the bourgeois who has fully been 'purified' of the *citoyen*-esque, which has become dominant today.

Before we describe him, let it be noted that the dominant burgher [*Bürger*] from the Renaissance to the present (with the sole exception of the Calvinist burgher) was always godless. Yet the bourgeois godlessness of today has become something different. The liberal believer in progress of the nineteenth century ceded faith to the people; as an optimistic burgher oriented to this life and educated in natural science and philosophy, he had no category left over for the metaphysical and the afterlife, even if, in order to keep up appearances and uphold religion for the people, he occasionally went to church. The pessimist without ideals of today is – no matter if he mimes Christianity or not – godless, because he no longer discerns any meaning in the world, this world no longer has any God for him. The dissolved relationship between ego and God enables the former to self-indulgently accommodate itself, precisely to this world that has become empty of meaning, just as it allows the devil to self-indulgently feel at ease in hell. Here the godlessness has other roots: in contrast to the once erstwhile natural scientific optimism, today's decadent nihilism. If it is correct to say with Marx, 'Religion is the sigh of the oppressed creature', neither the dominant optimistic liberal of old nor the dominant nihilistic pessimist of today has any need of this sigh.

The condition in which the bourgeois, detached from the *citoyen*, currently finds himself is the condition of comfortable and self-indulgent disgust characteristic of all decadence, i.e., the condition of simultaneous negation of the world and accommodation to it. However, this relationship to the world exclusively mediated through disgust is not bearable in the long run. For the final consequence would be suicide. It is no coincidence that in the ranks of the existentialists much is philosophised about suicide. Therefore in the uppermost strata of our society, in the bourgeois elite, to whom that disgust is nearest, a sort of flight, in the form of the return to interiority is taking place at the moment: the self-indulgent accommodation to the world that has become empty and meaningless, to the world of the useful swamp, turns under the condition of extreme bourgeois individualism at a certain point into the 'art' of individual self-perfection, which is supposed to bestow the consciousness of enhancement of one's own person and superiority over others, over the 'masses' [*den Massenmenschen*].

Yet precisely because, by this opposition to the world, no real tasks are posed to the ego, the nurturing of interiority degenerates into empty ecstasy, which goes in circles and never arrives at real satisfaction. Thus the disgust is only increased, at best repressed into the unconscious, in order to preserve the appearance of soaring. The dead *citoyen* feigns life. The result is the simultaneous negation as well as the affirmation of this world: nihilistic negation in favour of interiority, in order to secure it from the grasp of the progressive and optimistic forces, and self-indulgent affirmation, in order to dominate and exploit it. The bourgeois, as the counterpart of the *citoyen*, with whom he wants nothing to do, arrives at his highest perfection.

Only socialist democracy, which will be the democracy of a classless society, will be able to overcome these contradictions. In the following, however, socialist democracy is not what shall be discussed, but rather the central phenomena of bourgeois democracy, or more precisely, the phenomena and complications that result from the contradiction between the further existence of class antagonisms and the proclamation of a democracy that is equally valid for all members of society. It will become apparent here that this democracy is differently understood by the propertied classes than by the working classes. It signifies for both, as will be shown in detail, the loss of their original and actual political substance: for the bourgeoisie the loss of the bourgeois democratic 'face', for the working classes the loss of the socialist democratic 'face'. Both end up in the situation of the tragicomic hero, who is in denial about his face, but who is seen through by the sympathetically smiling audience. Depending on the historical moment, sometimes the tragic prevails, at other times the comical. In quiet times the 'worker's representative' appears to the people as the tail of the bourgeoisie, from whom he wrests a smile, the representative of the bourgeoisie as the keen gambler who gambles away his democratic assets; in times of historical or social tension the relationship reverses to the effect that the burgher out of fear for his purse acts out the most comical impulses, while the 'revolutionary' allows the practised cleverness of his opponent to deal with his advantage piece by piece. At any rate, the loser is always the working people for under all these conditions the bourgeoisie holds authority firmly in its hands.

France minted the greatest revolution of the bourgeoisie. The rising 'bourgeois', as he designated himself, found in the great revolution the term '*citoyen*' for daily intercourse with others. The ambivalence of the designation, in itself a coincidence, soon proved to be a thoroughly suitable means of recognition of the contradictory character of the bourgeois individual. The result of this apparently only terminological process was the surprising insight that the bourgeois had betrayed the *citoyen*. It proved that the equation of *citoyen* and bourgeois only takes place in the illusory ideological consciousness of the bourgeois class, but not in historical reality.

Citoyen is burgher-citizen [*Bürger-Staatsbürger*], in contrast to the mere subject of the Middle Ages, formally endowed with full bourgeois freedoms; he experiences himself – originally according to a transfigured model of the ancient city-states – as part of a free whole, which he serves in order to gain from it. Conversely, the bourgeois. This bourgeois experiences himself as an egoistical being, who unconcernedly pursues his individual interests in the space of the struggle of all against all, which terms itself 'free competition'; his relation to the whole is that of the beneficiary, of the recipient, who only grudgingly serves.

In truth, the *citoyen* and the bourgeois live like hostile neighbours in the breast of each burgher, not without coming into conflict with each other at every moment. If, however, the *citoyen* prevails over the bourgeois or the latter over the former, that is decided by the respective historical and social situation. At the time of the bourgeois revolution the *citoyen* oppressed the bourgeois, since then the tide has turned. In every case he appears as a one-sided being, as an angel or devil, as having alighted from the heaven of paradisiacal equality or the hell of devilish selfishness. Yet in both cases he deludes himself about himself, for he is, in fact, both at the same time, albeit not in the form of agreement, but that of contradiction. As *citoyen* he participates in public affairs, feel responsible for the whole; as bourgeois he uses the whole for his own purposes – he is a private individual.

Until approximately 1848 the *citoyen*-esque enthusiasm smouldered on for all that 'which bears a human countenance', and from then on, particularly since the proletariat began in that year to form themselves into an independent force, it became increasingly extinguished. The *citoyen* dropped his flags and took flight. Not without soon returning to live out his private happiness and surrender the happiness of others to the state, the police, welfare and social legislation.

This does not mean that the civic soul, the counterpart of the bourgeois, has completely died away in the breast of the burgher of today. Not only does he go vote every four years and rejoices over the successes of 'public life', he also keeps his civic consciousness alive in other ways. If he is afflicted with grief over the constant casualties of his 'order', he anxiously turns again to politics, in which there are very diverse possibilities, direct and indirect, open and hidden, even if he only monitors the 'politicking' [*politisieren*], as he likes to say, of those he commissions and pays well for their services.

The problem of the relation of the *citoyen* to the bourgeois is a serious sociological problem. Whoever wants to think through the problem of freedom in our society to its conclusion must pose the question: Which freedom does one actually mean, that of the *citoyen* or that of the bourgeois? Freedom and freedom are not the same under all conditions: the freedom of the *citoyen* is democracy, that of the bourgeois is liberalism. This remains to be demonstrated, but it is programmatically declared so that the notion that democracy expressed a constitutional form, and liberalism, by contrast, a form of society, penetrated into our heads from the reference books, does not entrench itself right at the beginning. Instead of extrapolating from the terminology of the reference book to reality, one should more reasonably extrapolate from reality to the terminology.

There are certainly still a few *citoyens* with democratic consciousness in the bourgeoisie, still a few real 'fellows'. However, they are the last, standing forlorn at their posts and hoping nevertheless to still be able to carry on the realisation of the great bourgeois humanist ideas of old. In their own ranks, the bourgeois ranks, they are seen as black sheep who are not taken seriously. The spirit of the *citoyen* has left the bourgeoisie and has sought a new home. This new home is the people, to whom the bourgeoisie do not belong. Democratic convictions today live on alone in the people, where it opposes convictions that are accustomed to calling themselves 'liberal democratic', but in truth represent merely liberal, in distinction to democratic, convictions. The victory of the bourgeois over the *citoyen* in the breast of the burgher has alienated him from democracy, and thus also from the people, who in this manner have become the sole refuge of democracy. Present-day society consequently fragments with regards to its prevailing political mood into two parts quite clearly distinguished from each other: into the liberal part, whose core is formed by the bourgeoisie, and into the democratic part, whose core essentially consists of the proletariat.

With conscientious investigation this neoliberalesque ideology reveals itself as an amalgam of the old liberalism and the elements that have grown up from the soil of the monopolistic development of capitalist society (in particular that which developed between the two World Wars), theoretically denying classes and thus a total romanticism, orienting itself to the estates-based and medieval. Adam Smith and Othmar Spann here join their hands. On one side: allow to continue to exist the monopolistic powers with all the perilous inclinations that reside in them for the revival of fascism in some sort of 'better' form – since democratic convictions have put down powerful roots in the people after the defeat of fascism and in the face of the terror of the Stalinist dictatorship, capitalism only defends itself, if at all, with liberal principles and arguments. Therefore the new orientation of bourgeois ideologues to the liberalism of old, albeit with the necessary constraint and distinction from its 'vulgar' optimism. On the other side: precisely this continued existence of the monopolistic and by their nature reactionary powers, whose influences and moods flow through a thousand veins in the intellectual circulation process of society, urges these neoliberal ideologues, whose historical task it is to give to this bourgeois class, extensively dominated by these powers, a 'modern' ideology adapted to the conditions, onto the path of a consistent anti-democratism, although under the appearance of recognition of democracy: i.e., with verbal affirmation of the people's desire for a society with a truly democratic form of life.

Neoliberal ideology is thus nothing other than the expression of a re-liberalisation of the public of society after the defeat of fascism under the condition of the retention of essentially monopolistic traits of this society. That individual liberal theorists, such as the anti-trade unionist Röpke, make an effort to mitigate economic and 'bureaucratic', i.e., state monopolism, does not signify much, since this problem cannot be negotiated with mere words. The 'critique' that they make is instead only suitable for giving their liberalism a democratic veneer and thus make it more palatable to the audience. We do not say that this lies in the subjective intention of the liberal scholars, but that it is the only objective effect.

The great crises in the history of humanity always appear at the transitions from one social order to another. They are marked by regressions into conditions of human barbarism that have already been overcome. The ideologue who wants to demonstrate that it is completely nonsensical to believe in progress in history clings to them. In such historical moments, when both the ruling classes as well as the classes striving for greater freedom often employ the most 'illegitimate' means in their struggle and when history shows its grim face, it may appear as if the dark moments of the crisis-ridden passage of society to a higher form of its being were the essences and history merely verifies this in them. The pessimists appear to be proved right and win the upper hand in the social consciousness of their time.

Today these theorists of liberalism are among the most influential bearers of this pessimism. Their influence reaches deep into the democratic organisations that otherwise treat liberalism with reserve, not least in the trade union organisations, without anyone here becoming conscious of it.

Only the consciousness of the progressive tendency of history, which we have to recognise as a complicated sequence of ever higher stages of freedom, may call itself democratic with good conscience. Every other conception of history that negates the concept of progress in historical development with an understanding of human 'essence' that constantly remains the same and is judged as inherently negative may otherwise call itself whatever it fancies, but it stands in obvious contradiction to any genuine democracy. Where the concept of individual freedom in the sense of a spontaneous and arbitrary being for oneself (*Aufsichgestelltsein*), that of the laissez-faire individual, remains the dominant idea, it might be meaningfully joined with bourgeois democratic beliefs – but this joining becomes impossible as soon as the foundation of any genuine democratic conviction, namely the affirmation of progress in history in the sense described above, is missing and gives way to a pessimistic view. In the former case, the *citoyen* and bourgeois are identical, in the case of pessimism-tempered neoliberalism, the *citoyen* and bourgeois end up in unending opposition to each other.

The course of development put inside historical being, which is supposed to justify neoliberalism's pessimistic idea of man and society, pursues the purpose of reconciling the process of human development with the static notion that basically nothing happens, and in this manner tries to remove the revolutionary sting, i.e., the revolutionising of conditions, from the concept of freedom, naturally with the claim of its sole validity for individualist and egoistic society. Of course, the movement of history is not denied; if anything it is rhetorically emphasised. Yet it appears in this thought as the mere unfolding of something already existing, it becomes here an illusion [*Schein*]: it basically does not change at all! Stasis is raised to the actual principle of interpretation of history [*Geschichtsbetrachtung*], no matter how little it agrees with the real image of previous human development. However, stasis and democracy exclude one another. A 'conservative democracy' is a contradiction in itself. At best, there is a conservative liberalism. Liberalism certainly gains the appearance of being democratic from the formal existence of democratic rights in the constitution and legislation: it however also gains this appearance from the Stalinist and totalitarian threat, which the democratic people fear just as much as a bourgeoisie unrestrained by democracy. Against this danger of a totalitarian Stalinist threat, a 'united front' of society and the bourgeoisie in the Western nations, which disguises the contradiction between the republican and democratic understanding and the liberal and bourgeois understanding, from which the bourgeois parties undeservedly profit at elections.

Pursuant to the structural contradiction between democracy and liberalism, the concept of freedom also differentiates itself into two irreconcilable modes of appearance, as when it is still presented as a bourgeois (and not as a, say, socialist) concept. One says that every bourgeois concept of freedom, or that which circulates on the ground of bourgeois class society, cannot do without formalism, because every attempt at thinking it through to its conclusion will bump against the limits of the capitalist order. This is certainly correct. However, it is easy to overlook the fact that, despite the serious difficulties that the further existence of capitalist private property at the large and socially decisive manufacturing facilities creates for the realisation of democratic desire and action, the world of democracy is a different one than that of liberalism, both in the setting of ideological goals as well in the practical attempts at their realisation. This is better demonstrated by the practical consequences that this will have for the validity [*Geltung*] of various forces within the established order, from the trade unions and cooperatives on the one side to the exponents of management [*Unternehmertum*] on the other.

Bourgeois and *citoyen* consider themselves equally free, yet each, despite the mutual affirmation of bourgeois individualist freedom, in specifically different ways. What initially stands out is that the liberal bourgeois understands the freedom of the individual in the realm of the bourgeois class order as absolute, while the democratic *citoyen* understands it as relative. This relativity consists in the fact that the democrat does not allow individual freedom to only become self-sufficiency, but rather understands it as the precondition of an only anticipatory fulfilment of a higher state of freedom of man and society. The democrat is not always clear about what is understood by that, since the desire for the fulfilment of complete freedom is indeed critical of existing property and class relations, but not in a way that recognises the necessity of their abolition. That is precisely why he is and remains, despite the sharpest antagonisms with the mere liberal, an essentially bourgeois democrat, even if his class affiliation is that of the worker or his role that of the trade union official – formally a representative of the workers striving beyond the bourgeois order. Thus his democratic mode of thinking, on the one hand, going beyond the merely liberal standpoint, on the other, however, remaining in the bourgeois standpoint, receives a tug into the illusory, since it harbours utopian expectations regarding the possibility of the further development of the bourgeois capitalist order to highly developed humanitarian conditions.

However, it would be completely erroneous to conclude from this that genuine civic democratic thought, which we already stated at the beginning has found its new home at the present moment in the working people and its organisations, would have no important social task to fulfil. The opposite is the case. It fulfils the task of confronting the mere pseudo-democratic liberalism with critical sharpness, removing its pseudo-democratic mask and thereby invigorating and consolidating the consciousness of the necessity for further development of society beyond its given state. The representatives of democracy certainly soon find themselves, precisely because they are not free of illusions about the possibility of such a social development up to the desired points within the capitalist order, faced with the alternative of either falling back into the mere liberal mode of thinking or striving beyond the framework of the bourgeois order, and giving thought to the future shaping of society. The danger of resignedly submitting oneself to liberalism is very great under present-day conditions [*Bedingungen*]. However, because this tendency of democracy to turn one's back and give in to conservative liberalism is so strong under present-day conditions [*Verhältnissen*], is precisely also why the *citoyen* has become so rare in the ranks of the bourgeois class, and democratic thought has passed over to the non-bourgeois classes.

In contrast to the concept of freedom of the democratic *citoyen*, that of the liberal bourgeois is absolute, i.e., self-sufficiently confined to the formal freedom of action of the individual and emptied of all genuine objectives concerning higher social development. The liberal bourgeois concept of freedom has no illusions save one – to stop history and establish a halfway smoothly functioning society that constantly turns itself in circles. The liberal catchphrase of 'socially-tempered capitalism' is only another expression for this illusion. Everything should roughly go on as before, not excluding a few 'reforms' that should gloss over the darkest spots of the capitalist order of life. What has hitherto been integrated into the order, has 'stabilised' in it, such as the 'stabilised trade unions' of Professor Goetz Briefs, and should remain in the interest of preserving 'balance', i.e., in the interest of preserving the appearance as if there was anything remotely like such a balance between those forces – those who hold tremendous agglomerated power in their hands, and those genuinely democratic ones striving against them. The democratic constitution that guarantees this 'balance' should remain inviolate, because it has at the same time proved itself a splendid means of securing the predominance of these forces. As once in medieval Florence, whose history Davidson so splendidly researched, where the rulers had developed the art of veiling their rule with a democratic constitution misleading the people, so it is no different in our time, despite the miscellaneous advances that have been made and which must be taken seriously. Thus one can say today that the democratic rules of the game are only still observed by those who believe in them: the working people and their organisations. Liberalism and democracy part here in clear terms.

Nowhere, however, does the opposition between liberalism and democracy emerge so clearly as in the question of workers' participation in decision-making [*Mitbestimmung der Arbeiterschaft*] in enterprises. It is well-known that the idea of workers' participation arose in trade union practice in Germany within the context of a very limited array of questions, namely the need for administration of manufacturing facilities at the end of the war that had become ownerless. In addition, of course, the idea of workers' participation retains a fundamental significance for the further development of any given state system [*Staatswesen*] in a democratic direction. Quite often in history, an idea that under 'normal circumstances' no one dared to conceive has been born from the necessity of the time, in order for it to be retroactively proven fundamentally significant for further social development.

The fundamental nature of the question of workers' participation in decision-making in capitalist enterprises arises from the acute problem of the continuation of bourgeois society, previously held by the rule of the liberal bourgeoisie in merely liberal forms, to the the height of its democratic form, i.e., the highest possible form of social coexistence within capitalism. It has previously penetrated the consciousness of those involved that such diverse forms as fascism and democracy can alternate on the same basis of a single capitalist society, but it still has hardly been understood that liberalism and democracy amongst themselves express further social orders of magnitude [*gesellschaftliche Ordnungsgrößen*] that can come into opposition with each other. The reason lies in the fact that we have, as will soon be shown, almost no examples of really democratic political systems [*Staatswesen*] – only on the margins of our present-day society – so that a political and scientific consciousness which uncritically reflects reality is inclined to regard what calls itself democracy as democracy, even though it is mere liberalism.

If one has understood that the question of workers' participation is still not at all about the opposition of capitalism and socialism, which moves on an entirely different plane, but rather only about the expansion of liberalism to democracy in the framework of capitalism, then one is also protected from the utopian misunderstanding that has not infrequently been spread in trade union circles, as if workers' participation in decision-making in enterprises were the first step to socialism. Such a utopianism endangers, on the one hand, the clear vision of socialists who give into the illusion of being able to realise socialism in capitalism. It has not escaped notice that not only numerous trade unionists, but also practitioners and theorists of the newer socialism, think themselves very clever if they succumb to the illusion of hollowing out capitalism from the inside and taking it by surprise. It is not exaggerated to determine that under the conditions of alienation the immediate contact of the socialist trade unionist with the problem of workers' participation, having surprisingly moved so near and become acute, leads to a dangerous weakening of his socialist consciousness. On the other hand, a non-socialist, for example, Christian trade unionist feels affected by this hasty and mistaken equation, not seen through by him, of the struggle for workers' participation and the struggle for socialism, and therefore pushes to distance himself from the consistent demand for workers' participation, and to regard a 'moderate' form as completely sufficient. Just as the socialist, through an overestimation of workers' participation and the belief that it plainly represents a philosopher's stone in the solution of the social question, expects everything from it and winds up pursuing a false radicalism, so the non-socialist trade union official by the same token believes he has much to fear from it, which pushes him onto the path of an equally false moderation.

There is nothing dormant in history. Capitalism is not finished once and for all, as long as it has still not been replaced by the next historical epoch. This assessment holds especially true with regards to its present concrete form. Capitalism is also situated in a state of constant movement and change. Its complex system possesses a certain structure that can only be fundamentally changed with the replacement of the capitalist social order. Yet within this field of force new tensions and problems emerge. One such problem is the incorporation of the workforce into the responsible bodies [*Funktionskörper*] of enterprises, arising from postwar development, and the ever more acute need for a transition of the bourgeois liberal order to a bourgeois democratic one, exacerbated by the fact of the looming one-sided monopolistic development and its associated power politics of social life in favour of the ruling classes.

Workers' participation thus has nothing to do with the future-suffused objective of the transition of capitalist property to social ownership. Positively, the task falls to workers' participation to secure and expand the achievements of the workforce, to restrict management's [*Unternehmertum*] exploitation of its economic position, to reduce management's previous advantage of an exact knowledge of proceedings within the company through acquisition of precisely this knowledge and, finally, to be that school for the representatives of the workforce through which inferiority versus management can possibly be overthrown.

The prevention of the 're-fascisisation' [*Refaschisierung*] of public life, the danger of which is still strongly underestimated, likewise belongs to this array of questions.

The question of workers' participation is not a question of the realisation of socialism, but rather the democratisation of bourgeois order in the sense of continuing its previously only liberal form of life in a democratic one.

Rhetorically, the bourgeois liberal also does not deny the necessity of a certain measure of workers' participation in the enterprise. Yet if one looks closer, his concession turns out to be a trick. Workers' participation for the liberal ideologues amounts to a highly formalistic right to be heard for the purpose of feigning democratic rights in the service of that doctrine coming from America, although minimally sincere, on the alleviation of tensions in the relationship between management and workers with the aid of an external system of 'humanisation' of the atmosphere in the company. We are dealing here with an offshoot of the old teaching that class peace is possible without fundamental transformation of social relations. The point is not to deny that with a cleverly devised method a certain external alleviation of tensions for a certain period can be attained in the relationship of the 'social partners'. However, this does not change anything about the condition of alienation and dehumanisation. On the contrary, it only consolidates itself all the more and becomes a means of impeding the democratisation of society. Not only the problem of workers' participation, but any component problem of social life in our time would demonstrate how correct it is to speak of a democratic workforce and a liberal bourgeoisie. The workers are those who are yearning for democratisation, while the insistence on and adherence to what exists stands for the possessing bourgeoisie as the guarantee of the preservation of its social privileges. The bourgeoisie's standpoint is hopeless, seen in the long run; since there is no history without movement.

Yet how to complete the movement, if the ruling and powerful social forces use all the weight of the means of the state available to them, school, university, press, culture, etc., in order to help the liberals to victory against the democratic forces? Can the weaker progressive classes in this situation, for whom all these means are only available in limited measure or not at all, be content with waiting for the great historical miracle that sometime something will happen? Are they not instead compelled to look around for other means, for democratic means, which arise as a result from the social position of the worker and are therefore the most important he can avail himself of? However, even such a thought is considered by the representatives of liberalism as a shameful betrayal of 'democracy', even though this thought is far more suited to serve the development and consolidation of democracy than all the pseudo-democratic ideas of liberal theory put together. The liberal bourgeoisie and its theorists fear nothing more than the resolve of the working classes to serve democracy with all the peaceful means available to them and in their way. Therefore they defame such means as protest, demonstration, or even the strike as undemocratic, because they fear nothing more than democracy.

The argument over whether demonstrations and strikes in all their forms, including political demonstrations and political strikes, are legal or not, is only possible in a state that is democratic according to its constitution, but in substance remains stuck in liberalism, and in which the *citoyen* is subordinate to the bourgeois. Which methods liberalism is accustomed to employing when it goes against democracy is already demonstrated by its language when it justifies its attempt to limit the right to strike with the necessity of 'protecting the democratic decision-making process', as if in contemporary society it was only a question of protecting perfected democratic harmony, equal rights, and mutual trust against the attempted disturbances of the 'monolithic' dictatorship-craving trade unions. In light of the one-sided class rule of the bourgeoisie, which has been perforated in some places thanks to the encroachments of democratic forces in our century, but is far from being shaken, the Heidelberg scholar Alfred Weber bravely posed the question of whether it is not more necessary to demand more democratic decision-making from business and the parties and organisations dependent on them.

Goetz Briefs, however, talks as if there were no longer any serious problems of bourgeois democracy, as if the contemporary social form of capitalism par excellence completely coincides with democracy, i.e., its conceptual content. The topic of his book, he says, was not merely dedicated to the trade unions, but rather 'primarily to the worker, his wife and his children, for it is about their worth and dignity, about their future as persons and as members in an intrinsically ordered society'.[1] Since this is the case, the spokesmen of the trade union movement do not have the right 'to advocate for extra-parliamentary struggle against a democratically-elected government with transparent sophistry'. One can only stop dead with astonishment at the sophistry of the theorists of liberalism. The poor working-class family raped by the trade union, while it is in a state, after all, 'with a democratically-elected government', enjoying all conceivable social, human and cultural rights and has nothing left to demand beyond protective laws against the assaults of the trade union movement. The sophistry, however, becomes perfidy, when Goetz Briefs undertakes to feign the appearance of justification for his arguments by imputing to the trade union the intention of 'seizing power' and attempts to convince the reader that the trade unions 'are indifferent to all democracy when it is a question of their power and your interests'.

This recalls the following historical incident. When in the thirteenth century the Inquisition was founded for the extermination of the harmless and peaceful sectarian movement that was preparing to spread from northern Italy and southern France across the whole of Europe, it was shortly afterwards handed over by the Pope to the Dominicans for implementation. The reputation of the Dominican Order, whose monastic habit only permitted the colours black and white to be visible, sank from then on in the eyes of the people who, in phonetic distortion, made out of the word 'Dominican' the phrase 'domini canes', i.e., the hounds of the Lord. The persecuted, in particular, only spoke after this of the inquisitors ironically, as the black and white mottled tracking dogs of the Lord. However, the Dominicans of that time, who anticipated the liberals of today, knew how to fend for themselves. They had images painted in chapels showing how the black and white mottled dogs protected the vineyard of the Lord from the cunning heretical foxes who coveted the grapes. All of a sudden the persecuted thus became the dangerous assailants and the inquisitors the defenders of the perfect and inviolate order in church and state, an order that revealed all its foulness under the onslaught of the reformation on the church and revolution on the state and collapsed like a rotten tree.

Only now are we in the position to answer the question of where democratic state systems [*Staatswesen*] which cannot not be spoken of as socialist, are to be encountered in this world. The completion of democracy is incumbent upon the forces to the 'left' of the bourgeoisie. Where these have attained control

---

1 Briefs 1952, p. 10.

[*Herrschaft*] in the state, only there are we dealing with really bourgeois democratic political systems, with bourgeois democracies. Only the terminologically exact distinction between democracy and liberalism allows us to give a satisfactory answer, free of contradiction, to the important question of where we actually encounter a completed bourgeois democracy.

If we look more closely at the states ruled by socialists in Europe's north, this is what can initially be stated: these states would only be societally socialist if the raw materials and staple goods enterprises engaged in large-scale production were converted to social ownership, thereby withdrawing the decisive foundation for capitalism. This is only minimally the case in these states. In this respect they are not socialist. At the same time, they fundamentally differ from the purely bourgeois-governed capitalist states through their popular [*volkshafte*] and dynamic way of government: They are what embodies the fully bourgeois democratic form of life in contrast to the merely liberal one in our time. Additionally, our insight arising from the analysis of our society is vindicated in them, namely that in the process of the sociological divorce of the *citoyen* and the bourgeois, democracy at present essentially focused on the lower popular classes, so that democracy in the practical arena only gains life and shape where the political representatives of these classes, thanks to a favourable historical constellation, have arrived in government earlier than in other bourgeois states. Where the working classes have succeeded in helping socialist parties to power [*Herrschaft*], but where at the same time the path to socialism is not pursued, only there do we have in front of us true democracy in the civic liberal [*bürgerlich-freiheitlichen*] sense. If we require some sort of convincing confirmation of this thesis, let reference be made to the fact that precisely such phenomena as mass demonstrations and the right to strike, which in our liberal states are still objects of endless disputes and spiteful animosities on the part of the leading [*maßgeblichen*] circles and governments, no longer represent a serious point of contention in the really democratic states of the north, no object of class struggle from above.

It is Goetz Briefs, again, who hastens to excuse the grim sides of liberalism with reference to the 'human situation' and to the inevitably of 'disappointments' in human life. The meaning of such references can only lie in enervating and devaluing all serious references to the real and concrete, the historically shaped, and to a definite 'situation' of man towards capitalist society, suffused by a set of problems to be solved concretely.

In the chapter 'American Industry and the Human Factor', Georges Friedmann sketches a very specific human situation, that of the worker in the highly-industrialised capitalist enterprise. Can this situation be changed and improved? Friedmann provides concrete details, of which one should be highlighted by way of example, showing how fundamentally human situations can change: 'The reduction of the working day and the overcoming of the opposition between city and country indicate paths full of hope for the future'.[2] Friedmann employs an entirely different language and his perspectives on the human situation are not only permeated by an optimistic spirit, but also have the character of concreteness. Even where Friedmann goes into the psychological side of the 'human situation' problem, he remains concrete, explaining its modes of appearance not from any sort of abstract concept of 'situation', but rather from man's being as observed by him and scientifically analysed. He lets it be known that the situation of man in our time has nothing to do with any sort of eternal character traits bestowed by nature, but rather results from capitalist society's way of existence. He writes:

> In any event, one indeed speaks a lot of relationship, of alleviating tensions and the necessity of relieving internal strain [*Verkrampfung*] ... as the economic boom already demonstrates for the real and so-called 'psychoanalysts', among whom many controversial – and dangerous – charlatans are found. Another symptom the sociologist must not overlook: the number of works brought out in large print runs with outstanding sales that suggest and recommend various means and 'cures' for attaining peace of mind. *The Peace of the Mind* is the name of one of these handbooks, among which Dale Carnegie's is the most widespread, teaching millions of Americans (and Europeans, since the translations were also pronounced commercial successes in Europe) the art of acquiring happiness [*Freude zu gewinnen*].[3]

Such accounts arise from a fundamental cognisance of the situation of man in our time and provide not the slightest justification for speaking of any sort of 'situation' of man 'in general'. The opposition between the two conceptions of the 'human situation' – the historically concrete one and the abstract one disregarding history – likewise express the existing opposition between democracy and liberalism in the reality and thought of our time.

The historical and sociological optimism does not deny the profoundly tragic note in all human being. Yet for this optimism it is no empty 'psychological' assessment, but rather comprehensible from the concrete contradiction of social areas of tension, from whose constant resolutions and recomposi-

---

2 Friedmann 1953, p. 81.
3 Friedmann 1953, p. 79.

tions the historically new and higher is born. The tragedy of this development does not solely lie in the stagnations and regressions accompanying them, by which the lone individual is affected and falls into a tragic situation. The tragedy of the historical individual lies in the fact that his goals and acts collide against the concrete historical space and are rarely realised according to what was intended. Moreover, it is precisely the significant individuals who, thinking far beyond their own time in their objectives and 'dreams', only rarely see the life's work they have set for themselves fulfilled, and therefore often end up in that condition of bitter resignation that is tantamount to the tragic collapse. At the same time, however – and this must not be overlooked – their life is also fulfilment, since it fulfils their hope that their thought and action may become levers of the historical progression of humanity. Abstractly making this context into an empty 'human situation' directly bypasses the essence of the tragic and history, and overlooks the dialectical tension that also bring something positive, something sublime [*Erhabenes*]. It especially overlooks the role of the tragic in the process of historical progress. Certainly, tension is predominant in human life. Yet this tension results in the field of the crossroad [*Kreuzung*] of struggle for survival, passion, sorrow, enjoyment, ideal striving, fulfilment, etc. Above all, it is shortsighted to conclude that human life must be something simply negative, dark – more precisely, hostile to progress. The great expert in human nature [*Menschenkenner*] Goethe saw more deeply when he once depicted in the following way how he had enjoyed life: 'I have gloriously enjoyed a little sampling of the motley activities of the world: vexation, hopes, love, work, hardship, adventure, boredom, hate, tomfooleries, follies, joy, expected and unexpected, shallow and deep, as the dice fall'.

The individualistic and alienated liberal mode of thought is not in the position to comprehend the complicated context. It does not understand that in the face of the shallow optimism of the old liberalism that understood the higher development of society as a straight line and without contradictions, the role of the tragic in history must be recognised; and, conversely, that in the face of today's dominant neoliberal pessimism, it must be underlined that history is nothing other than a chain of ever new problems posed and being solved at an ever higher level. Because liberal ideology represents an extreme form of alienation of consciousness in our time, it not only encounters democratic aspirations and struggles without any understanding, but also obstructs its own path to the recognition of the essence of the historical in general. What is particularly difficult for it is the grasping of the various historical phenomena as aspects of a comprehensive and contradiction-filled process, or, in concrete application of this insight to our problem, the recognition simply of the role of the democratic in history. Liberal ideology becomes reactionary.

As a whole, neoliberal doctrine proves itself to be a disguised doctrine of class struggle of the most unrestrained type. Class struggle today on the terrain of monopolistically-inclined capitalism has taken the form of the struggle between neoliberalism and democracy, whereby the question of the further development of society into a form overcoming capitalism plays a complicated role. In possession of social privileges and powers, the liberal bourgeoisie propagates class peace, the voluntary submission of the working classes under their rule. In the case of noncompliance with their views, they threaten with state measures. Their doctrine is thus nothing other than a doctrine of class struggle against class struggle, or as the liberal ideologues like to express it, against the 'doctrine of envy that is class struggle'.[4] One is therefore not surprised that an otherwise so reserved and conciliatory author as Karl Mannheim feels himself compelled to say: 'This, the reactionary, attitude more or less complacently accepts the existing forms of social and political oppression and does not seek to change the social techniques in use'.[5] As little as it may be clear to liberal minds: this is also class struggle – today being fought between liberalism and democracy.

However, this answer to the question of the character and reality of bourgeois democracy has nothing to do with the question of the essence of socialist democracy, and the mature socialism to be realised in the eventual future. The question of socialism transcends in every respect that which is directed to bourgeois democracy. This must be properly understood. For otherwise that ever so shameful muddle comes into being which is rooted in the confusion of the struggle for the utilisation and completion of bourgeois democracy against mere liberalism and its modern monopolistic excesses with the struggle to overcome the bourgeois class order, and thereby also bourgeois democracy in favour of socialist democracy.

As a result, let it be said that only in the process of the completion of the bourgeois conceptual world did that internal contradiction come to light which we have exposed, by means of depicting the contradiction between the declaration of popular sovereignty and the denial of the right to vote to the workers, as already inherent in the revolutionary bourgeoisie of the past and in its innermost essence. Here it becomes clear that bourgeois thought, in which the vulgar materialist equation of person and proprietor, of man and material disposition, remains the insurmountably dominant conception arising from the

---

4 See *Gedanken zur sozialen Ordnung*, published by the Bundesvereinigung der Deutschen Arbeitgeberverbände, 1953, Section IV.
5 Mannheim 1943, p. 147.

social being of the bourgeoisie, unable to change its spots. Further development proves that under the new conditions of winning the participation of the people in certain democratic rights – that incidentally the bourgeoisie understood how to manipulate very well, and despite the shamefaced concealment of this still dominant conception – this conception represents today as before, the last determinant of bourgeois consciousness. Therefore, bourgeois liberalism cannot be democratic simply because its own undemocratic concept of man prevents it. Even the newest slogan, which amounts to helping provide every worker with property, cannot honestly mean it, since the bourgeoisie knows very well that in bourgeois class society, individual freedom with all its consequences for the achievement of a completely changed condition of life for the individual only begins where the necessity of selling labour power stops. What it does not know, however, is that in the world based on the division of labour, which already deforms and alienates individuality in its simplest manifestations of life, even sufficient property will not liberate man, so that the aforementioned slogan, for this reason alone, even with its feasibility hypothetically assumed, cannot lead to any satisfying result. The equation of man and property-owner becomes an impediment for the equation of man and freedom.

The optimistic notion of the old bourgeois humanists, particularly of the eighteenth century, already suffered in particular from being completely uncritical of capitalist property. What moved them and had to move them as revolutionary individualists was their dream that man, on the foundation of future economic harmonisation, would obtain the possibility of developing his individual strengths, facilities, and talents to the height that they called 'personality', in a sense non-exclusive, but democratic. However, their idea of the future participation of all in the economic prosperity of society was abstract and indeterminate. Just as they saw the astoundingly developing division of labour in front of their eyes only as a wealth-increasing force, but overlooked its inhuman effect, because it destroyed the entirety of the individual personality – apart from a few ingenious approaches in Rousseau, Linguet, among others – they overlooked in the same manner the undemocratic consequences lying in the capitalist enterprise. They saw only the formal equality of the self-determination of the individual in the form of the 'free contract', but not that 'the republic of the market conceals the despotism of the factory'. The thinkers of the Enlightenment understandably could not yet escape the dilemma between blind capitalist materialism and far-sighted humanist idealism. All the same, their merit of having established humanist optimism remains indisputable, resting on the three pillars of prosperity, freedom and personality.

At any rate, the magnificent image that the humanists painted of future man shattered after the revolution against the internal contradictions of bourgeois order. The bourgeois class, having long deteriorated into a one-sided practical [*praktizistischen*] egoism, even in the thought of their ideologues, sneer today at the eighteenth century as one of 'shallow reasoning' [*vernünftlerische*], 'unhistorical' [*unhistorische*], sinking into 'shallow enlightment' [*Aufkläricht*], they deny their own parents. They do not do it without reason, but in order to be able to better shield themselves against all humanism and against all democracy.

The Progressive Elite [1959]

Considered on a surface level, the progressive elite, which will be discussed in the following, does not exist, since they are found nowhere as a particular, sharply demarcated group.* They also do not represent a specific part of a class, like the ruling elite. They are instead composed of many different elements that not infrequently oppose each other in outlook, ambition, and habitus, which barely pay attention to and do not know each other. Looked at more closely, they are a shapeless mass with strongly fluctuating tendencies.

The progressive elite of the epoch of bourgeois decadence is the result of two historical components, one negative and one positive: on the one hand, the decomposition of the once impressive and respected role of the socialist workers' movement and its world of humanist ideas as the tribune of the people and, on the other, the continuing effects of an anti-nihilism and humanism smouldering everywhere in the ashes of capitalist decadence and nihilism. The spirit of resistance in all classes (even the bourgeoisie) ever rising up anew, in the domains of various worldviews and religious orientations, where in greater or smaller numbers, people are to be found who think independently, who can settle for neither the spirit of the nihilistic amalgamation nor the highfalutin, hollowly libertine and aristocratic anti-popular subjectivism. Thus alongside the main line between socialism and anti-socialism runs a varying dividing line straight through the traditional social and ideological fronts, which is significant for understanding modern historical disputes. Thus the badge of the socialist, which some wear in the button hole out of good old tradition, is no longer a reliable sign of having truly progressive views. Many a socialist and many a trade union official have long 'integrated', that is, without being fully conscious of it, have fitted themselves into the bourgeois capitalist apparatus's structure [*Gefüge*]; and others, only in part convinced socialists, sometimes even encounter socialist thought with critical wariness. Not infrequently the mind disappointed by socialist practice retains for itself, out of a deep animosity against all inhumanity and alienation, its independence of thought and the strength for the humanist No, which is not to be confused with the nihilist one.

History, which leads man up to ever higher stages of freedom, does not let itself be deceived. It is in its entirety cleverer than its individual exponent, for when it is deceived by the individuals called to accelerate its process, where

---

* [Originally published as "Die progressive Elite" in: *Periodikum für wissenschaftlichen Sozialismus*, Heft 6/1959, p. 61 onwards.]

revolutionary forces fail, it creates a replacement, to whom the task of securing the transition falls. In our time the progressive elite is this replacement. Yet it is a replacement and not a surrogate, and therefore a force to be taken seriously, which has become an important factor in public life, simply by virtue of its existence, not to mention the virtue of its effective actions, even if often only realised with cautious reluctance and in silence.

Their representatives can be found, often fearfully concealing themselves, rarely putting everything in the balance, anywhere there are institutions: in the local councils, the schools and educational institutions, the religious organisations, the cultural associations, the political and non-political societies, even occasionally in the ministries, and obviously one finds them among independent writers, artists, and academics, for which the physicists in recent years have provided a striking example in taking a prominent stance on the question of nuclear armament.

The progressive elite cannot, however, replace the workers' movement historically called to transform society. It remains merely a temporary replacement for this movement in the intervening periods of its degeneration, an indispensable ferment that preserves society from the rigidity of death. Yet, on the other hand, it is not superfluous in times of the reliable functioning of the workers' movement, for in such moments it becomes an integral component, particularly in the public impact of this movement.

In times of decadence, the progressive elite does not let life come to rest: it preserves life from death. It is everywhere that you least expect it, admittedly – and this is one of its most dangerous contradictions – not without the tendency to stay away where one assuredly expects it. It tends to be consistent in its inner stance and inconsistent in its external stance. This reflects its unhappy origin, its character as an aggregate and the circumstance in which it is not backed by a definite historically emergent class. Its strength is not its origins, not its social basis, but rather its incorruptible desire for the creation of truly human conditions. From this desire stems the compassion with simple working people, those most struck by the blows of alienation, and therefore it often demonstrates – albeit, in turn, in strong gradations – a social revolutionary streak.

From the extensive arguments about what was actually to be recognised as an elite, let us highlight for our purpose the voice of Prof. Ernst Steinbach. At a convention organised by the Evangelical Academy in Bad Boll, he said:

> The elite is first and foremost characterised by the fact that it keeps itself strictly disciplined. Someone who is not able to make decisions for the sake of consciousness of certain values, who is not in the position to

reject advantages that are offered to him for the sake of a good cause, this person does not belong to the elite, because every elite is ascetic. What further pertains to this elite is that one in every moment of the whole responsibly knows that one does not proceed from consideration of the next day, but thinks through a matter and responsibly makes a decision.

This standpoint, as much as it correctly applies with reference to *certain* (we think of several revolutionary and religious) elites, is too greatly influenced by formalism and too little by sociology. Thus a consistent application of his formulation would exclude the ruling decadent elite: it would have no place in the modern problematic of the elite. As a result, the true historical situation would only be obscured.

What appears most important to us, however, is differentiation from Steinbach's connection of elite and asceticism. To be sure, we support his suggestion that every ethically superior elite must be ready at any time for self-denial, must be incorruptible. Hence, we find many in the ranks of the progressive elite in particular, who pursue their work under extreme self-denial of life's comforts. However, pleasure does not fundamentally contradict the essence of the progressive elite, since it is understood as an aspect of relief and release of forces for other tasks.

In the distinction between the progressive and any other elite, the determination of incorruptible readiness, to take responsibility on, does not suffice. Fascism, for example, thoroughly understood how to groom ascetic elites ready for action that defiled the human species. If an elite in Steinbach's sense, that is, in a true and real sense, should exist, then it can only be a progressive and humanistic one. Yet what does that actually mean: progressive and humanistic? Without being able to examine here the concepts in detail, we also cannot quite get around this question.

The progressive elite is, despite its miscellaneous internal differences and wherever one might seek its limits, the one true guardian of the primary validity of the great, universal problems of humanity, which kept in mind the totality of life, and the past, present and future as an inseparable coherence. It places itself against the specialised perspectives of the decadent elite and of the intelligentsia who follow them, which are based on the division of labour, and which obstruct the view of the whole, and thus constantly succumb to the inhuman tendencies of class society, directly glorifying it or indirectly romanticising it 'in a philosophical manner'. This is the source of the hatred of the ruling elite against the progressive elite, who lead a pariah existence not only for (partly) material reasons, but for social ones, an existence, however, which is accompanied by the pride of those who know the hidden things of human and social existence.

The incorruptible desire for humanist freedom drives the thought of the progressive beyond the present into the future, into utopia. The internal tension that is typical for the progressive elite, between the inclination to a subjective utopianism and its constant correction according to a criterion of a far-reaching, but realistic and rationally derived future-oriented thinking, which coincides with the sensibly restricted utopianism as an unavoidable historical impetus of action, is excellently reflected in Herbert Marcuse's significant work, *Eros and Civilization*.

Marcuse energetically underlines that at the present level of immense wealth, the possibility of changing into an order without repression and without alienation draws near. As splendid and correct as these perspectives are, which Marcuse sketches with all necessary rational acumen, his conceptions are not free from utopian exaggerations, as is typical of the progressive elite of our time. The state of the society without oppression awaited by him, freedom without repression, distinguishes itself – at least at certain points in his remarks – by the fact that man will near a state of blissful nirvana in 'timeless' contemplative enjoyment. On the one hand, Marcuse quite correctly sees that the fundamentally revolutionary effect of the reduction of working hours will not spontaneously entail the overcoming of the repressive reality principle, but rather that only the complete overcoming of oppressive labour can lead to the path of its revolutionary transformation into 'play', into free activity, into true freedom. Yet, on the other hand, he seems to succumb to Freud's seductive thesis that 'there is no original instinct of workmanship', that man suffers from a 'natural human aversion to work', and therefore under all circumstances 'unhappiness and work' are identical.[1]

From this uncritical encounter with Freud and in overt distaste for the notion that man is to be defined 'anthropologically' as an 'active' being, Marcuse lapses into the extreme of equating freedom with timeless contemplation. He mistrusts the claim that repressive labour is transformable into free activity. He so fears the danger that man could be misled for the purpose of his submission only to new forms of oppression, that he almost claims that play must be unproductive. A utopian tension thereby arises that, if one thinks further, ultimately must lead to the construction of a society of fully unproductive contemplative nirvana, purely taken care of by machines. If one compares this with Marx, it becomes clear that for Marx, 'activity' and 'productivity', which are

---

[1] Marcuse 1974, p. 81.

simultaneously freely creative and painstaking, facilitating and pleasing individuality in all directions, must not be mutually exclusive in any way; rather, the opposite is the case.

Marcuse's affinity with Freud and his notion that *all* cultural creation is the result of inhuman self-denial (which in Freud coincides with the self-denial of instinctual gratification), pushes him to conclude that freedom and productive activity a priori exclude each other. If it remains indisputable that until now, i.e., in class society, all culture was paid for through the oppression and the sacrifice of the great majority of the human species, by the same token it also cannot be disputed that great cultures such as those of slavery were created by the slavery of the ruling strata and not their slaves, by not only completely free bearers of culture, but also those that, in contrast to Freud's notion, led a life of all-round *unsublimated* enjoyment, i.e., enjoyment without any denial of drives and pleasures, that is, in spite of their extensively applicable situation of unlimited eros, they were extremely productive in cultural respects. Despite certain correct perspectives, the psychoanalytic theory that cultural goods can only be produced by the sublimating sacrifice of pleasure remains a scientific myth.

The principle of rational control is also familiar to Marcuse. Despite certain fluctuations that we have shown, he emphasises the positive role of reason, thus also he says:

> Utopias are susceptible to unrealistic blueprints; the conditions for a free society are not. They are a matter of reason.[2]

In connection with the problem of the elite, what Marcuse contributes to the illumination of the essence of art is also of the utmost importance. That decadent formalisation and emphasis on the hereafter are at all possible is something for which art itself, exhibiting a contradictory essence, is not blameless. In the clarification of this circumstance, Marcuse proceeds from the interpretation of phantasy as a mental [*seelischen*] sphere acting independently of all *repressive* rationality, which lives from the memories of the joyous primeval ('paradisiacal') conditions passed from generation to generation and dreams in uninhibited freedom of a realm of restored harmony between individual and species as well as within individual life. '[P]hantasy insists that ... behind the illusion lies *knowledge*'.[3] Yet as much as art hereby adopts a progressive function, it is

---

2 Marcuse 1974, p. 225.
3 Marcuse 1974, p. 143.

however its aesthetic form that leads to a reconciliation of the retarding needs of the oppressive society with the revolutionary content of all genuine art, making the critical function of art bearable for society, and finally condemned to ineffectiveness. For art, by virtue of its aesthetic guide, enables its contents to be 'enjoyed' and thereby 'forgotten', is granted a jester's license, and becomes harmless or even a decadent means for the ruling elite's self-aggrandisement.

We have said that the progressive elite primarily distinguishes itself through its fundamentally humanistic and anti-nihilistic attitude. The progressive optimism resulting from this does not, however, remain undimmed. The deep contradictions of high capitalist society do not unconditionally and under all circumstances lead to an open resistance of the people against the disintegrating effects of alienation, but rather cause, for the time being, i.e., as long as no sufficient progressive consciousness-raising is possible due to the decadence of the workers' movement, a still stronger, still more tragic and still more disintegrating bond to this alienation. The progressive elite, which is not organised into a coherent force and with no firm political power behind it, easily reacts to this fact with a mood of deep despair and resignation. To be sure, the progressive elite adheres steadfastly to its humanist ideal, but under the impression of the rising erosion, bestialisation and capitalist materialisation [*Vermaterialisierung*] of man, the increasing weakening of the people's power of resistance and the expanding emptiness and lethargy, the progressive elite all too easily shifts the ideal into the utopian, beyond realistic sense and activity oriented to the present. The lethargy of the people transfers to the progressive elite and elicits here a similar proclivity to wait and see, which is to be understood as an expression of their despair over the existing conditions. On their part, this mood of despair does not remain without repercussion for their humanist optimism. Where the ideal, inhibited through despair, cannot be fully lived out, but only appears broken, as though it could only be realised in the far future, it experiences a colouring co-determined by despair which can be called irony [*Ironisierung*], not dissimilar to the well-known 'romantic irony' but differing from it, however, in its markedly humanist and, in the historico-philosophical aspect, optimistic basic attitude.

We rediscover all these contradictory aspects in the art of Bertolt Brecht, even if resolved and worked into a coherent aesthetic theory. Brecht points to the sign posts of the humanist ideal only in the form that he allows *existent*, although optimistically understood, man to demonstrate and prove true in his justification. The means to this for him is the positive popular figure that forms the central point of his great theatre. However, because this figure does not stand outside of, but rather inside, class history, not outside of, but rather inside alienation – even appears to be largely alienated – it embodies the ideal not in its full purity, but rather only straight through this figure behaving brokenly. Thereby a problem of irony also emerges in Brecht that, however, fundamentally differs from the romantic through its realistic character; it follows from historical reality itself, from its laws [*Gesetzlichkeit*], that the ideal can be realised. In this view, not only is the optimistic ideal ironic, but in dialectical interaction the irony coming out of despair is also optimistically broken. We cannot expand on it here, but can only note that Brecht is not unfamiliar with the mood of despair, particularly as a result of his experiences with the workers' movement and fascism. It remains, however, merely an integral element of his dialectically understood optimism, which represents itself as ironic optimism.

Even if in a form artistically thought through to the end, this perspective corresponds to the spontaneous consciousness of the progressive elite. Denoted with this reference, however, is not only the wavering of this elite between optimism and despair that in spontaneous reflection is only rarely elaborated to a dialectical mediation (like in Brecht himself), but also its realistic sense is strengthened through its incorruptible humanist orientation. For the making ironic of one's own ideals means nothing further than the practical understanding of the optimistically interpreted man, just as he is and must be in capitalist reality, while the destruction of the ideal in light of this practice is nevertheless avoided. The constant correction of utopianism through realism prevails here – in terms of tendency – just as, conversely, the constant correction of one-sided realism, which easily leads to blind practicality through the utopian hope in goal-oriented idealism, is asserted. That we in reality are dealing here with a mere, albeit strong, tendency, for different members of the progressive elite to behave very differently, and that this tendency is thus simultaneously threatened, often opening out into a naked wavering between optimism and despair, is something that belongs to the peculiarity of the elite under discussion, which can be explained by its peculiar, complicated and contradictory social situation. Brecht's ideological position differs from that of the progressive elite in that the merely spontaneous reflections are thought through to the end and brought to an ideal unity.

Brecht's positive folk figures are positive, because they prove that in a world of human depravity, egoistic lack of character and brutality have retained a high degree of independence and attitude, that they individually embody the ultimately resilient, because they contain the unspoilt [*Urwüchsig*] forces of man that belong to the human essence. From this contradiction between alienation and unspoiltness [*Urwüchsigkeit*] arises a dialectical tension tinged with the tragic between the everyday negative and the everyday superior positive features of the popular figures standing in the foreground on Brecht's stage, with which the problem of guilt in Brecht's art is closely related.

It is primary to this contradiction that it does not entirely let the ideal arrive at its breakthrough, does not allow figures that purely embody this ideal. It causes the heroic, selfless, lofty and worthy to only appear before the spectators in ironic disguise. Since however this heroic, selfless, lofty and worthy at the same time expresses an ideal that is not merely opposed to reality in an unmediated and abstract fashion (as with reactionary romanticism), and is not understood as a merely conceptual supplement for an 'eternally depraved' reality, but rather the other way round, in spite of all contradictorinesses, in spite of all the gloom and tragedy distilled out of it, in Brecht it can never become an expression of an abstract romantic despair, but remains on the ground of a fundamentally humanist optimism. Whilst the optimistic tendencies prevent a sinking of the irony into despair and the ironic tendencies prevent the seduction of a vulgar straightforward optimism, reciprocally and to the benefit of a sophisticated and dialectical arrangement of the art, a third orientation, mediating the contradictions, moves in this art, in the direction of the humanist desire simultaneously suffused by pain and hope. Brecht does not go beyond desire anywhere, in his most mature epoch from his emigration in 1933, to which all his great pieces (with the exception of the *Threepenny Opera*) belong, he nowhere offers 'solutions'. That has occasionally been made into an accusation against him. It is difficult to clearly decide whether this behaviour is explained by artistic ingenuity, which does not want to repel those who think differently through obviously revolutionary 'solutions', or perhaps by the mood of the progressive elite, which, corresponding to its inactive character, gladly steers out away from conclusions calling for practical action. Perhaps both play a certain role.

Like all realistic art, Brecht's is also naive; like all progressive forces of history, the modern ones, including the progressive elite, also behave naively. Expressed negatively, that is, in sharp distinction to the attitude of modern nihilistic art and the decadent bourgeois elite connected with it, naivete at first glance means as much as standing in opposition against every process of onesidedness and subjection, every formalisation and emphasis on the hereafter. Positively expressed, naivete, which bourgeois classicism also took part in, signifies life in its comprehensive totality, life's diverse contradictions and mediations, life as it really is. Thereby avoiding naturalistic and superficial unmediatedness, opening oneself to life, exhausting life in its whole breadth and depth. All one-sided psychologising and mythologising of thought and art that contradicts naivete also contradicts truth.

Naivete and democratic convictions belong indivisibly together, no matter whether in the spontaneous ideological reflection on life of the progressive forces, whether in rational theory or in art. Thus, for the progressive elite there is no opposition between elite and 'mass', but rather only an opposition between classes. Its democratic convictions manifest themselves most plainly here. Notwithstanding its contradictions and weaknesses, it represents an important and not to be underestimated pillar in the structure of the progressive bloc of our time, which naturally is not identical with this elite and under other conditions cannot be.

In the long run, the attitude of contemplation and passive negation remains not without consequences for the further arrangement of elite consciousness. Since this passivity virtually excludes the acting out of optimism and humanist desire in areas of practical activity, irony not infrequently turns into despair, pushing the progressive individual to the edge of tragic collapse and, in weaker characters, effects a change into complete apathy, and, if only in exceptional cases, into direct participation in bourgeois Sodomism [*Sodomismus*].[4] In stronger and more persevering natures, however, the propensity to utopianism pushes itself to the fore, not to be taken on without the note of the irrational, dreamy and playful. Thus, a deep cleavage often arises between the rational and astute, in the strictest sense of a realistic assessment of current events, and the world of utopian reveries. Under more favourable, more encouraging conditions, a retrograde process of critical inspection of utopian ideas and concepts tends to be deployed, with the effect of a rational alignment of the concepts of a goal, oriented towards the future, to the preconditions of social practice, to the law-bound tendencies of historical reality. At the same time, this demonstrates the superiority of the progressive elite over the progressive bureaucracy, who are constantly active yet sunk into mere pseudo-activity without visible progress and success, from whom in the best period of the workers' movement the effective tribunes of the people recruited. It expresses itself in the progressive elite's inclination to involve the more or less utopian future goal in its judgement, so that it finds a reliable corrective in the assessment of daily goings-on in the area of social and political contestation.

The progressive elite's sense of realism, despite all inclination to utopia, preserves it from giving itself over to myths, from which the bureaucracy only remains preserved because it is not capable in its practical aridity of mustering up any imagination. No concept, no term is so threatened by mythological distortions as freedom. How immediately it suggested itself for this elite, so contradictory in itself, to give itself over to the 'revolutionarily' gesturing exaltations about freedom, like the existentialists – among whom are some who, in

---

4 The term *Sodomismus* was used in the 1950s – by Kofler and others – as another word for bourgeois decadence (trans. note).

contradiction to their philosophical position, themselves belong politically to the progressive elite, like Sartre. This individualist streak, explainable from the disorganisation and the amorphous character of the progressive elite, immediately suggests a concept of freedom that claims, in its individualist exaggeration, that each is as free in each situation as they want and can be, e.g., in the short span of time before death by firing squad. The progressive elite's holding fast to a social and collective concept of freedom, a freedom that first creates the condition for individual freedom, testifies however to the incorruptible nearness to reality of the progressive elite, to its critical and incorruptible sense.

Yet the existence of the progressive elite can become, without its intention and awareness, a regressive aspect in the structure of modern decadent society. This is the case if, due to its inclination to pause in cautious and wait-and-see passivity, it appears harmless and the ruling powers concede a jester's license to it, with the very conscious intent of demonstrating democratic freedom precisely through the existence of a progressive opposition. Hardly any other social stratum is more suited as a fig leaf for the repression that is supposed to prove consummate freedom than the progressive elite, who appear in their dispersal over all areas of activity and culture as the personal embodiment of the possibility of dissent, of oppositional critique in public consciousness. Material need, material ruin, socially and culturally, often even isolation that embraces employment, the fate of becoming discreet, of character assassination and the derisive relegation to the no man's land of the 'genius' jester appear opposite this possibility as the self-inflicted consequence of a radical overzealousness. Public opinion is so well prepared for participation in the persecution of the braver and more stubborn elements of the progressive elite that public opinion experiences the progressive elite's 'normal', i.e., more reserved parts as the most certain expression of a dominant freedom, not suspecting how it is only tolerated at the moment because the decadent order requires it for self-justification. The recalcitrant university teacher, the critical lecturer at an adult education centre, the employee at one of the few opposition organs that still remain, the official who doesn't toe the line in everything, the councillor who doesn't say yes to everything, the audience member who occasionally defiantly discusses, the person interested in politics who organises events with well-known members of the opposition, the schoolchild who blabs the opinion of their father and puts the teacher on the spot, the priest who interprets the Bible progressively, and so on – they all, if they do not transgress certain limits of thought and action, may more or less move freely, for without them all appeal to bourgeois freedom would remain empty words. This also belongs to the contradictions in the mode of operation of the progressive elite. Its nonconformism has two sides: an unconsciously regressive one next to an intended progressive one. Only where this elite connects itself with the most advanced ideas, with the most unrelenting critical consciousness and with advanced forces, will it fulfil the task history has intended for it.

The Concept of Society in Historical Materialism
[1956]

The sociological character of the problem at hand was first recognised by Marx and Engels.* It is true that the social philosophy of the eighteenth century already showed some rudiments of this recognition, especially in Helvetius, who went beyond the thesis of the dependence of society on non-human factors, such as climate and geography, and assumed the factor within society of 'social milieu' as the determining factor. Other thinkers also attributed importance to the 'economic factor' before Marx (e.g., Schlözer and Kant); likewise, French historians have underlined the importance of class before Marx (Mignet, Thiers, Thierry, Guizot). But it was Marx and Engels who first recognised the self-contained relationality of the social process, which in their opinion was derived primarily from the relationality between individuals in the labour process; they raised the question of the totality of the social process as a problematic and tried to solve it.

Hegel's philosophical methodology of illuminating those universal relations that can be understood as totality had been of decisive service to them in this respect. For the conception of society and history, Hegel's *subject-object theory* has proved to be particularly fruitful. In summary, it can be characterised as follows: in their actions, the human individual (the subject) 'produces' actions and materials which, in their totality, condense into an ordered system (object), which in turn confronts man as something independent (in turn as a subject). The objective, his 'environment' 'produced' by man, thus becomes in turn a subjective by exerting a determining influence on man (his will and action), and degrades him into an object. But man, by virtue of his ability to think and act with consciousness (that is, to be a subject), reaches ever higher forms of freedom, and thus remains the true subject of history. History appears here as man's self-realisation on the path of realising ever higher levels of freedom. With this, Hegel founded the historical concept of progress, which Marx adopted.

Marx once remarked that his view of history is essentially concerned with the 'self-criticism of bourgeois society'.[1] According to Marx, bourgeois soci-

---

* [Originally published as "Die Gesellschaftsauffassung des Historischen Materialismus" in: *Handbuch der Soziologie* (eds. W. Ziegenfuss et al.) 1956, p. 512 onward. Reprinted in *Zur Dialektik der Kultur: Sechs Beiträge* (1972), in *Geistiger Verfall und progressive Elite: Sozialphilosophische Untersuchungen* (1981) and in *Zur Kritik bürgerlicher Freiheit* (2000).]

1 Marx 1986, pp. 42–3.

ety is distinguished from all other preceding social formations by its formal principle of *individual freedom*, which in turn is an inevitable corollary of the capitalist commodity structure. In commodity society, each individual appears socially as the owner of some kind of commodities, from the simplest products of labour to the intellectual products that they 'offer', to mere labour power as commodity, and in this form as an autonomous – 'equal and free' – contractual partner. This formal equality and freedom, which finds its most incisive expression in bourgeois law, becomes the basis for the unfolding of the entire social process, though not in a vacuum, but under the condition of capitalist property and class relations. Individual freedom, however, means the relative, i.e., only hindered through structural aspects, detachment of the simplest building block of the social structure, namely the individual, from every external bond, and thus the methodical facilitation of the process of the transformation of the subjective into the objective, which is inherent in all social phenomena, in its undisturbed purity.

But this constitution of a comparatively pure and thus simple process of social *subject-object relationship* based on individual freedom is, at the same time, mediated by a complicated and contradictory process, contrasted with that highly differentiated and not easily legible totality of social events that can be subsumed under the concept of *alienation*. Here, alienation is to be understood as the combination of complication, impenetrability, separation from individual action, uncontrollability and hostility, with which man's own social product, namely the social process, confronts him as something alien, as a self-acting power. The *darkness of alienation* in bourgeois society is what has seriously posed the problematic to the inquiring mind in the first place, and has made possible the modern theory of society, which reveals the ultimate nature of the social. This nature lies in the relationships of 'base and superstructure', of 'practice' and 'theory', of social being and social consciousness, generating the totality of social being. At the same time, however, the success of this theory of society is only ensured because the simplest precondition of social construction, namely the individual within the *general subject-object relationship*, emerges undisturbed in the form of bourgeois freedom, thus making for its part the penetrability of the alienated process itself possible at all. The dialectical contradiction between the concrete reduction of the social process to its simplest categories and the simultaneous emergence of its most confused and tension-filled problems became the starting point of dialectical social theory. The fact that subjective aspects, such as the location of the observer, interest in certain discoveries, impartiality with regard to the question of social progress, etc., must be added to the actual enabling of this recognition is only noted in passing.

In all its forms, and particularly evident in modern bourgeois society, social being is synthetic, i.e. all aspects are drawn into its process and here knotted into a 'unity'. The unity consists in the irrevocable dependence of the aspects on each other and their mutual determination through each other. The essence of the process is that, as a result of the constant change of the 'circumstances' and 'conditions' of the concrete social being, the phenomena of which this being is composed also change, without the unity being destroyed by this change. The society held fast in a specific moment of its development and posited as something static can easily be understood as a total unity; all that is needed is a description of the hierarchy of the interdependence of the aspects. The difficulty only begins in the realisation that it is never static. Rather, it is part of the concept of society to be uninterrupted movement, self-generation in ever new forms. But if this is so, then the principle must be revealed through which movement, the process, proves to be the force that makes totality possible as the 'mediation' of the contradictory and seemingly mutually exclusive into unity. This means: in order to discover in its essence the process by which the social whole as a whole is to be produced, it is first necessary to discover the principle which in turn produces the process.

Historical materialism recognises this principle in the fact of labour. The comprehensive determination of work, its determination of consciousness, the transformation of its subject character into object character, its social functionality, and so on, runs through the entire work of Marx.

The situation is such that in and through work man not only produces things for the profane satisfaction of needs, but via the indirect route of this profane activity produces himself as a man, albeit not 'merely' that, but as a social being. In other words, it is labour that generates what we call 'society'. With this view, Marx clearly distinguishes himself from the flat materialistic views that explain society on the basis of the family, that is, as biologically determined – although the historical connection to the family need not be denied – or from geographical and climatic conditions.

The astonishing work of labour to uninterruptedly produce sociality is based on the fact that labour as such can only exist if it uses a means that is alien to the animal – consciousness. Only the working man has conscious being, and only the man endowed with consciousness works. Working, therefore, does not merely mean putting sinew and sweat into action for a specific purpose, but working with consciousness. The modern materialism of Marx strictly rejects the idea of 'animal labour', because it considers work to be irrevocably linked to consciousness.

With this insight, it becomes clear that the conscious being of the labouring individual means something fundamental to the relationship between individuals. Animal species are essentially biologically conditioned, they are therefore not a 'society'; the society of humans is formed by conscious activity. The biological and familial being of man loses its priority here and becomes the object of social precedence.

In the conscious activity of work, man gets into a 'relationship' with his fellow man in a way that corresponds to a certain purpose. To be sure, man is an individual who both consumes and produces. But it is only the producing, the productive activity that produces sociality. However, production, in accordance with the necessity of serving life-sustaining consumption, refers to the items into which man, by shaping the raw materials of nature according to his purposes, 'externalises' [*entäußert*] his powers, facilities and abilities. This 'externalisation' [*Entäußerung*] makes the separation of production and consumption, i.e., the appropriation of products by non-producers possible, and thus class society.

The essence of the social process viewed factually [*sachlichen*] is that subjective acts have a constant interaction with each other and therefore something arises from the diversity of subjective aspirations that was neither intended nor could be foreseen by the individual: the objective that now confronts the individual in its supra-individual violence. This shift of conscious activity into unforeseen objectivity is what Marx primarily means when he speaks of the role of the 'unconscious' [*Unbewussten*] in history. The objective in its totality forms what we tend to call the 'circumstances' or 'conditions' of social existence, which in its totality includes institutional and ideological phenomena. This constant shifting of the subjective into the objective and vice versa, which is equivalent to the constant transformation of 'circumstances' and 'conditions', constitutes the fundamental determination of history, because this is what makes history possible in the first place – the constant shifting from one state of social being to another – which is also the case within a 'social order'. As in labour, one can also speak of 'externalisation' with regard to the described formation of the objective in the social process: here, in this extended sense, 'externalisation' means the fact that the activity of man 'externalises' itself in the product of the supra-individual social conditions, in the objective.

In the course of history, 'externalisation' [*Entäußerung*] becomes 'alienation' [*Entfremdung*] when the subjective purposes conflict with the objective circumstances. Under such circumstances man then also misses the ultimate purpose of all his activity, namely that of 'self-realisation'; in life and culture he comes into conflict with the given possibilities of a meaningful use of his powers, abilities and capacities, i.e., conducive to 'self-realisation', while at the same time this state of loss of the capacity for self-realisation in all its various historical forms can in turn become an inevitable point of passage on the contradictory path of the human species and thus of the individual to self-realisation and freedom.

However, inasmuch as labour is first and foremost in the service of satisfying needs, the task of engaging with nature falls to it. But by virtue of the endowment with consciousness of those who work, labour does not mean choosing from and transforming with, by chance and arbitrariness, the infinite variety of natural objects, forces of nature, and both with extremely differentiated characteristics, but to subject both the choice and the type of approach to a set purpose. The labourer, Marx says in *Capital*, makes use of the mechanical, physical, and chemical properties of some substances in order to make other substances subservient to his aims.[2] Contrary to a vulgar and mechanistic assumption, Marx points out that even the worst architect, in contrast to the best of bees, must have his plan finished in his mind before he executes it in reality.[3] And: 'At the end of every labour process, we get a result that already existed in the imagination of the labourer at its commencement'.[4] In the labour process, therefore, man's activity, with the help of the instruments of labour, effects an alteration, designed from the commencement, in the material worked upon.[5] It is thus said that in the human there is no simple determination on the part of nature as in the animal. Rather, man confronts nature as an independent power, in his actions he confronts himself, as the active subject, as an object.

He owes this power over himself in turn to his endowment with consciousness. However, this consciousness also gives him authority over his fellow man. With the help of the consciousness that becomes a practical force in labour, man subjects not only objects and forces of nature to his purposes, but also himself and his fellow man, who for their part behaves in the same way, so that this subjection is not, at first, one of bondage, but of simple mutual dependence – the merely preexisting social relationship. This relationship does not come about abstractly, not in empty space and arbitrarily, but again according to the purposes that humans set themselves 'in the production of their life' and under certain self-created conditions. Nowhere is the circle of consciousness and thus of that which is subject to human 'activity' broken, but within this circle, in which, following Engels, everything must 'pass through the human mind', the determining factor is not the abstract idea, but rather 'practice'.

---

2 Marx 1996, p. 189.
3 Marx 1996, p. 188.
4 Ibid.
5 Marx 1996, p. 190.

It is implicit in the concept of labour for it to be 'activity', i.e. movement, change; therefore labour, as a principle constituting sociality, can also have a transformative effect on social relations. At this point, the misunderstanding tends to arise that while the objects and forces of external nature are not socially determinative, the products of labour become so. Marx already protests against this interpretation, noting: 'It is not the articles made, but how they are made ... that ... distinguish[es] different economic epochs'.[6] But these economic epochs, as soon as they exist in a certain form, become, for their part, the primary social condition for the further development of labour, more precisely, of the means used in labour, the 'means of production', the forms of the forces of nature used in them, the 'productive forces'.

In Marxist theory, the totality of the social relations that develop in the described process of changing from subjectivity to objectivity and vice versa are called relations of production, because their roots are found in the domain of the social labour process and from here they receive the impulses for further social development. In terms of content or structure, these social relations always appear ordered according to the historical form of the control over the means of production, which is determined by the development of the productive forces. The overall social control over the means of production results in the primitive communist society and the socialist society of the future, which will continue at the highest level of previous development; where the power of disposal over the social means of production is reserved for only a part of society, we are dealing with class societies. It is not, therefore, the different levels of ownership of consumer goods, which existed in certain epochs of primitive society and will exist in socialism – provided, however, that everyone is provided with the richest supply of all the necessities of life – which divides society into classes, but the power of one class over the important means of production to the exclusion of another.

If historical materialism equates 'class relations' with 'property relations', this is meant in this limited sense. In the formulations of Marx and Engels themselves, however, the concept of 'relations of production' does not find a very clear definition, which is related to the method of dialectics. It is possible to take both narrow and broad meanings: depending on the theoretical context meant, 'relations of production' is understood in the narrower sense as the totality of property and class relations plus the means of state organisation and legal stipulation for securing this, and in the broader sense it extends these facts into the manifold ideological forms. According to Marx, at certain

---

6 Ibid.

stages of maturity in social development, the productive forces, which have become more abundant and developed in the meantime, come into conflict with the existing relations of production, which now become fetters for further historical development. At such historical moments, society enters a stage of increasingly open contradictions, tensions, fierce political and ideological clashes and the revolutionary upheavals that result from them.

From what we have seen so far it is clear that in the Marxist system everything without exception that concerns man in historical scope is understood as the 'product' of man himself. 'Theory ... demonstrates *ad hominem*, and it demonstrates *ad hominem* as soon as it becomes radical. To be radical is to grasp the root of the matter. But for man the root is man himself'.[7] Marx takes this sentence seriously with complete consistency. Nowhere does Marx enter into the contradiction of looking 'behind' the sphere of human and social being for something that determines man from there. According to Marx, man is an 'active and suffering' being in the sense that, on the one hand, he can only be subject to such bonds that he 'makes' himself, but that, on the other hand, the 'determining' phenomena are never of an objective nature, but always only social. But for Marx the material [*dinglichen*] products of man do not simply stand as 'such' beside the social ones, rather, in truth, there are only *social products of man*. The 'products' are to be understood as the objectification of human powers and relations and as such must be unveiled by science. The material [*dingliche*] so-being [*Sosein*] of the products, as it presents itself as such to everyday understanding, is mere appearance; in it lies the social relationship of labouring individuals that constitutes its essence. What Marx means by this is that the products only acquire social significance as an expression of human-social behaviour and by no means for themselves, that is, in their mere representational nature, quite in the sense, for instance, that he once remarked that a Negro is a Negro, that is, a mere natural thing, and only becomes a slave under certain social conditions.[8] Thus, Marx excludes not only the natural or natural and objective thing as such from the circle of those factors to which he attributes a determinative effect on social being, but also those objective products of man himself that acquire meaning as objects and means of interpersonal action.

This unique radicalism, to attribute the role and essence of all factors without exception in the domain of social events to pure sociality between individuals, corresponds in Marx's economic theory to the scientific endeavour of proving that such 'material' [*dinglichen*] categories, such as *capital, commodity*,

---

7 Marx 1975, p. 182.
8 Marx 1977, p. 211.

value, price, money, etc., are potentialities that are nothing but an *expression of the social behaviour* of individuals or groups, a behaviour, to be sure, that revolves around things and which we therefore call 'economic'. Marx writes, for example:

> However, capital is not a thing, but rather a definite social production relation, belonging to a definite historical formation of society, which is manifested in a thing and lends this thing a specific social character. Capital is not the sum of the material and produced means of production ... which in themselves are no more capital than gold or silver in itself is money.[9]

Or: 'The (economic) categories are only the theoretical expression of the relations of production', the totality of social relations. They express 'mystification of the capitalist mode of production, the conversion of social relations into things ... It is an enchanted, perverted, topsy-turvy world, in which Monsieur le Capital and Madame la Terre do their ghost-walking as social characters and at the same time directly as mere things'.[10] As an important determination: the economic categories appear as fixed 'natural forms' where they in fact only represent 'forms of thought', i.e., they ideologically feign at objective form.[11] In response to the objection that materialism dissolves here, one may refer to a statement by Marx himself, in which he gives credit to Feuerbach, who had founded 'true materialism' by making 'the social relationship of man to man' 'the basic principle of theory'. The materialism of Marxist social theory is based on the fact that here in the social 'practice' derived from the phenomenon of labour the root of the totality of social events and the explanation for the essence of the phenomena of this totality, also the ideological totality, is found.

In his concrete investigation, Marx, despite his critical dissolution of the reified categories, temporarily allows the individual to act theoretically in a way that is peculiar to the world of alienation and reification, in order to be able to follow each of his steps into even the most distant branches of his consciousness, but again only to prove this behaviour, which is inscrutable and incomprehensible to the individual himself – which the individual therefore experiences as 'natural' – as being subject to alienated and reified appearance. When Marx, for example, investigates the 'contradiction between subjectivation and reification' in the state of consciousness of capitalist individuals, he

---

9   Marx 1998, pp. 801–2.
10 Marx 1998, p. 817.
11 Marx 1996, p. 87.

first identifies two poles in the practical behaviour of these individuals, which, however, at the same time mean distortions in their mental reflection of social facts. Yet by accepting the reified appearance of the object world confronting the individuals for the purpose of describing the factual way in which the individuals react to them as such, i.e., by not immediately destroying the reified structure of capitalism as a stage on which the practical movement of humans occur, but by allowing it to exist as a moment of a total process, the erroneous opinion can arise, if not enough attention is paid to the special nature of Marx's method of investigation, as if precisely with Marx 'technology' was not understood on the basis of the 'person', as is required.

Under the two 'last', i.e., no longer derivable, preconditions of the constantly revolutionizing self-generation of man at work and the associated constant change of the social foundations, *man and society* reveal themselves as subject to constant change, or, meaning the same thing, as thoroughly *historical phenomena*. For the conception of historical materialism there is no more 'man' as such or an unchangeable 'essence' of man than there can be a transhistorical 'sociality as such'. To exist humanly here means essentially to exist in a concrete and changeable relationship to one's fellow man in the concrete social space, and that means again to exist as a historically active being, equipped with a changeable way of thinking and imagining. What man is in this respect historically, that is what he really is, that constitutes his actual existence.

Here it should be noted that historical materialism does not deny general characteristics that are valid for all human existence. However, here they gain the validity of merely formal provisions, i.e., those which express the general preconditions of human existence in general and therefore do not directly determine the factual preconditions. One can also express it in this way: The formal presuppositions make human existence possible without entering into or coinciding with its actuality. The formal preconditions include: 1. that man is a natural being, lives in nature and must constantly engage with it. 2. the physical organisation of man. 3. the mental structure of man, probably to be distinguished from the environmentally conditioned contents of the mental process. 4. the fundamental rationality-endowed faculty of man, which represents a natural product of development and is to be regarded as a natural fact.

Under these general, formal preconditions, concrete human history unfolds, i.e., concrete human existence [*Sein*] in its movement, which alone expresses human existence [*Sein*]. This movement is characterised by epochs that are characterised by a structure that has evolved from it but is essentially different from it. Only the inner 'understandable' and therefore 'lawful' contexts of individual epochs, which can be seen from the totality of interpersonal relationships of a structurally ordered epoch, have validity in expressing the concrete, i.e., expressing the true 'essence' of human existence [*Sein*]. The fact that such fundamental, abstract conditions, as the general theory of historical materialism calls them, are simultaneously repeated in them is connected with the fact that under the enumerated formal preconditions of human existence, *certain forms of concrete existence* are repeated, because they flow from the irrevocable concrete conditions of historical being (work, the transformation of subjectivity into objectivity, the development of productive forces and their constantly emerging contradiction to the relations of production, etc.). This repetition of certain forms of concrete existence does *not* mean, however, that the concrete historical contents are repeated: and these alone constitute the real and actual being of man; being is in an uninterrupted process of change.

As far as the general determinations that are not formal but relate to concrete and historical being, i.e., are summarised for abstract validity, are concerned, they express, in so far as they themselves are narrowed down to the very last abstract determinations, that which one could call 'anthropological', according to the modern concept. The 'anthropological' characteristics are very different from those which we have formally named on the one hand, and which we have assigned to the narrower theory of historical materialism on the other. While the formal statements comprise the most general natural preconditions of human and social existence at all, and while historical materialism makes the most general statements about the nature of the social and historical process itself, the 'anthropological' describes those characteristics by which man under formal and historical conditions develops as a being of his own [*Eigenwesen*], whereby, however, again only very abstract insights are gained, which can only be verified by the concrete historical process itself. The 'anthropological' determinations, listed here in an otherwise inadmissible rationalistic sequence, are therefore the following: 1. Man is a labouring being. 2. Man is, in a way determined by the fact of labour, a being necessarily related to his fellow human beings, as a social (socialised) being. 3. Man is a being that is both self-oriented (individual) and socially-oriented (socialised): he is a contradictory being. 4. Labour, and in a broader sense all human activity, is expressed in physical or mental products; man 'externalises' himself in them by virtue of his ability to work. 5. In the context of the fact of 'externalisation' in labour, the contradiction between the self-orientation and the social orientation of human beings gives rise to the dialectical capacity to be in agreement or opposition with one another in concrete historical space, which is the 'anthropological' precondition for the fundamental possibility of the historical formation of antagonistic (class-divided) or harmonious forms of social coexistence. However, only under concrete social conditions does this possibility become concrete reality in the manifold forms corresponding to these conditions. Pay attention here to the difference between precondition [*Voraussetzung*] and condition [*Bedingung*]! 6. Man realises himself only in historical and social space, so that his previously enumerated most important 'anthropological' characteristics, although they are the irrevocable precondition of all human existence, have to be constantly generated in the historical process. A 'pure' anthropological existence of man, independent of his historical being, is therefore an unfeasible notion for the dialectical conception.

The dialectical mediation between generality and specificity makes it understandable that history, on the one hand, contains what is generally valid, and on the other hand, is expressed exclusively in specific features, concretised into 'epochs' and 'social orders'. The specificity of a social order is characterised by its 'relations of production'. Therefore, Marx can say: '*The relations of production in their totality constitute what* are called *the social relations, society*, and, specifically, ... a society with a peculiar, distinctive character'.[12] Accordingly, historical materialism breaks down history into different, distinct epochs, and this for the purpose of making each of these epochs understandable in its totality, structured and determined by the relations of production; its approach is a consistently historical and 'individualising' one. This historicisation and individualisation of the process does not stop at the epoch, however, but also embraces all the content of the circumstances of each epoch. At the same time, this 'individualisation' is not one-sidedly rationalistic, but dialectical: the 'individual', i.e. the individual phenomenon, such as a personality, an action, a form of thought or an event, is regarded as an element of a certain social formation, is here not subsumed under a 'law' according to the concept of natural science; rather, it retains its individuality by co-creating the context, which is understandable in its inner dynamics – what is here called social 'law' and is fundamentally different from the law of natural science – and is for its part essentially determined by this context as unrepeatable and qualitatively abundant individuality.

As far as the epochs according to Marxist theory also represent 'individualities', they are nevertheless encapsulated for the sake of clarity in major epochs of mankind that are based on a general 'economic structure'. Five such epochs are distinguished, excluding the 'actual history of mankind', as Marx says, which lies in the distant future and is not recognisable. The primitive society of 'primitive communism', in which there is already individual property, but no ownership of what the whole society lives on, namely the basic means of production (soil, forest, water, game), is followed by the epoch of slavery. This

---

12   Marx 1977, p. 212.

originates from the increase in economic productivity from the initial division of labour, whereby the use of force in the subjugation of foreign tribes provides an external expedient. It represents the first form of class society. From the next feudal one, bourgeois or capitalist society develops, which in turn features very different historical epochs within it. The epoch of industrial capitalism is the highest within class society. It is characterised by numerous contradictions arising from the contradiction between the establishment of general individual freedom and the simultaneous retention of economic dependence. The capitalist commodity structure signifies both and forms the basis for an undreamt of development of social wealth, but also, for the first time in history, for a complication of the social process that is no longer comprehensible to the participants. Economically, and in certain periods of ascent also culturally, the ruling bourgeois class fulfils a tremendous task that overturns all previous conditions and opens up great possibilities for the future, albeit on the back of the proletariat, which exhibits the highest degree of human, moral and spiritual alienation [*Verfremdung*] possible in modern culture, and by its tragic condition draws all the other classes into the alienation, whereby in turn the context concerning this process proves to be extremely complicated. On the economic role of the bourgeoisie, Marx says: '[The bourgeoisie] has been the first to show what man's activity can bring about. It has accomplished wonders far surpassing Egyptian pyramids, Roman aqueducts, and Gothic cathedrals; it has conducted expeditions that put in the shade all former Exoduses of nations and crusades'.[13] At the same time, this magnificent development of the capitalist productive forces becomes an obstacle at a certain point; the bourgeoisie 'cannot be rid of the spirits it has summoned'. Yet even apart from the devastating *human* situation of the proletariat, the labouring man does not have a sufficient share in the immense wealth development of society; i.e., even in a one-sided economic assessment, a type of assessment Marx strictly rejects, the modern labourer falls short:

> A house may be large or small; as long as the surrounding houses are equally small it satisfies all social demands for a dwelling. But let a palace arise beside the little house, and it shrinks from a little house to a hut. The little house ... however high it may shoot up in the course of civilisation, if the neighbouring palace grows to an equal or even greater extent, the occupant of the relatively small house will feel more and more uncomfortable, dissatisfied and cramped within its four walls. ... Thus, although

---

13   Marx and Engels 1976, p. 487.

the enjoyments of the worker have risen, the social satisfaction that they give has fallen in comparison with ... the state of development of society in general. Our desires and pleasures spring from society; we measure them, therefore, by society and not by the objects which serve for their satisfaction.[14]

We see here too, by the way, that Marx attributes the material to the social and not vice versa.

However, Marx is not only concerned with the economic situation of the labourer, which interests him only as a precondition for the liberation of the *whole* man, this precondition also being understood by him as an irrevocable and fundamental one, as, by the way, was already the case with the great bourgeois humanists of the eighteenth century up to Lorenz von Stein and the 'lectern socialists' [of the 'German historical school', *Kathedersozialisten*]. He calls the human situation of the labourer, understood in its totality, 'pauperism', in radical contrast to the usual purely economic conception, which for him does not mean poverty [*Armut*], but rather misery [*Armseligkeit*], that is, the being of man that is remote from the development and realisation of human powers, abilities and talents, namely, the being of man that is subject to human misery. This state of 'pauperism' is aggravated by ignorance of one's own human situation, which even economic improvement cannot change. The liberation of man from 'pauperism' can only be that of the *whole* man. How much Marx is concerned with the whole and not merely with the 'economic well-being' of man is proved by the harsh criticism, always approached anew, of the devastating effect of the division of labour by which man becomes a 'one-sided' being, his copious powers no longer that of a potent being and in this sense also a 'subjugated' being. The devastating effect of the division of labour is to be alleviated by the shortening of the socially necessary working time and 'pauperism' is to be overcome by the educational and cultural organisation of extended leisure time.

From the socially emerging tendency to solve the contradictions of the capitalist order, the urge towards socialism arises on the favourable economic basis created by capitalism itself. Socialism is thus the fifth of the major epochs of humanity discernible so far. Because man was, according to Marx, half animal, half man due to his previous essentially economic (material) determinacy, his previous history is to be regarded as the mere 'prehistory' of humanity. With classless society begins 'actual history', in which society becomes master of its

---

14   Marx 1977, p. 216.

'laws' and man develops himself in full freedom. This society is classless not because all in it 'live approximately equally' – such an idea, which is imputed by the capitalist way of thinking to Marx, is alien to him – but because man can no longer become the instrument of man.

Seen as a whole, the historical development can be recognised as that of progress. It is true that within class society each epoch brings forth new forms of inhumanity, but at the same time, judging from the overall development, an ever higher form of freedom is realised in it.

It is not easy to see history as the progressive self-realisation of human freedom. The external image of history rather confirms the opposite. This confirmation, however, is illusory, even though most historical subjects are subject to it and take it to be the essence. They do not understand that even the negative, tragic, gloomy moments in the historical process, the subjective and objective errors, breakdowns and relapses are in many cases inevitable moments of transition, born of concrete contradictions, in the evolution of history towards a new, higher history. In the beginning, man was still strongly subject to the randomness of what nature commanded. Man could only take the decisive step beyond his immediate dependence on nature when he was able to make use of man himself, provided that a certain division of labour was established. This means that slavery, the most terrible of all forms of class oppression, represents a highly contradictory but unavoidable moment of transition on the path of history towards ever higher levels of freedom. It is also the deepest stage of unfreedom in class society, so that from here every future stage can be determined as a relatively progressive one. The difficulty in defining the historical concept of freedom results from the fact that in class society there is no form of freedom which is valid for all members of society, and thus it is not possible to find the uniform criterion by which all are equally able to describe a state of affairs as free or not. But this difficulty is a subjective one, i.e., it arises from the wrong perspective on the totality of events.

In the sense of historical materialism, the state of affairs is as follows. Because in class society there is no form of freedom that is equally valid for everyone, every stage of freedom in it is a highly contradictory entity, or in other words, it is also a stage of unfreedom. The contradiction is expressed in the fact that only the ruling class constantly enjoys the fullest historically possible extent of freedom, whereas the ruled classes only participate in this partaking of freedom to a certain degree, within the domain of the historical form of being ruled. The development of humanity towards ever higher levels of freedom does not, therefore, entirely pass the oppressed classes by. Yet the higher the level to which society has climbed, and the more the dominated classes have tasted the aroma of freedom, the more fervently it thirsts for its consummation, and the higher humanity – provided the corresponding economic, spiritual and political conditions are met – ascends to the point at which the relative form of freedom turns into (relatively) absolute freedom, the highest form of class society into the lowest form of classless society, afflicted with 'inevitable' major 'defects' according to Marx.[15] The absoluteness of this socialist freedom consists in its truly universal validity for all members of society.[16] The slave very seldom remembers his human dignity, the serf, close to him in this, first needs to be awakened by urban society in order to dare to undertake his uprisings, which are at once pathetic and magnificent; the clanging of arms of the artisan associations and city district organisations in the Middle Ages is already unending, the rising but oppressed bourgeoisie is carrying out the greatest revolutions the world has ever seen, setting an example for modern society in which the powerful organisations of the working class threaten to shake the fabric to its very foundations.

According to Marx, thought, 'consciousness' in all its forms, 'correct' and 'false consciousness', plays a decisive role in this process. It is not 'outside the world'. Marx's view is radically opposed to the mechanistic and materialistic point of view, according to which thought is only able to look retrospectively (contemplatively) at what has already been accomplished 'according to laws', i.e. is not able to gain any influence on the course of events 'according to natural laws'. Here, the participation of thought in the historical process becomes a self-deception of the subject; e.g. in Hobbes, Spinoza and the French materialists.

It is significant that Marx, precisely in disassociating himself from the neglect of the subjective and active and thus also the mental side in the assessment of the essence of the historical process, even accuses Hegel of letting the Absolute Spirit not consciously and actively, but unconsciously accomplish the real movement of history, i.e., in a mechanical way and according to natural law, as it were.[17] Marx says here – and later he repeats his notion that man makes history with the help of his thought, in the most diverse variations – that Hegel lets the 'Absolute Spirit make history only *in appearance*'. Equally revealing for the theory of historical materialism is the reasoning he gives: Under the precondition of the correct insight that history must be consciously formed, thinkingly and actively 'made', the philosopher of history must show how the mental process (also as Hegel's Absolute Spirit) turns into objectivity at *each* of its steps,

---

15   Marx 1989, p. 87.
16   See Kofler 1970.
17   Marx and Engels 1975, pp. 85–6.

thus itself becoming a tool, a subject within the historical subject-object relationship, within the dialectical self-making of history [*Sichselbstmachens der Geschichte*] or, which is the same thing, within 'practice'. In contrast to this, however, Hegel allows the philosopher, in whose head the absolute spirit allows itself to come to the consciousness of itself or of historical being, to attain this self-consciousness only *retrospectively*; the absolute spirit has until then only 'made' 'mechanical' and 'unconscious' history. 'For since the Absolute Spirit', writes Marx, 'becomes *conscious* of itself as the creative World Spirit only *post festum*, ... its making of history exists ... only in the speculative imagination' and not in reality.

What Hegel calls the Absolute Spirit, i.e., that principle that expresses what is active in the historical process, is understood in Marx's critique not only as something absolutely practical, but at the same time as something intellectual, as thinking action or acting thought. From this it becomes clear how Marx, regardless of the other acknowledgement of the fundamental difference between the two types of behaviour, also understands thought as an element of the deed, as a fact in the process of man's making history himself. This making of history by thinking does not, however, consist in the fact that it 'acts' on history from outside, but rather that it itself represents an irrevocable condition of historical existence in general. Thought does not merely 'participate' in history, but makes history possible in the first place, i.e., it is such a decisive aspect of the historical process that it is not possible without thought. That thought can take over this task results from the fact that it does not produce its thoughts in the 'space' of nothingness, in order to let them descend from there into the space of historical being, but that it is the thought of this being itself, 'identical' with it: it is nothing other than the right or wrong 'self-knowledge' of this being that necessarily belongs to being and its movement.

The far-reaching significance Marx ascribes to thought can also be seen in the fact that he even attributes to it the power of transforming the subject. The historically effective subject (individual, society, class, etc.) is different in each case, depending on which thinking is suitable for it. It is on this insight that Marxist class theory, with its important distinction between the class 'in itself' and class 'for itself', is essentially based. It says that the economic conditions of a class, its position in the overall economic structure of society, only becomes a historically active and thus history 'making' power as soon as a 'consciousness' (correctly or falsely) recognising this situation attains development, with which a factual change in the relationship of the classes to each other is already effected. The structural change of society tends to be the further consequence. Thought, as Georg Lukács teaches in the sense of Marx, is what makes the next historical step possible in the first place.[18] A fact that should be particularly emphasised is the possibility of subjective decision in the space of the formation of the 'ideologies' of a social epoch, including the aftermath of intellectual traditions, that is, what is called 'intellectual freedom'.

> The general theory of social consciousness can, of course, focus only on the typical average. However, Marxism is not a 'sociology' that would interpret this determination [*Bestimmung*] as a fatalistic determination [*fatalistische Determination*] or – as is the custom with the modernists – as an abstract, registering typology. On the contrary, it gives the flexible structure of these connections, the real social-historical leeway, within the limits of which the individual development of consciousness proceeds individually and at the same time fits into this typology.[19]

So-called 'false' ideological consciousness, i.e., ideological consciousness that does not correctly reflect reality, is by no means based on the mere 'interest' of a class, but conversely, this ideologically manifested class interest can only prevail on the ground of the preceding failure to negotiate the subject-object process and the resulting ideological distortion of reality. Ideological consciousness, which is the result of a certain position in society and a limited perspective on society, under the pressure of contradictory and conceptually unnegotiated reality, first of all deceives itself, and only when this happens can this ideological consciousness believe in the primacy and the validity 'for all people' of its interest. The equation of the capitalist-egoistic with the general interest has its roots here. This is why Marx asks, in the *German Ideology*, in what way interest can become independent of reality. Additionally, in the *Theories of Surplus Value* he notes: 'Hodgskin regards this as a pure subjective illusion which conceals the deceit and the interests of the exploiting classes. He does not see that the way of looking at things arises out of the actual relationship itself; the latter is not an expression of the former, but vice versa'. That, however, under this once existing precondition of the phantasmagorically distorted reflection of real conditions, space is then also gained for conscious deception and for the assertion of a consciously egoistic interest, only clarifies the problem, but does not abolish it.

Social alienation is always also alienation of consciousness; both are identical in the specifically Marxian sense. As true as it is that the objective process

---

18   Lukács 1973.
19   Lukacs 1951, pp. 109–10.

does not merely appear to become independent of the individuals, but really becomes independent of them as something alien to them, it is just as true that this process, as a result of the contradiction of individual functionality within it, is understood neither in its social origin, i.e., as the product of subjective activity, nor in its totality of the dialectical subject-object-relationship, and therefore presents itself to thought in a distorted way. As soon as it is present, this apparent consciousness becomes a condition, on the one hand for practical action that 'analogously' adapts to the real conditions (of the commodity society), on the other hand for a further development of the ideological current up to the scientific systems. In concrete terms, however, this process must be examined anew from case to case.

It can be seen that the process of the formation of social consciousness shows two currents merging into each other. The more developed ideological (philosophical, political, juridical, etc.) institutions [*Gebilde*] do not apply unconditionally and necessarily, i.e. not in such a way that they have to manifest themselves in a very specific form; they are in a constant flow, can be individually shaped and are always interchangeable with related ideologies. On the other hand, the ideological institutions that originate from the lowest level of social existence show a more solid, unchangeable form. The reason is that they represent the form in which the economic categories present themselves. They therefore arise spontaneously and show an unchangeable unambiguity: commodity, value, price, capital, money, profit, economic rent, etc., appear as material conditions [*dingliche Gegebenheiten*], whereas they are only ideological forms of certain social relations of production, as we have already shown. The understanding of the relation between the totality of social 'practice' and the whole ideological process – in the analysis of the modern capitalist epoch mediated by the intermediate of the just described reified (or as Marx also says 'fetishistic') elements of being and imagination – constitutes what is called the ideological theory of historical materialism.

The Three Main Stages of Dialectical Social Philosophy [1966]

For thousands of years, the average structure of the social process had been transparent to those who witnessed it, but nevertheless abstract.* One is reminded of the fact that although man lived in class society through long periods, class was first discovered in the French Revolution (Marat) and only in the nineteenth century was it elevated to a concept by utopian socialists as well as the liberal and conservative French historians (Thiers, Thierry, Mignet, Guizot, Michelet). Abstractness consisted both in the reflection of historical events as a jumble of coincidences and in the idea of the primary influence of the subjective, i.e., the more or less powerful personality. Where it was opposed by the notion of a 'destiny' above the subject as an ideological form of the notion of objective forces, it could likewise only be understood in abstract terms, mythologically as in antiquity or with the help of astrology as in the Renaissance. The reason for this ideological attitude is to be found in the predominant naturalness, simplicity and slowness of the development of economic conditions, primarily of the productive forces. Such conditions therefore appeared as mere and passive objects of human effort, of subjective will. A knowledge of their power to determine society and history could not emerge.

The French Revolution finally shook this imaginary world. It made us aware that history is not merely composed of coincidences and subjective actions, but is permeated by the universality of an upward development that is pushing from stage to stage and by an encompassing dependency of the parts on each other that transcends away from the coincidental. The image of an objective, albeit contradictory, reasonableness of the historical event imposes itself upon the consciousness of time. The fragmentation of the order of the estates, based on apparent randomness, its seemingly exclusive dependence on the will and decisions of powerful persons and groups – only the difference between people was regarded as predestined by nature and God – was replaced by the image of a historical dynamic that does not respect this will, and by the bourgeois claim of elevating all historical existence to the level of purposeful shaping of life according to rationally justifiable and therefore reasonable principles. Even subjective egoism, freed from the fetters of the Middle Ages, presented

---

* [Originally published as "Die drei Hauptstufen der dialektischen Gesellschaftsphilosophie" in: *Kürbiskern*, Issue 2/1966: 103 onwards.]

itself as an aspect of the realisation of reasonable 'natural laws' in human life that transcended all randomness. What always prevailed, behind the still veiled knowledge of earlier epochs, as a historical connection organised to totality, as a result of the simple circumstance that man makes his own history and therefore in every social epoch the dialectical relation of all its aspects to each other shapes this epoch, became recognisable as a general (formal) principle of all history and imposed the need for philosophical treatment. Yes, even more than that. It imposed itself with such vehemence on the contemplative mind that it was often experienced by this mind as the most general world law, for which we find the most extreme expression in Hegelian philosophy. In understanding these phenomena, Hegel went far beyond the statements on these phenomena by eighteenth century philosophy, which, by referring to the external conditions of nature, set only a very external framework for the event, because the dialectic, which Hegel took from historical observation, although transposed into the world spirit of the synopsis of the natural world and the human world, the dialectic of subjective activity and objective process (totality) and, as a further consequence, of the individual and the whole, became present to him. At the same time, he was only able to grasp these relations in their philosophical generality, due to the immature economic situation, and it was only with the overcoming of this in the following epoch that what was behind them and what drove them in their subjective as well as in their 'natural law' domains became visible (and we will return to this later), namely the contradiction between the application of productive forces and the prevailing relations of production, the contradiction that constantly pushed towards its overcoming and constantly opened up anew; in short, the economic conditions. It was only with the real effects of the industrial revolution after Hegel's death that it became apparent that what for Hegel was still called abstract totality was given its concrete structural and boundary-setting definition through the relations of production, and that the conceptual instruments with which this concept of totality can be approached must be derived from the dialectical concept of the economic base. It should be added that it was only through this real and cognitive basis that not only the historically concrete joining themselves together of the infinite and contradictory variety of phenomena of an epoch into the dialectical unity of totality became visible in abstract and real terms, but also the problem of the relationship between the subjective and the objective, activity and process, thought and being could be brought to a satisfactory solution.

While for Hegel the mystery of reality was the totality of reason, for Marx the mystery of reason was the totality of reality. Yet by conceiving of reality and reason as a totality identical to one another – and we have seen for which historical reasons – Hegel directs his attention to the inner dynamics of this totality, which as such, if thought through to the last, reveals the secrets of its essence, albeit initially and entirely in the sense of the metaphysics of reason in its metahistorical and therefore abstract philosophical form. In this abstractness, however, the world spirit is, at the same time, extremely concrete in so far as the determinations of the negation of the negation that permeate it (in truth taken from history), the identity of the self-contradictory, the concept as being, the whole as truth, the appearance as illusion and, at the same time, the essence that appears (translucent) in the mediation to totality – which already points to the centre of the later Marxist problem of ideology – and so on are the determinations of real history itself. With Marx and Engels, under the impression of the real emergence of the deus ex machina of the 'world spirit', namely the economic and social process, reversing Hegelian determinations and stripping them of their metaphysical shell, they climb to that stage of historical and philosophical thought from which there is only a theoretical progression on the same theoretical level or a regression.

Two forms of this regression can be observed in our time: that in the mechanical materialism of the eighteenth century, albeit with all the limitations that no longer permit a total regression behind Marx and Engels; and that in Hegelian world spirit idealism, albeit with all the limitations that likewise do not permit such a regression. We will only concern ourselves with some phenomena of the latter in the following. It should be said here, however, that we do not totally reject the results of this orientation, especially because their inner differentiation and complexity allows for positive features precisely where their representatives still feel committed to Marxist dialectics.

The third stage of the development of the dialectical philosophy of society declines into the epoch of bourgeois decadence. The most obvious representatives are Theodor Wiesengrund-Adorno, Herbert Marcuse and Günter Anders. We will not deal with the latter, since we have already done so elsewhere.[1] Their peculiarity is the return to a system of generalising quasi-philosophical definitions of socially relevant phenomena and concepts, which is, however, hindered by Marxist reminiscences, as well as an energetic and, in some areas, fruitful combination of this attitude with aspects of depth psychology. This attitude is to be characterised as *quasi*-philosophical because it only inclines toward the form of a tendency to neglect individual phenomena to a large extent and to combine them into general determinations, while the content of the statements remains within the framework of socio-theoretical and socio-psychological problems. A conceptual apparatus in the sense of Hegelian philo-

---

1 See Kofler 1974.

sophy, for example, is not developed. Among themselves, they do not agree on everything, especially not in their assessment of so-called 'possible practice', i.e., action to revolutionise the bourgeois order, and also not in their estimate of the utopian element in this action. Their merit lies in having drawn the new phenomena of modern society into a critical light; their barrier, on the other hand, is that they mythologise the tendencies of reification and fetishisation, which are extremely apparent in the high bourgeois epoch, in a quasi-philosophical manner to the general, or, expressed sociologically, to the negative fate of inescapable violence, and therefore they either do not care about the multitude of individual phenomena at all or, from case to case, only care about them to the extent that they seem to confirm their theses. Phenomena such as the state, bureaucracy, bourgeois and progressive intelligentsia, the modern proletariat, the petty bourgeoisie, managers, trade unions, associations, crime, today's youth, etc., are neglected by them in favour of the general trend, which they interpret in the sense of a 'second nature' of almost independent and mechanical violence. Which, if it is seen in the living mediation to the contradictory totality, has much that is correct about it, but which is falsified through a sudden coming to a halt with it.

The 'philosophical' manner of their analyses takes on the character of a quasi-world spirit, clearly traceable in Adorno, more covert because it is not transposed into the overall historical as in the case of the former, in Marcuse. Adorno's world spirit ideology, which he lays down primarily in his 'dialectic of enlightenment', represents a kind of reversal of Hegelian world spirit philosophy. If for Hegel the world spirit is identical with reason, for Adorno it is identical with unreason. Since Adorno is more modern and tries to extrapolate history not from the world spirit, but rather his own world spirit empirically from history, everything here is not quite so uniform, but more contradictory, more ventilated. Although much more reserved than Marcuse, he does not fundamentally exclude the possibility of utopian aspirations becoming practical. However, he vigorously denies 'possible practice' today from an alleged empirical insight into the present. *In Adorno's case, however, the empirical insight is that of insight into the general of the reified process, excluding insight into the individual facts*, so that the occasional admission of the possibility of the opposite, of escaping, of resisting the given state of total reification, remains only of dialectical formal significance. In the matter, Adorno is an extreme pessimist with a nihilistic sting in the tail [*nihilistischen Pferdefuß*]. Adorno's 'negative dialectic', as he himself describes and establishes it out of aversion against 'premature' intention towards classless society and the like, forms the methodological prerequisite for the preposition of 'always the same' [*Präposition des 'Immergleichen'*].[2] Despite all the valves he keeps open for a relaxed interpretation of his view, the curse of irresistible progress, irresistible regression, remains with him.[3] According to Adorno, the dialectic should not be carried out in any other way than concretely. Yet there is no concrete carrying out of the dialectic in the domain of 'always the same'. Nowhere in Adorno's writings is there a clear indication that there was also a history of freedom within class society, nowhere does he examine the dialectic of history and repression and that of the partly quite successful struggle for freedom. Adorno's rejection of any 'system' that seeks to capture reality in a grid of predetermined [*vorgegebener*] ontologisation ('idealism') is of little help. For the identification of the domination of nature and oppression, of 'Enlightenment' knowledge, which he understands as a process of all of history, and of inhuman application, of progress and regression, of humanistic ideology and myth, means the diremption of historical totality towards the merely negative and thus the new positing of a system, namely a world spirit, and a pessimistic one.

The devastating effect of this theoretical position on Adorno's disciples and sympathisers could be confirmed by many examples, but space forbids this here. A Jürgen Habermas, a Karl Markus Michel, the circle around the Frankfurt student newspaper *neue kritik* in part, and loners such as a Karl-Heinz Neumann vehemently defend doing nothing as the only possible 'way out', mock humanism and avoid criticism in a cowardly manner from such powers as the trade unions and parties, who would historically be called upon to help break the vicious circle of reified ideology. Against this argumentation the objection is usually raised that the power of integration, of 'sedimented structures' and of social as well as psychological 'mechanisms' proves that even with criticism nothing can be done. But if we have shown elsewhere that it is not so much the proletariat but rather its organisations that have become bourgeois, then, with the appropriate energy and perseverance, the critical effort would be able and obliged to make their object, namely, precisely these organisations, adapt themselves again to the actual mentality of the working masses they serve and turn themselves to critical consciousness as well as to its practical consequences.[4] The writings directed against the various refined forms of repression and integration are available in sufficient number and could be evaluated with the help of the organs set up for this purpose. Proof of this possibility can be found in the equally surprising and widely observed fact that many functionaries, especially of the trade unions, familiarise themselves

---

2 On the analysis of Adorno's philosophy of history, see Tomberg 1963.
3 See Horkheimer and Adorno 2002, p. 28.
4 Kofler 1960, p. 198 onward.

'privately' with the critical investigations, but do not speak about them and the consequences arising from them, because they fear being slandered as 'communists'. The millennia-old oppression through slander does not fail to have its effect even today. What has been said several times elsewhere about this should not be repeated here. A pseudo-critical and resigned coming to terms with what is given, a 'conformism camouflaged by nonconformism', as Georg Lukács puts it, therefore remains characteristic of most of the adherents of this direction. For example, when the Adorno student Michaela von Alth defends his point of view by pointing out that 'practice', and that means progressive practice in this argumentation, is not possible at the present time, in order to substantiate this thesis she does not seriously proceed to criticise the opposite or at least modified point of view, but stubbornly insists on what has been proclaimed, which of course does not provide any proof. A closer look at the texts of Lukács and Kofler would show that they too are aware of the great difficulties for a progressive practice in the present, but that the latter, for example, has shown in multiple analyses how much the modern proletariat itself, even in its extremely reified and integrated form, is participating but not becoming bourgeois, that it ideologically refrains in a special way (which cannot be presented here), etc. Participating is not yet to become bourgeois – but this does not go into the minds of the theorists of 'mechanisms' (a favourite expression of many Adorno apologists). Where 'mechanisms' prevail, there is no gap through which to escape for the helpless victims standing in practical life, even as a distant prospect, not even for those who consciously see through and reflect on this situation. At least this is how the state of affairs is reflected in their self-conception. Contemplative distance from the events in irresponsible passivity gives, in view of the alleged impossibility of all 'possible practice', the reassuring feeling of not having to risk anything because there is nothing to risk. The opposite point of view is then called 'vulgar Marxism' in this perspective, although it does not recognise any 'mechanisms' of total violence according to quasi-natural law. Claiming for itself purity from all defilement through practice, this orientation is defeated by its 'reified mechanisms' to such an extent that one has trouble discovering here the last remnants of the dialectic; claiming for itself therefore freedom from all ideology, it turns out that the ideology of non-ideology is also one.

The root of this modern decline to a conceptual relationship to reality, as was already present in the form of Hegel and overcome by Marx, is to be found in this reality itself. The deindividualisation and making uniform of life, which has become prevalent in the field of modern reification and massification [*Vermassung*], creates the appearance of an all-encompassing 'second nature', which, although it is only appearance, becomes a valid reality for those who experience it. The extreme totalisation and hardening of the process of reification and fetishisation in the twentieth century cannot be denied. Yet the question alone – as one among many – whether the anti-socialist trauma that terrorist Stalinism has left in the consciousness of Western peoples has not made the greatest contribution to unnerving the humanist opposition to this process and putting it in an inhuman light in the eyes of the public, along with the closely related question, whether under other political circumstances the parties and trade unions historically called to oppositional criticism could not have brought up to date a developed consciousness of its inhuman nature in order to affect the proletarian masses, who are inclined to criticism anyway – this shows as a *possible question* that obstinately restricting oneself to the description of the phenomena of reification is unjustified. For political impulses of the opposite kind can, tomorrow or the day after tomorrow, turn the discussion of the reified way of life of modern capitalism, which is already widely offered today in literature and art, into a political moment in itself, into an element of the dynamisation of the frozen fronts as a consequence of a humanistic enlightenment that starts out from the critique of this way of life. Yet first of all, and this is the primary task of our day, such a humanistic enlightenment would be quite sufficient; it itself becomes a priority! Enlightenment *is* practice respectively. Or, according to Adorno, does world history merely remain at its present state? Does 'second nature' have the power to render history irrelevant? Is such a standpoint not eschatology in reverse, not an (unintended) implication of the idea that the final state is not set in the future but now?

Under the impression of what is undeniably extensive fetishisation, the Adorno movement can be misled into treating the reified structure of the social process in a quasi-natural philosophical sense. Admittedly, every social process can to a certain extent be regarded as if we were dealing with a natural phenomenon, which is what makes social science possible in the first place. Even Marx, who is concerned with illuminating the 'contradiction of subjectification and reification', does not immediately theoretically destroy the reified structure of capitalism as the stage on which the practical movement of individuals occur, but first places himself on the ground of the reified appearance of the object world confronting the individuals, in order to prove it as appearance from there. Certainly since Marx, reification has intensified, it has become total, something that other critics of capitalism have already noticed before and independently of Adorno. The mistake of the Frankfurt current lies less in its preoccupation with this phenomenon, on the contrary, in this is founded their superiority over all non-dialectical orientations, who either content themselves with the flattest empiricism or throw themselves into the arms of the most arbitrary construction that is supposed to protect them from it, and this with the sole effect of uncritical or pseudo-critical devotion to what already exists (König, Geiger, Topitsch, Dahrendorf, etc.). The error of this orientation lies in getting stuck in the abstract generalisation reflecting unmediated reification of quasi-natural philosophical relevance. This abstractness, in turn, has the effect that too little attention is paid to individual phenomena which, despite the violence that reification does to them, display a certain differentiation. Yet they must be considered if the whole social process is to be grasped in its real character. In the dialectical area of tension between reification and the different ways in which that same reification works case by case, this 'case by case' is of decisive importance. It is precisely in the phenomenon of the modern proletariat, on which is poured out the whole unwillingness of the Frankfurt Marx critics (e.g., Habermas) to accept the proletariat's 'anti-societal affect', which is still observable today and which must be denied for the purpose of verifying one's own social philosophy of nature, that it is possible to see how carelessly Adorno's theory proceeds. The same is true for certain strata of the intelligentsia and even bureaucracy, e.g., the trade unionists. Even as elements of general reification, as those integrated into the commodity structure and its reified ideologies, they each have a separate quality and must therefore be considered separately. What one says about them will only be inadequate if they are merely thought of, as in the analysis of 'second nature', as homogeneous drops in a uniform river. Critique must be critical not only in its generality, but even more so in its specificity, through which it becomes truly critical. The mediation of the 'second nature' with oneself is not. Only the search for the many qualities and their mediation by a fetishistic whole makes them the real thing. To disregard this is the weakness of modern dialectical social philosophy. However, this weakness itself is mediated by the whole of the fetishistic process and can be explained, for its part, with the criticism of ideology [*ideologiekritisch*].

This weakness is repeated, albeit mitigated, in the writings of Herbert Marcuse. Overall, his thought is more differentiated. This becomes evident, for example, when he speaks of a not to be underestimated role for oppositional intellectuals. Even a sentence like the following would be unthinkable in Adorno, even in Habermas: 'Even today, the songs that were sung for and in this struggle [in Spain, L.K.] are for the young generation the only remaining reflection of a possible revolution'. While he is very close to Adorno in many respects, characteristically in the undialectically one-sided evaluations of 'absurd literature', as a font of apt criticism, he aims far more concretely, and in addition he occasionally allows himself to make concessions with regard to a 'possible practice', as for example in the discussions that took place in Yugoslavia and in Salzburg in 1965.

However, since Marcuse, in accordance with his basic attitude that is similar to Adorno's, also tends to neglect individual phenomena, he too falls into the abstract and universal. For this reason, despite all the loosening up, the pessimistic strain is unmistakable. Yet this pessimism does not degenerate here into nihilism. The energetic affirmation and analytical treatment not only of the necessity but also of the possibility of taking a step beyond the boundaries of bourgeois society, a possibility, however, whose realisation is judged pessimistically, gives Marcuse's attitude a more neutral colour. He does not turn his pessimism into a worldview, a philosophy of world spirit. However, there is a tendency to philosophise problems, supported by an equally strong tendency to psychologise them.

First of all, evidence of the latter is offered. In the essay collection *Culture and Society II* he says:

> These changes [the ego-limiting external influences, L.K.] reduce the 'living space' [*Lebensraum*] and the autonomy of the ego and prepare the ground for the emergence of the masses. The mediation between the self and the other gives way to immediate identification ... In the psychic structure, the ego shrinks to such an extent that it no longer seems capable of maintaining itself as a self, distinct from the id and superego.[5]

Marcuse's definition of a truly adequately functioning ego thus goes in the direction of sharply distinguishing it from the superego (the social). The purely psychological (Freudian) determination of the ego contradicts, however, the historical development; it is dogmatically and undialectically conceived. It is not only conceivable, but it was indeed the case in a prehistoric epoch that, precisely because of the total identity of ego and community, the most comprehensive formation of this ego conceivable under the conditions of the time and the most complete satisfaction of individual needs was achieved, beginning with erotic needs and extending to the areas of activity coinciding with 'play'. An order without class and without repression encourages such an identity, whose special character of harmony between the interests and needs of all also achieves the highest degree of satisfaction. Marcuse's critical determination applies fully and entirely to class society, but it is forcibly elevated to the general level because certain entrenched psychological theories need to be

---

5 Marcuse 1968, p. 89.

verified. This is also the reason why Marcuse never talks about the primeval epoch, which has been sufficiently proven by modern science, in which the satisfaction of drives required by Freudian psychology was fulfilled. The recognition of this epoch would mean the abandonment of the psychological dogma of the sufficient realisability of the ego only in contrast to the superego (and the id); it would mean an improvement of Freudian theory with all the inevitable consequences of its change in other points as well. But it would also mean a new assessment of the future free order in the sense of the recognition of a freedom in which the individual ego derives its power, its creativity, even its independence (!) from the fact that it has become identical with the other egos. Such an identity would be directed all the more towards the formation and maintenance of all possibilities of satisfying erotic needs such as playful creative activity – defined by its contrast to repressive activity, labour – above all in the engagement with nature, in the shaping of communal living together and in the development of artistic abilities, without which life would be without beauty, comparable to the currently repressive one. It would be an order in which the 'principle of reality' as such would not appear at all, because it would be identical with the unalienated inclinations and forms of realisation of life of all.

With Marcuse, the scientifically already confirmed insight into the once harmonious society of the recent Ice Age, which lives on in the primeval memory of the human race as 'paradise' or as 'golden age', is replaced by the completely unproven and purely mythological assumption of the Freudian primal father order. This myth makes possible the untenable assumption of judging the 'weakness of the ego' at the beginning of the human race as negative and persevering with this assumption. Freudian formalism, seemingly supported by a 'historical' construction, is made the criterion of all society, including the future free one. What is certainly true of the repressive order is elevated to the status of a generality, and history is judged solely on the basis of whether or not the ego can refrain from identification with the other. Yet it is precisely this theoretical attitude that defames all possible and future history, in which, without weakening the forces of the ego, identification with the whole further increases these forces. However, this fact cannot be deduced in a purely psychological way.

What is also striking about modern social philosophy and criticism, which has turned to social psychology, is the lack of insight into the actual dialectics of progress and freedom. Adorno's historically pessimistic philosophy allows utopia to flare up on the margins as a possibility of real future development, e.g. in *Minima Moralia*, but without a real dialectical reference to the course of history. In the words of Herbert Marcuse: 'If absence from repression is the archetype of freedom, then culture is the struggle against this freedom'.[6] Here is to be asked: all culture, are there no contradictions, no counter-tendencies? If a historical epoch coincides with what is called its culture, and if this culture is nothing other than a struggle against freedom, then, indeed, in none of the previous cultivated epochs, nor at the stages of their succession, can there be anything like a historical development towards ever higher stages of freedom, real freedom. That is historically pessimistic nihilism, one that denies all contradictory and dialectical development in the sense of just such progress. The exaggerated generalisation of the culturally critical aspect taken from Freudian psychology destroys the inner diversity of historical events and forces the interpretation of these events as if they were on a single rail. Whereby this interpretation is supported and receives its apparent confirmation from the one-sided identification of the individual, who is free in an anthropological sense, with the satisfaction of drives in an effort to define man. As infinitely important and decisive as the elaboration of the understanding of sexuality and its repression is for the critical successes of sociological and social psychological theory – and it is one of the commendable achievements of the Frankfurt movement to have drawn attention to it again – as inadequate is the demonstrable tendency to define man by the mere structure of drives, i.e., the unilaterialisation of this definition to one of mere instinctual psychology.

For the anthropological definition of human essential being also includes the fact of being active, the understanding of man as an irrevocably active being and of free man as a being who realises himself through 'playful' active, corresponding to the theory of Marx. Here, it will be necessary to differentiate very sharply between the repressive forms of activity and the free forms of play (not of empty playfulness) that the determination of the latter must initially turn out to be negative as the opposite of all repressive activity per se. Marcuse himself suggests that a order fit for human beings is compatible with an activity that 'offers a high degree of libidinal satisfaction, which is pleasurable in its execution'. He is thinking primarily of artistic activity. He says: 'artistic work, where it is genuine, seems to grow out of a non-repressive instinctual constellation and to envisage non-repressive aims – so much so that the term seems to require considerable modification if applied to this kind of work'.[7] Only that we can no longer speak of work here, since work without drive-sublimation is not work. In my book *State, Society and Elite*, I undoubtedly did not do justice to Marcuse when I accused him there of only being able to imagine a future

---

6   Marcuse 1974, p. 15. In the English version, Marcuse used *civilisation* instead of *culture* (trans. note).
7   Marcuse 1974, pp. 84–5.

free society in the form of mere idle contemplation and of considering it to be solely compatible with a non-repressive condition of the all-round satisfaction of human needs. Yet Marcuse does not see that being active, even if anthropologically occurring in a different corner of human existence than the instinctual constellation, is as original a determination and as important to the definition of man as this constellation. What should be emphasised in any case is the interplay of the two, depending on whether the pleasure principle belonging to the instinctual sphere affects activity in a repressive and sublimating way or in a creative and liberating way and vice versa. The concept of activity must be included a priori in the concept of man; it is not enough to let it appear a posteriori and behind it via the theory of sublimation, because the appearance of the non-repressive real 'play' cannot be overlooked and forces its treatment at a later place of derivation, instead of what is only correct, at the beginning and with the same justification as the pleasure principle.

Ideas from Greek mythology help us to represent the applicable anthropological process in an abbreviated form. We formulate the problem in question as the opposition and dialectical unity of the Apollonian and Dionysian. In their dialectical relation to each other, in their unity, these two principles define man. The Apollonian is the principle of activity (as an outflow of man's endowedness with consciousness and the resulting constant urge to mastery [*Bewältigung*] and transformation of the world) and the Dionysian is the pleasure principle (as an outflow of man's endowedness with instinctual dispositions for delight), whereby both sides bring themselves to the essence of their being only in their mutual penetration – more about this in my essay 'The Apollonian and the Dionysian in the utopian and antagonistic society' – so the overemphasis of the pleasure principle out of Freudian distrust of activity leads to a distortion of the concept of man.[8] This can already be seen in the extent to which, in the one-sided light of the pleasure principle, all historical progress in matters of freedom disappears if one equates the realisation of this principle with the realisation of freedom in general. Here the differences between the slave and the serf, between the serf and the proletarian, between the early industrial worker and the modern worker, and between the epochs in general, vanish, since they were all equally in the condition of repression of the instinctual demands. It is still an open question whether even the latter is true. Certainly, all class society has strictly respected the limit set for the progress of freedom, where it reaches the point of destruction of that society itself, which has always been reflected in the limitation of the requirement for

---

8   Most recently in Kofler 1981, p. 26 onward.

pleasure [*Lustanforderung*]. Yet the struggle of the human race for more freedom was not meaningless even within class history. By fighting for ever new forms of increasingly freer social and individual activity in the alternation of advancement and decline, ascent and decadence, the claim to freedom of the erotic was also increased and in part satisfied. Even the period of decline of capitalism, characterised by reification in all directions, shows the contradiction of having strengthened this claim and at the same time hindering its satisfaction. What becomes of this contradiction depends largely on the progressive forces that recognise it. They have a chance if no decadent 'opposition' and no Marxo-nihilism, both of which, at least as far as seeing through the 'mechanisms of reification' is concerned and keeping access to critical theory open, stand in their way; and they stand in their way less by their ignorance than on the contrary by their knowledge of these mechanisms and by their pessimistic and nihilistic interpretation of them, which is fed not only by ideological roots but also by the theoretical part of the one-sided Freudian concept of man. When Marcuse speaks of 'compromised freedom, gained at the expense of the full satisfaction of needs', he neither shows what the partial satisfaction of needs consists of nor that a piece of freedom is reflected [*sich ... niederschlägt*] in it: a freedom that is constantly withdrawn and threatened, but which, even in its formal form, in the form of political emancipation, as Marx says, implies a possibility of being more free in comparison to earlier epochs, which makes escape conceivable despite all the dangerously refined forms of manipulation of the individual.[9] What the repressive order cannot manipulate are the concrete circumstances in their manifold contradictions and in their unpredictable change. It depends in turn on the forces that are powerful in critical theory and propagate its results with perseverance whether certain favourable circumstances are utilised or not. The tempo does not matter; world history has always had a slow pace for human expectations, slowed down even further in our time by Stalinism, an integrated 'opposition' and modern forms of domination. Yet the development points to a condition soon to be reached, in which a long leisure time will enable both contemplative enjoyment and, at the same time, free activity in close interwovenness for the mass of people. Whether the humanist slogan, which realises this possibility, will prevail depends on many things, but not least on the energy and perseverance of the humanist elite. It is here, in this area surrounding events, that the real competition between East and West will take place in the future; it is here that the true fate of the human race will be decided in the next epoch of world history. Neither the slogan of mere

---

9 Marcuse 1974, p. 18.

idleness, which is theoretically derived from the instinctive human disposition and practically taken from the symbols of life of the ruling class, nor the slogan of mere activity – 'Work makes life sweet' – which is theoretically derived from insight into the nature of man as an active one and practically comes from the symbols of life of the domination of servitude, can be the solution for itself, but only the Apollonian-Dionysian in its mutual determination and unity. Freedom understood in this way or a relapse into barbarism, that is the perspective of the future, which is appended with a huge question mark. All the more are we obliged to help prepare the future with the help of a *daring* critical theory and to reject all Marxo-nihilism; we have no right to make pessimistic preliminary decisions, but as humanists we are bound, in the face of the possibilities opening up that Marcuse has energetically emphasised, to do our duty, each in his own way and in his own place.

However, we must not only take insight into the generality of the events, but also into the diversity of the particular, because only here today can tendencies be detected where progressive humanistic criticism can start for the purpose of not remaining mere criticism, but preparing for change through humanistic enlightenment. The ingenious analysis of the complicated forms of modern alienation, which is conducted primarily with the help of insights from depth psychology, must not be driven so far into the generallly 'philosophical' that a quasi-natural philosophical picture of the social process emerges through the associated neglect of individual problems. This generalisation, driven into the quasi-natural philosophical, ultimately forces the authors in this orientation to align all occurring factors according to a uniform measure. This can be observed more precisely in Günter Anders. But Herbert Marcuse also uses – and not merely for the purpose of preliminary empirical description, as we shall see later – a language that comes quite close to that of reified ideology. Critical intention changes little about this; one should not forget that even in reified consciousness the 'critical' aspect is not absent, even if it is provided with the tendency to come to terms with the object, for instance, in this way: everything is evil, but man is powerless against objective forces. Note, for example, the following sentences from Marcuse: 'The products indoctrinate and manipulate; they promote a false consciousness which is immune against its falsehood'. 'The means of mass transportation and communication, the commodities of lodging, food, and clothing, ... carry with them prescribed attitudes and habits, certain intellectual and emotional reactions ...'[10] The 'products' could be used by a person who sees through the totality of repressive class relations, without

---

10   Marcuse 2002, p. 14.

renouncing them, he could escape 'their' influence. For the products themselves do not achieve anything! But Marcuse does not allow himself to be stopped from continuing: 'The instruments of productivity and progress (of the technological, L.K.) determine, organised into a totalitarian system, not only the actual, but also the possible use'. So the products also determine the possible use, not society.

The mania to consider everything in a quasi-natural philosophical manner, and not for a merely introductory purpose, but for the sake of the matter, also has theoretical consequences. The individual who has come to enjoy home ownership, supermarkets, department stores, etc., Marcuse writes, keeps his consciousness so occupied with the appearance of freedom and happiness that the concepts of freedom, equality, and happiness no longer appear as demands.[11] 'This society has mastered [bewältigt] its ideology', Marcuse concludes, 'by implementing it in the reality of its political institutions, its homes ...' This false consciousness actually conceals the factual economic asceticism and the screaming human misery of the masses. In this respect, it can be said that high capitalist society has mastered its ideology. However, the question remains open as to the extent to which it would be able to master it, if the opposition parties and trade unions were to put their enormous energies into the service of the Enlightenment, to which it would be the task of critical theory to force them through critique. Instead of the proof that nothing can be done anyway, the proof of the critical power of critical theory would have to arrive. But Marcuse draws a curious conclusion from his definition of the high capitalist ideology as one that has been mastered, namely also that 'the concept of alienation seems to become questionable'.[12] It becomes questionable, according to Marcuse, because the 'individuals identify with the existence which is imposed on them'. This identification is also presented as a kind of 'mechanism' of a quasi-natural philosophical kind. As all tension with reality as a result of mastering ideology is removed, the tension between individual and alienation also disappears. Marcuse explains his point of view in the following way: 'The people recognize themselves in their commodities; they find their soul in their automobile, hi-fi set, split-level home, kitchen equipment. The very mechanism [!, L.K.] which ties the individual to his society has changed, and social control is anchored in the new needs which it has produced'.[13] 'Onedimensional thought' emerges.[14] The word 'mechanism', popular with all rep-

11   Marcuse 1964, pp. 339–40.
12   Marcuse 2002, p. 13.
13   Marcuse 2002, p. 11.
14   Marcuse 2002, p. 14.

resentatives of the Frankfurt School, already indicates the quasi-natural philosophical approach. This is confirmed by an effort to include even that which by its very nature must remain outside the generalising scheme: the *criterion* for judging what is called ideology or alienation. Such a criterion is not to be found in the social process itself, and certainly not in the historical event totalised into a quasi-natural process, but only outside, namely by answering the question of the original nature of the non-alienated man, who is therefore managing without false consciousness (which Marcuse equates with ideology), in the anthropological determination of this man. Whereby this determination perhaps only coincidentally, but in any case fortunately, finds historical confirmation in primeval epochs of human history.[15]

Apparently Marcuse wants to say that because today's society has mastered its ideology in a highly ideological way, because false consciousness has become identical with the apparent needs of apparent satisfaction [*scheinhaften Bedürfnissen der Scheinbefriedigung*], therefore the fact of alienation has been erased from this consciousness, it has become 'irrelevant' [*gegenstandslos*]. Marcuse would be right if his assertion were applicable in this totalising form. Even in an epoch in which the individual is driven in the manner described by Marcuse to 'voluntary' identification with the existing repressive order, the pressure of the alienated form of life is certainly felt by the masses – but only felt and not raised to full consciousness. There is unlimited evidence for this, which we unfortunately cannot deal with in this place. A hint must suffice: the constant complaining about 'massification', about the 'rule of technology', about the 'devastating effects of the mass media', the widespread discontent and lethargy about the fact that 'nothing changes anyway' and 'it has always been like this', about 'those up there' and 'us down there', etc. – all of this in a peculiar dialectical relationship to the phenomena of identification that Marcuse has brilliantly demonstrated – in general, the widespread pessimistic attitude to life, which stands in a strange contradiction to the almost smooth integration into the existing, proves that the dialectic of today's ideology is more complicated than it appears at first glance. Again, it must be emphasised that criticism has a double task: on the one hand, to subject the organisations that have grown out of the tradition of the labour movement and still exist today to a persistent critique, and on the other hand, to force them to bring up to date the critical mood that exists among the masses *in nuce*, in the direction of breaking open the hard ideological shell of identification with what exists. In many cases, this tendency to identify is not only rooted in the 'consumption mech-

---

15   Kofler 1964.

anism' and the 'psychological mechanism' (Adorno) or similar 'mechanisms', but just as much in resignation, in a mood of hopelessness [*Ausweglosigkeit*] and helplessness. Anyone who gets around a lot and is used to staying in contact with the broad sections of the population knows this. So although Marcuse sees the right things in the large trend and formulates them aptly, he generalises his observations too much to the 'one-dimensional', which gives his analysis a quasi-philosophical character of a fundamentally pessimistic colouring. In the system of total 'one-dimensional' identification of individual and order, of order and ideology, of ideology and alienation, all movement ossifies into nothing, world history becomes irrelevant. The classless eschatology which Marx wrongly assumed with optimistic intention is here transformed into a class society eschatology of pessimistic significance.

The Anthropology of Consciousness in the Materialism of Karl Marx [1983]

> They do not know it, but they do it.
> KARL MARX

∴

Anthropology within the framework of Marxist theorising is rejected by most Marxist theorists.* The reasons for this are quite understandable.

First, traditional, and that means bourgeois, anthropology manifests the tendency to detach man from the historical space in which he is subject to constant changes in his way of being and to impute to him a metaphysical and unchangeable 'being'. We indeed also accept such an unchangeable 'being' as a condition for human changeability (!), but in the Marxist view it remains purely formal, i.e., it remains a condition, but has no influence whatsoever on history and on man acting in it.[1]

Secondly, apart from all material contexts, man is interpreted in a purely idealistic manner as a spiritual being, for instance by following Scheler's example. Where the modern biologically determinist variant à la Gehlen prevails, only a new, idealistically (e.g., ethically or elitist) dressed-up vulgar materialism emerges out of an albeit intelligent, yet highly questionable construct of ideas. The danger lies in the fact that Marxist theorists can be found who, by varying this biological determinism, fall for it because it appears 'materialistic' to them.

The demonstration of a Marxist dialectical anthropology would have to precede this contribution, which, however, the (prescribed) space does not permit here. There are many anthropological conditions in historical materialism – e.g., labour, teleological positing, determination of consciousness, socialisation, etc. What remains decisive here is the fact of the anthropological dependence on consciousness – 'transcendentality' – of the human social being and all his material as well as ideal expressions. Decisive, because man, also according

---

* [Originally published as "Die Bewusstseinsanthropologie im Materialismus von Karl Marx" in: Ossip K. Flechtheim (ed.), *Marx heute. Pro und contra*, Hamburg: Hoffmann und Campe. 1983, p. 155 ff. Reprinted in Kofler 2000, p. 207 onward.]
1 See my work *Aggression und Gewissen*, among others.

to Marx, defines himself by this fact of consciousness and thereby, in a dialectically identical manner, by *telos*, labour, perception and language.

Against all the misunderstandings and inaccuracies in the reception of Marx's theory, it should be made clear that here we are not talking about consciousness as the ideological content of historical societies, but about the fundamental anthropological ability to think, to set goals, to work in service of these goals, to enter into social relationships, to form and speak of concepts. The occasional assertion that labour and language already existed before man can only be a reference to the realm of sophism biased by biological determinism. For if man defines himself through consciousness, labour and language, then logically he begins precisely at that point of intersection in development where work and language first appear.

At the same time, all anthropological terminology must be understood as supra-historical and formal, i.e., as terminology that, although it unconditionally presupposes certain possibilities of human behaviour, never in itself generates historical content of any kind. What is responsible for the generation of this content is exclusively the historical conditions themselves. In the course of working out my anthropological views, I already emphasised many years ago: 'A "pure" anthropological existence of man independent of his historical being is therefore an impracticable concept for the dialectical term'.

The anthropological problem of consciousness continues in historical materialism. Even the practically ('economically') active person cannot be thought of anthropologically in any other way than as a person who is active with the help of the mind, i.e., as a person endowed with consciousness. Engels remarks in *Ludwig Feuerbach*: 'In nature ... there are only blind, unconscious agencies acting upon one another ... In the history of society, on the contrary, the actors are all endowed with consciousness, are men acting with deliberation or passion, working towards definite goals; nothing happens without a conscious purpose, without an intended aim'.

However, it is also momentary needs and circumstances that move the individual to choose this or that goal. In the first place, purposeful activity turns out to be an element of immediate practice, and in the second place it turns out to be a derived interest, namely ideological. What is remarkable here is that even the social conditionality of the choice of the goal and the action based on it represents a general anthropological 'law' valid for *all* society and *all* history, which precisely because of its anthropological and formal universal validity can neither be increased nor weakened in its effectiveness, but applies 'absolutely' or 'generally'. Only history itself fills it with concrete and infinitely differentiated content; only history itself is responsible for the actual effects of this anthropological 'law'. Yet this 'history itself' is in turn nothing other than the completed realisation, under causal conditions set by it itself, of the anthropological and formal possibilities that are given to man *as such*, defining him as such, in his anthropological being. To fully comprehend this dialectic of the anthropological and formal and the historical and substantial opens the door to the real and all-round understanding of historical materialism.

If Marx, in his famous comparison between the architect and the bee, points to the fundamental difference between man and animal that expresses not merely a quantitative but an absolutely qualitative fact, then the architect or the active man (the 'labourer'), but also the slave or the serf or the guild journeyman are completely arbitrary to him; in the context he meant, they form only exemplary symbols for each individual in his activity. Here he refers to anthropological facts. In this view, the well-known quotation reads differently than a quotation that is merely related to economic theory, which it *also* is. We reproduce it completely. We pay special attention to the expression 'from the outset' [*vornherein*], which means as much as 'in principle', 'supra-historically' or, in our language, 'formally':

> But what distinguishes the worst architect from the best of bees from the outset is this, that the architect raises his structure in imagination before he erects it in reality. At the end of every labour-process, we get a result that already existed in the imagination of the labourer at its commencement. He not only effects a change of form in the material on which he works, but he also realises a purpose of his own in those materials ...[2]

This passage from the first volume of *Capital* expresses more than just an anthropological fact, it also expresses a theoretical perspective that characterises the core of all historical materialism and which we emphasise here against all those who have still not understood the real qualitative contrast to mechanistic vulgar materialism: the really important thing in Marx's conception of historical materialism is not so much its simple opposition to any idealism – although this is important enough – but something completely new in the modern history of the mind, namely the dialectical abolition of the opposition of one-sided, undialectical idealism and one-sided, undialectical materialism against each other. It is the dialectic of 'ideal conceptions' and active and economic 'changes of form in the material', this dialectical unity of the ideal and the material, that makes up Marx's materialism.

---

2   Both major translations of Volume I of *Capital* render this passage without an English equivalent to *vornherein*, thus necessitating a modified translation here (trans. note).

The active realisation of the practical goal envisaged in the 'imagination' [*Vorstellung*] (Marx) is labour. The animal knows no conscious purpose and therefore also no labour. The 'material' aspect of work consists of three things: 1. labour must be oriented according to the objects of labour, 2. according to the means with which it makes and transforms the objects of nature into its objects, the tools ('productive forces'), and 3. according to the relationships that individuals enter into in work. Here, in contrast to a misunderstanding that is still to be found, the stopping at the objective conditions of labour as the allegedly last determining factor is to be classified as a relapse into mechanical materialism, as a blatant violation of the dialectic of ideal and material. While the tools and the conditions between individuals are factors that have become historical, the objective conditions, insofar as we encounter their still unspoilt, not-already worked out form, are constant factors that assume anthropological significance in their relationship to man.

Their anthropological character can already be recognised by the fact that they precede social existence and represent mere formal possibilities. From them (as the ancient scientific materialists believed) social dynamics cannot be deduced. It is one of the most important discoveries of historical materialism that economic legality nowhere exceeds the framework of social conditions, indeed that both are identical. That is why Marx dissolves the conditions, which appear to be determined in a material way, into purely social conditions, or even more radically: into 'forms of thought'.[3] Not having understood this produces the most hopeless accusations against Marxist theorists, here, for example, against Lukács:

> The fetish character of the commodity is thus primarily seen as a process of distortion of consciousness ... rather than as the real domination of the commodity producers by the things they themselves have made.[4]

The thesis of the domination of 'things', even those we have made ourselves, is a relapse into the most vulgar form of materialism. In the scientific ambit of historical materialism there is nothing that is not an expression of the relationship of *consciousness-endowed* individuals among themselves, that is, nothing that is not 'ideological'. Among other things, Marx also counts the laws of movement of capitalist economy among what he literally calls 'ideal conditions of existence' in *Capital*.[5] Even more precisely: according to Marx, economic cat-

---

3 Marx 1996, p. 87.
4 *Theorien über Ideologie*, Argument-Sonderband, Berlin 1979, p. 50.
5 [It does not seem Marx ever literally phrased it this way. (trans. note).]

egories appear as fixed 'natural forms' – 'things' that dominate us, according to the conception of the author of the above quotation – whereas in reality they only represent *forms of thought*.⁶

Marx succeeds in such an interpretation by theoretically dissolving the economic relations of things as categorical phenomena of reification (he speaks explicitly of 'categories'), that is, the ideological degeneration of social relations in labour to 'things' (money, capital, machine, commodity, value, profit, ground rent). It is always the relations entered into by people 'in the social production of their lives', and these are always 'ideal' relations or 'forms of thought' within whose boundaries reification is constituted. Man always acts ideally, 'according to his purpose'.

What is most important to us in this context is the idealistic determination (the 'transcendentality') of all social, and thus also economic processes in consciousness, with which we come across a fundamental anthropological fact.

With which consequence Marx lets the 'materials' [*Gegenstände*] as objects [*Objekte*] of work recede in relation to the latter itself can be seen particularly clearly when he says: 'It is not the articles made, but how they are made, and by what instruments, that enables us to distinguish different economic epochs'. The 'what', the thing, has no power over man. 'In the labour process, therefore, man's activity, with the help of the instruments of labour, effects an alteration, designed from the commencement, in the material worked upon'. Designed from the 'commencement' [*Von 'vornherein' bezweckte*]! If 'labour is', according to Marx, 'in the first place, a process in which both man and Nature participate, and in which man of his own accord starts, regulates, and controls the material re-actions between himself and Nature', and 'compels them to act in obedience to his sway', then this 'of his own accord' ['*seine eigene Tat*'] is only possible as a social action [*gesellschaftliche Tat*], for man is, as Marx says, a being 'that can be individualised only within society'. The anthropological principle by which man enters into a necessary and indissoluble relationship with his fellow man lies in the already demonstrated anthropological identity of consciousness and work, through which man defines himself. People make use of the 'possibility', which is not understood here as a concrete possibility originating from a certain historical process, but rather as a formal possibility, which, for example, also makes surplus labour under capitalist conditions possible: 'Favourable natural conditions alone, give us only the *possibility*, never the reality, of surplus labour' (my emphasis).

---

6   Source: see above.

That Marx also assesses the principle of socialisation not merely historically, but in a fundamentally anthropological manner, is proven by such formulations that do not refer to any specific social formations that have become historical, but to *all* history, to history in general: 'In the production of their life, human beings work not only upon nature, but also upon one another. They produce only by working together in a specified manner and reciprocally exchanging their activities'. In what 'specific' manner human beings work together and what 'form of society' he means, Marx does not and cannot say, for his train of thought means nothing less than the anthropological fact of the socialising character of *all* production.

Marx radically emphasised the fact that all phenomena of the social and historical existence of man, without exception, are bound to consciousness, which in its essence is to be defined as anthropological, and also does not omit the fact of the senses, which is in itself purely biological and only gradually distinguishes man from animals. In relation to the overall picture that we anthropologically form of human beings, the senses are the tools for the satisfaction of drives and needs. However, it is precisely as tools, as a means of satisfaction that they are used differently in humans than in instinct-controlled animals, namely by means of conscious reflection.

What needs to be rectified as a consequence of a misinterpretation of Marx's concept of the 'development of the senses' is the following. On the one hand, that the network of senses has a strictly anthropological and formal character: the possibility, for example, of using the sense of touch in a conflict to produce pain does not coincide with the historical cause of the intention to produce pain. On the other hand, and precisely because of this formal anthropological essence of the senses, their essentially unchangeable character must be emphasised. What changes and 'develops' in the senses is not themselves but, as with all anthropological conditions and possibilities of their existence, their application, which has social causes. The dialectic of anthropological, unchanging possibilities and the historically changing reality of human existence becomes particularly clear in the phenomenon of the senses.

Accordingly, when Marx speaks of the 'development' of the senses, this statement means nothing other than that the historically active person learns to use the senses (sensuality), primarily in the supersession of historical periods and in engagement with the environment, in love – note the variation of forms in promiscuity, polygamy, polyandry, monogamy, homosexuality, lesbian love and asceticism, in which forms the senses always remain the same in their formal and biological consistency – in art, in technology up to the most extreme forms in the imagination, intuition, speculation and ecstasy in an increasingly differentiated way. Or, saying the same thing: to constantly change the contents by including the activity of the senses in the reflection of consciousness according to certain teleological positings.

Precisely with the latter undertaking, to warn against the one-sided historical interpretation of biological and anthropological preconditions, the opposite warning against the biologically determinist misuse of anthropological insights is closely linked. Not infrequently, biological and anthropological insights are used to explain social phenomena. This can also be observed among Marxist theorists. This happens to them mostly unintentionally and as part of an insufficient epistemological foundation in the claims of Marxist theory. The relapse into anthropologising biological determinism [*Biologismus*], however, is no less a danger for a theory that ultimately wants to serve practice than the denial of the necessity and possibility of an anthropological foundation. A misunderstood materialism, namely a biologically deterministic and mechanistic one, is at the end. Scientific materialism, apparently long since dismissed, has only shifted from physics to biology. Marx himself goes even further in the anthropological determination of man. If Marx uses the term 'play' in both the *Grundrisse* and *Capital* as an expression of the many-sided 'life forces' that oppose any division of labour, he does so not only in a positive sense but also in a thoroughly anthropological one. With the introduction of the concept of play, Marx hints at the other level, dialectically mediated to the economic one, which opposes the level of repressive work: that of the erotic. For man does not live from work alone, but also from the erotic bread (pleasure), which first gives meaning to work by putting itself at its service. Work on its own, isolated from erotic needs, has no meaning at all, not even that defined neutrally as 'activity', and certainly not that which is repressive.

The activity of the 'mental and bodily forces of life', as Marx says in *Capital*, equating it with 'play', is more accurate to the concept of Freud's libido than Freud's, because Freud grasps it too one-sidedly in a way that is fixed on the sexual. In this way, Marx's anthropology, which precedes economics and historical materialism factually and logically ('formally'), undergoes that expansion and rounding off which provides the actual occasion for a further development of anthropology on a basis that is identically Marxist and that of the theory of consciousness.

In addition to the concept of 'play', the concepts of 'species-being' and 'self-realisation' are central to Marxist anthropology. Both concepts are often conceived in an empirical and positivist way, in that they are assumed to coincide with the expressed interests of the proletariat and the overall interests of the society striving towards it, which leads to the concept of the 'species interest'.

As early as the 1960s, Ralf Dahrendorf, a critic of Marxism, insisted that the expressed interest of the proletariat is identical with its real interest. Such a statement wants to say, in opposition to Marx, that there is no such thing as a 'species interest' hidden behind the everyday interest of the proletariat as expressed. Insofar as this 'species interest' is not defined with the help of a differentiated anthropological derivation based on the concept of 'play', but is economically and practically deduced from the existing condition of suffering of the proletariat, the expressed interest that flows from it can never be proved to be the 'right' one and contrary to 'self-realisation' – to which must be added that under the ideological and seductive consumer influence of capitalist society the expressed interest is actually contrary to the 'human' one. Outside the dialectical anthropological relationality of 'play', 'self-realisation' and 'species interest' it is in principle quite possible to falsely characterise class antagonism, domination, exploitation, surplus value, profit and many other things – consciously or unconsciously, anthropologically – as appropriate to human life, yes, to man himself, which happens often enough (mostly in connection with the positing of the egoism, aggression and natural deficiency of man – for example, Gehlen – as anthropological characteristics). From the positivist or bourgeois anthropological point of view, why should class society and man's domination over man have less validity than classless society and self-realisation?! We can't get any further without a Marxist anthropology.

Marx also understood the relationship between labour and freedom according to the pattern of a formal anthropology. For Marx, the situation is such that all labour, regardless of the historically possible 'slavish', i.e., non-free forms, anthropologically includes the aspect of freedom in itself. We quote the *Grundrisse* as evidence:

> In the sweat of thy brow shalt thou labour! was Jehovah's curse on Adam. And this is labour for Smith, a curse. 'Tranquillity' appears as the adequate state, as identical with 'freedom' and 'happiness'. It seems quite far from Smith's mind that the individual, 'in his normal state of health, strength, activity, skill, facility', also needs a normal portion of work, and of the suspension of tranquillity. Certainly, labour obtains its measure from the outside, through the aim to be attained and the obstacles to be overcome in attaining it. But Smith has no inkling whatever that this overcoming of obstacles is in itself a liberating activity – and that, further, the external aims become stripped of the semblance of merely external natural urgencies, and become posited as aims which the individual himself posits – hence as self-realisation, objectification of the subject [externalisation in products is meant here, L.K.], hence real freedom, whose action is, precisely, labour. He is right, of course, that, in its historic forms as slave-labour, serf-labour, and wage-labour, labour always appears as repulsive,

always as *external forced labour*; and not-labour, by contrast, as 'freedom, and happiness'.

The difference between the anthropologically commonly accepted '[need for] a normal portion of work' and the 'historic forms as slave-labour, serf-labour, and wage-labour', i.e., between the formal and anthropological and the historic and substantial concept of labour, is clearly evident here. For Marx, just as for Hegel, labour is, according to its original anthropological principle, 'educating, deploying action', i.e., freedom. It only becomes unfreedom in its historical dimension.

On this point in the reception of Marx's text, a current among Marxists is to be objected to, which is, for example, excellently represented by Agnes Heller. Here it is assumed – succinctly and seemingly without any problems – that the Marxist anthropologists, as anthropologists, mind you, and not as sociologists or economists, raise the question of 'what work is'. In fact, this question is not even asked in the field of Marxist anthropological study. Rather, here the explicitly anthropological question is asked, i.e., abstracting from all 'historic forms as slave-labour, serf-labour, and wage-labour' (Marx), what human activity gains a logical and factual meaning *as such* [*überhaupt*], and this not for itself but in relation to the fulfilment of libidinous needs as such; or, as Marx says, to the 'self-realisation of the subject' (see above quotation).

The answer is that in the area of the – conceived or real – correspondence between activity ('labour') and libido, a form of behaviour becomes visible that can be called 'play'; this despite the fact that in the concrete historical space there are many forms of play that would be worthy of their own investigation. This concept of 'play', thus defined here, abstracts with anthropological intention from all forms of play that have become historical, insofar as it is noticeably opposed to the various forms of repressive labour, thus fulfilling a libidinous task – and this in complete agreement with Marx.

We have asked the question of what meaning human activity has 'as such'. The addition of the word 'as such' [*überhaupt*] refers to a usage that is not merely permitted, but indispensable in anthropology. The same can be found in the centuries-old history of philosophy, when, as is well known, we speak here of 'consciousness as such'. What is meant by this is that in abstraction from psychological and historical categories of consciousness, in terms of content as a whole, the question is to be answered as to how 'consciousness as such' relates to 'reality as such'. From the standpoint of Marxism, Engels and Lenin have given a detailed answer to this question. Moreover, the answer can be idealistic or materialistic, sensualistic, empirical or agnostic; in any case, it is a meaningful abstraction.

As far as anthropology is concerned, it can be shown in the course of further investigation how the anthropological theme [*Motiv*] of the dialectical identity of activity and self-realisation or libido gives way to alienated work under concrete historical conditions, and how the alienated forms of libidinousness assert themselves in different ways in the worker, petty bourgeois and bourgeois. 'Play' in its original anthropological meaning, i.e., identical with man and his needs, takes on a historical form for its part, but only in residual forms (especially in everyday life). It moves to the margins of life and, just like the imagination, is reduced to the secondary and incidental because of the libidinous claims that are indestructible in them, and often when the contradiction to the repressive demands of society becomes too obvious, even slandered.

Marx's word about the positing of man 'as man' also means nothing other than man who articulates himself in the context of 'self-realisation'. Here Marx does not think of a specific man produced by certain historical and social circumstances, but of one conceived in his anthropological and humanistic ('playing') being. The whole quotation reads: 'If we assume man to be man, and his relation to the world to be a human one, then love can be exchanged only for love, trust for trust.'

Long before Marx, Schiller, not without influencing him (which is obvious), had already understood man as 'by nature' bound to freedom, which is why he can demand: 'Man was nature and must become nature again'. The raising up [*Aufhebung*] of such thought processes into Marxism is one of the most outstanding theoretical tasks of our time. Away from anthropology, man's inclination towards freedom can be derived either subjectivistically, as for example with Camus – 'I can only prove my own freedom' – or metaphysically, as with Jaspers, who uses this label himself. And that means: only facing backwards.

If, finally, the identity of man, labour and freedom is to be brought to its most radical anthropological expression, it is none other than Marx who offered the 'blueprint' for this with the sentence: 'Only man produces according to the criterion of beauty'. The same applies to the concept of 'passion' [*Leidenschaft*] used by Engels: 'The actors are ... men acting with deliberation or passion'. A few remarks on both.

It must be understood that man produces according to the measure of beauty because beauty is the most extreme expression of the erotic. In the field of human existence mediated by consciousness, beauty is in turn the most extreme expression of the erotic because it opposes the effort of activity; it is 'useless', i.e., it rounds off and completes the libidinous without immediate necessity. Beauty belongs to the needs that leave the sphere of the useful, appearing to be expendable in the purpose of human action under certain conditions of necessity. A drinking cup, quickly folded by a wanderer lost in the desert due to the accidental presence of paper, does not claim to be pleasing in form or beauty.

On the other hand, in an already reasonably balanced everyday life, man strives for aesthetic design of the objects of daily use, whether he makes them himself or purchases them. Even in the early epochs of 'primitive' primeval times, such objects that we perceive as beautiful can be found in large numbers.

The reason for this basic erotic form of human behaviour, beauty, lies in man's ability to reflect on products of whatever kind and to examine and judge them not only for their 'useful' but also *erotic* servitude [*Dienstbarkeit*]. A decorated person is more pleasant than an undecorated one. Yet 'pleasant' means as much as: enriching the conscious and erotic experience. And nobody can deny that we are dealing with a basic anthropological phenomenon. Marx's reference to producing according to the measure of beauty, which in his opinion distinguishes man from all other living beings, thus implies a statement of radical anthropological significance.

With all of this it is also to be kept in mind that the fact of consciousness of beauty in the Marxist system is of the utmost importance because it contradicts all mechanism, economism and biological determinism, i.e., it raises the conception of man to that level of versatility and abundance where alone the concepts of 'self-realisation', 'species-esque' [*Gattungsmäßigen*] and 'progress' can be fully understood and exploited for practice; this both for political practice as well as the shaping of everyday life.

The situation of the concept of passion is similar to that of beauty. The teleological principle of all activity of consciousness, which sets goals and purposes in all activity, pushes the individual acting practically or ideologically towards realising the goal which he has decided on, with all available means and forces. However, while the choice of goal is removed from arbitrariness under the compulsion of limited, socially determined causal possibilities, which in their entirety constitute the 'conditions' – from which above all the well-known economic regularity results – the means remain, regardless of their being bound to the same possibilities, more or less variant. The latter because, in addition to the external objective means oriented to the social circumstances themselves, there are also those that belong exclusively to the subject (e.g., strength or weakness of will, greater or lesser skill, as Marx points out, etc.) and are therefore subject to greater randomness.

To make a final and decisive choice between the means available in the subjective realm, such as power of judgement, intensity, criticism or morality, requires the use of the whole personality, an 'attitude' that we call 'passion'. Thomas Mann remarks in *The Magic Mountain*: 'Passion is this: to live for the sake of life'. This life, in turn, is nothing but the passionate will for self-preservation and self-realisation. 'Self-forgetfulness' is what Thomas Mann lets wise Madame Chauchat say. If Friedrich Engels believes that people always act with passion when they have seriously set themselves a goal, they seem to forget themselves in the service of the realisation of that goal, which at the same time remains in the service of their 'life'.

In principle, passion is inherent in all activity, whether merely 'useful' or erotic (which includes art and science), to which it is imparted. In the society of property based on the division of labour, the means separate from the end (Schiller), activity becomes repressive 'labour', rational and dispassionate. In contrast, any activity identifying means and ends, that is, creative activity, is first and foremost, and in the true sense of the word, passionate and as such satisfies the individual right down to his everyday needs. Friedrich Engels's reference to the passionate nature of every action, when looked at more precisely, points to a general anthropological abstraction that looks beyond the concrete historical circumstances and their forms of deformation. It was certainly known to Engels and Marx that, for example, assembly line work (i.e., translated into its time, extremely labour intensive work) lacks passion. Like beauty, therefore, passion is an anthropological fact, and to disregard it would lead to Marxist theory becoming one-sided and impoverished.

To conclude, I would like to make one more point: in the light of the Marxist anthropology of consciousness, the preference for Bachofen's intuitivist mysticism over the 'dry-as-dust', as Marx occasionally says, rationalism of McLennan by Engels in the introduction to his *Origin of the Family* seems understandable.[7] Here the contrast between a dialectic, albeit still metaphysically fermented in Bachofen's work, on the one hand, and an empirical positivism that McLennan explains from his profession as a lawyer, on the other, is broken up. Marx's reference to the 'dry-as-dust' style of writing of many theorists does not aim at a mere external style, at a mere aesthetic shaping (as Ranke, for example, takes into consideration for historiography), but rather considers the substantive expressiveness that is caught in the contrast: anthropological-dialectical and empirical-positivist.

From all of this it is clear that anthropologically (and not ideologically) understood consciousness is a quality that primarily defines human beings, which is the basis of anthropology as a kind of pre-theory to Marxism. We have demonstrated that we encounter here the identity of consciousness and work,

---

7   The original misspells [John Ferguson] McLennan as Mac Lenan and misattributes the Engels reference to the *Peasants' War in Germany* (trans. note).

and further of consciousness, telos, work, socialisation, concept and language. We have done nothing else here but to proceed strictly according to the theoretical conception of Marx.

Bibliography

Adler, Max 1926 [1924], *Neue Menschen: Gedanken über sozialistische Erziehung*, second expanded edition, Berlin: Laub.
Adorno, Theodor W. 1991 [1958], 'Extorted Reconciliation: On Georg Lukács' Realism in Our Time', in *Notes to Literature, Volume One*, edited by Rolf Tiedemann and translated by Shierry Weber Nicholsen, New York: Columbia University Press.
Ahlberg, René 1976, *Die sozialistische Bürokratie: Die marxistische Kritik am etablierten Sozialismus*, Stuttgart: Kohlhammer.
Albrecht, Clemens et al. 1999, *Die intellektuelle Gründung der Bundesrepublik: Eine Wirkungsgeschichte der Frankfurter Schule*, Frankfurt am Main: Campus.
Althusser, Louis 1969 [1962], *For Marx*, translated by Ben Brewster, London: Allen Lane.
Anderson, Perry 1979 [1976], *Considerations on Western Marxism*, London: Verso.
Anderson, Perry 1992, *A Zone of Engagement*, London: Verso.
Balakrishnan, Gopal (ed.) 2003, *Debating Empire*, London: Verso.
Bourdieu, Pierre 2001, *Gegenfeuer 2: Für eine europäische soziale Bewegung*, Constance: UVK.
Brieler, Ulrich 2001, 'Eine Genealogie des kritischen Geistes: Über Leo Koflers Zur Geschichte der bürgerlichen Gesellschaft', in *Am Beispiel Leo Koflers*, edited by Christoph Jünke, Münster: Westfälisches Dampfboot.
Brückner, Peter 1978, *Versuch, uns und anderen die Bundesrepublik zu erklären*, West Berlin: Wagenbach.
Bürger, Peter 1984, *Theory of the Avant-Garde*, translated by Michael Shaw, Minneapolis: University of Minnesota Press.
Callinicos, Alex 1987, *Making History: Agency, Structure and Change in Social Theory*, Cambridge: Polity.
Cardorff, Peter 1980, *Studien über Irrationalismus und Rationalismus in der sozialistischen Bewegung: Über den Zugang zum sozialistischen Handeln*, Hamburg: Junius.
Colletti, Lucio 1970, 'The Question of Stalin', *New Left Review* I, 69: 61–81.
Demirović, Alex 1999a, *Der nonkonformistische Intellektuelle: die Entwicklung der Kritischen Theorie zur Frankfurter Schule*, Frankfurt am Main: Suhrkamp.
Demirović, Alex 1999b, 'Spannungsreiche Nähe', *Mitteilungen der Leo-Kofler-Gesellschaft e.V.*, 3: 34–45.
Deutscher, Isaac 2017 [1958], 'The Non-Jewish Jew', in *The Non-Jewish Jew and Other Essays*, edited by Tamara Deutscher, London: Verso, 25–41.
Eagleton, Terry 1991, *Ideology: An Introduction*, London: Verso.
Eagleton, Terry 1996, *The Illusions of Postmodernism*, Oxford: Blackwell.
Eagleton, Terry 2000, *The Idea of Culture*, Oxford: Blackwell.
Eagleton, Terry 2004, *After Theory*, New York: Basic Books.

Eagleton, Terry 2008, *The Meaning of Life*, Oxford: Oxford University Press.
Eagleton, Terry 2011, *Why Marx was Right*, New Haven: Yale University Press.
Fleischer, Helmut 1973, *Sozialphilosophische Studien: Kritik der marxistisch-leninistischen Schulphilosophie*, Berlin: Olle & Wolter.
Fleischer, Helmut 1974, *Marx und Engels: Die philosophischen Grundlinien ihres Denkens*, second expanded edition, Freiburg/München: Alber.
Fleischer, Helmut 1980, 'Sozialismus, Humanismus, Anthropologie', in *Marxismus und Anthropologie. Festschrift für Leo Kofler*, edited by Ernst Bloch, Dietrich Garstka and Werner Seppmann, Bochum: Germinal.
Fleischer, Helmut 1987, *Ethik ohne Imperativ: Zur Kritik des moralischen Bewusstseins*, Frankfurt am Main: Fischer.
Fromm, Erich (ed.) 1965, *Socialist Humanism: An International Symposium*, New York: Doubleday.
Geras, Norman 1983, *Marx and Human Nature: Refutation of a Legend*, London: NLB.
Hardt, Michael and Antonio Negri 2000, *Empire*, Cambridge: Harvard University Press.
Hardt, Michael and Antonio Negri 2004, *Multitude: War and Democracy in the Age of Empire*, New York: Penguin.
Hobsbawm, Eric 1995, *Age of Extremes: The Short Twentieth Century, 1914–1991*, London: Abacus.
Honneth, Axel and Hans Joas 1988 [1980], *Social Action and Human Nature*, Cambridge: Cambridge University Press.
Illian, Christian (ed.) 1997, *Leo Kofler: Materialien zu Leben und Werk*, 4th expanded edition, Bochum: Leo-Kofler-Gesellschaft.
Jakomeit, Uwe et. al (eds.) 2011, *Begegnungen mit Leo Kofler: Ein Lesebuch*, Cologne: PapyRossa.
Jameson, Fredric 1974, *Marxism and Form: Twentieth-Century Dialectical Theories of Literature*, Princeton: Princeton University Press.
Jameson, Fredric 1980 [1977], 'Reflections in Conclusion', in *Aesthetics and Politics*, by Theodor W. Adorno et al., London: Verso.
Jander, Martin 1988, *Theo Pirker über 'Pirker': Ein Gespräch*, Marburg: Schüren.
Jünke, Christoph 2007a, *Sozialistisches Strandgut: Leo Kofler – Leben und Werk (1907–1995)*, Hamburg: VSA.
Jünke, Christoph 2007b, *Der lange Schatten des Stalinismus: Sozialismus und Demokratie gestern und heute*, Cologne: Neuer ISP.
Jünke, Christoph 2014, *Streifzüge durch das rote 20. Jahrhundert*, Hamburg: Laika.
Jünke, Christoph 2015, 'Wie ein reaktionäres Häuflein versucht, den linken Sozialisten Leo Kofler auf rechtsaußen zu drehen', *Leo Koflers Philosophie der Praxis. Eine Einführung*, Hamburg: Laika, 151–175.
Kagarlitsky, Boris 1989, *The Thinking Reed: Intellectuals and the Soviet state, 1917 to the Present*, London: Verso.

Klein, Naomi 2001, 'Reclaiming the Commons', in *New Left Review* II 9: 81–9.
Kofler, Leo 1951, *Marxistischer oder stalinistischer Marxismus? Eine Betrachtung über die Verfälschung der marxistischen Lehre durch die stalinistische Bürokratie*, Cologne: Verl. f. Polit. Publizistik.
Kofler, Leo 1958, 'Orthodoxes Pfaffentum', in: *Funken*, 4:59 onward.
Kofler, Leo 1960, *Staat, Gesellschaft und Elite zwischen Humanismus und Nihilismus*, Ulm/Donau: Schotola. New edition in two volumes under the title *Vergeistigung der Herrschaft* [1986–7], Frankfurt am Main: Materialis.
Kofler, Leo 1964, *Der proletarische Bürger: Marxistischer oder ethischer Sozialismus?*, Vienna: Europa.
Kofler, Leo 1967, *Der asketische Eros: Industriekultur und Ideologie*, Vienna: Europa.
Kofler, Leo 1970, *Stalinismus und Bürokratie: Zwei Aufsätze*, Neuwied: Luchterhand.
Kofler, Leo 1971 [1944], *Die Wissenschaft von der Gesellschaft*, 4th edition, Frankfurt am Main: Makol.
Kofler, Leo 1971a, *Technologische Rationalität im Spätkapitalismus*, Frankfurt am Main: Makol.
Kofler, Leo 1972, *Zur Dialektik der Kultur: Sechs Beiträge*, Frankfurt am Main: Makol.
Kofler, Leo 1973, *Aggression und Gewissen: Grundlegung einer anthropologischen Erkenntnistheorie*, Munich: Hanser.
Kofler, Leo 1974 [1962], *Zur Theorie der modernen Literatur: Der Avantgardismus in soziologischer Sicht*, Düsseldorf: Bertelsmann.
Kofler, Leo 1983a, *Zur Kritik der 'Alternativen'*, Hamburg: VSA.
Kofler, Leo 1983b, 'Die neue Form des Klassenkampfes und die Grünen', in *Nicht links – Nicht rechts? Über die Zukunft der Grünen*, Hamburg: VSA.
Kofler, Leo 1986, *Aufbruch in der Sowjetunion? Von Stalin zu Gorbatschow*, Hamburg: VSA.
Kofler, Leo 1987a, *'Die Kritik ist der Kopf der Leidenschaft': Aus dem Leben eines marxistischen Einzelgängers: Ein Gespräch anlässlich seines 80. Geburtstags*, Hamburg: VSA.
Kofler, Leo 1987b, *Die Nation – Zukunft und Verpflichtung: Gedanken zum Tag der Deutschen Einheit*, Nienburg: Stadtarchiv.
Kofler, Leo 1987c [1964], 'Zum Streit um eine marxistische Ästhetik', in *Avantgardismus als Entfremdung: Ästhetik und Ideologiekritik*, Frankfurt am Main: Sendler.
Kofler, Leo 1987d [1986], 'Die "erotische" Universität – Leo Kofler über Wissenschaft und Selbstverwirklichung', in *Die versteinerten Verhältnisse zum Tanzen bringen! Beiträge von Leo Kofler in der Bochumer Studentenzeitung*, Bochum: Die Unabhängigen – Gruppe aktiver Fachschafter u. Fachschafterinnen.
Kofler, Leo 1989, 'Asiatische Despotie: Historische und soziale Wurzeln des Stalinismus', *Sozialismus*, 10: 11 onward.
Kofler, Leo 1990, 'Alltag und soziales Bewusstsein', *Marxistische Blätter*, 2: 75 onward.

Kofler, Leo 1992 [1948], *Zur Geschichte der bürgerlichen Gesellschaft*, 8th Edition, 2 volumes, Berlin: Dietz.

Kofler, Leo 2000, *Zur Kritik bürgerlicher Freiheit: Ausgewählte politisch-philosophische Texte eines marxistischen Einzelgängers*, edited by Christoph Jünke, Hamburg: VSA.

Kofler, Leo 2000a [1954–5], 'Marxistischer oder stalinistischer Marxismus', in *Zur Kritik bürgerlicher Freiheit*, edited by Christoph Jünke, Hamburg: VSA.

Kofler, Leo 2000b [1955], 'Ethischer oder marxistischer Marxismus? Zur Kritik einer neueren sozialdemokratischen Ideologie', in *Zur Kritik bürgerlicher Freiheit*, edited by Christoph Jünke, Hamburg: VSA.

Kofler, Leo 2000c [1957], 'Bert Brecht und die Neue Linke', in *Zur Kritik bürgerlicher Freiheit*, edited by Christoph Jünke, Hamburg: VSA.

Kofler, Leo 2000d [1965], 'Ist revolutionäre Praxis heute möglich? Zum Verhältnis von Theorie und Praxis', in *Zur Kritik bürgerlicher Freiheit*, edited by Christoph Jünke, Hamburg: VSA.

Kofler, Leo 2000e [1971], 'Anthropologische Erkenntnistheorie und Aggression', in *Zur Kritik bürgerlicher Freiheit*, edited by Christoph Jünke, Hamburg: VSA.

Kofler, Leo 2004 [1955], *Geschichte und Dialektik: Zur Methodenlehre der marxistischen Geschichtsbetrachtung*, Essen: Neue Impulse.

Kofler, Leo 2007 [1968], *Perspektiven des revolutionären Humanismus*, Cologne: Neuer ISP.

Kößler, Reinhart 2001, 'Asiatische Despotie oder Despotie in der Moderne?', in *Am Beispiel Leo Koflers*, edited by Christoph Jünke, Münster: Westfälisches Dampfboot.

Krahl, Hans-Jürgen 1971, *Konstitution und Klassenkampf: Zur historischen Dialektik von bürgerlicher Emanzipation und proletarischer Revolution*, Frankfurt am Main: Neue Kritik.

Krahl, Hans-Jürgen 1971a [1969], 'Der politische Widerspruch der Kritischen Theorie Adornos', in *Konstitution und Klassenkampf: Zur historischen Dialektik von bürgerlicher Emanzipation und proletarischer Revolution*, Frankfurt am Main: Neue Kritik.

Krahl, Hans-Jürgen 1971b [1969], 'Kritische Theorie und Praxis', in *Konstitution und Klassenkampf: Zur historischen Dialektik von bürgerlicher Emanzipation und proletarischer Revolution*, Frankfurt am Main: Neue Kritik.

Krätke, Michael 2001, 'Ökonomie und Ideologie: Wes Geistes Kind ist der moderne Kapitalismus?', in *Am Beispiel Leo Koflers*, edited by Christoph Jünke, Münster: Westfälisches Dampfboot.

Kulemann, Peter 1979, *Am Beispiel des Austromarxismus: Sozialdemokratische Arbeiterbewegung in Österreich von Hainfeld bis zur Dollfuß-Diktatur*, Hamburg: Junius.

Labriola, Antonio 1966 [1903], *Essays on the Materialistic Conception of History*, translated by Charles H. Kerr, New York: Monthly Review.

Lebowitz, Michael A. 2010, *The Socialist Alternative: Real Human Development*, New York: Monthly Review.

Lefebvre, Henri 1965 [1958], *Probleme des Marxismus, heute*, Frankfurt am Main: Suhrkamp.
Lefebvre, Henri 1995 [1962], *Introduction to Modernity: Twelve Preludes, September 1959–May 1961*, translated by John Moore, London: Verso.
Lefebvre, Henri 2009 [1940], *Dialectical Materialism*, translated by John Sturrock, Minneapolis: University of Minnesota Press.
Lepenies, Wolf 1971, *Soziologische Anthropologie: Materialien*, Munich: Hanser.
Linden, Marcel van der 2007, *Western Marxism and the Soviet Union: A Survey of Critical Theories and Debates since 1917*, translated by Juriaan Bendien, Leiden: Brill.
Löwy, Michael and Frei Betto 2015 [2003], 'Values of a New Civilization', in *Another World is Possible: World Social Forum Proposals for an Alternative Globalization*, edited by William F. Fisher and Thomas Ponniah, London: Zed Books.
Lukács, Georg 1969 [1957], *The Meaning of Contemporary Realism*, translated by John and Necke Mander, London: Merlin.
Mandel, Ernest 1971 [1967], *The Formation of the Economic Thought of Karl Marx: 1843 to Capital*, translated by Brian Pearce, New York: Monthly Review.
Mandel, Ernest 1989, *Beyond Perestroika: the Future of Gorbachev's USSR*, translated by Gus Fagan, London: Verso.
Mandel, Ernest 1992, *Power and Money: A Marxist Theory of Bureaucracy*, London: Verso.
Marx, Karl 1975 [1843], *Contribution to the Critique of Hegel's Philosophy of Law*, in *Marx & Engels Collected Works*, Volume 3, London: Lawrence & Wishart.
Marx, Karl 1996 [1867], *Capital, Volume I*, in *Marx & Engels Collected Works*, Volume 35, London: Lawrence & Wishart.
Marx, Karl and Frederick Engels 1975 [1846], *The German Ideology* in *Marx & Engels Collected Works*, Volume 5, London: Lawrence & Wishart.
Merleau-Ponty, Maurice 1969 [1947], *Humanism and Terror: An Essay on the Communist Problem*, translated by John O'Neill, Boston: Beacon.
Mulhern, Francis 2000, *Culture/Metaculture*, London: Routledge.
Mulhern, Francis 2002, 'Beyond Metaculture', *New Left Review* II, 16: 86–104.
Negt, Oskar 2011 [1988], 'Zur Bedeutung Leo Koflers für einen kritischen Marxismus', edited by Uwe Jakomeit, Christoph Jünke and Andreas Zolper, Cologne: PapyRossa.
Raith, Werner 1985, *Humanismus und Unterdrückung: Streitschrift gegen die Wiederkehr einer Gefahr*, Frankfurt am Main: Extrabuch.
Seppmann, Werner 2012, *Marxismus und Philosophie: Über Leo Kofler und Hans Heinz Holz*, Berlin: Kulturmaschinen.
Serge, Victor 2012, *Memoirs of a Revolutionary*, translated by Peter Sedgwick with George Paizis, New York: NYRB Classics.
Soper, Kate 1990, 'Socialist Humanism', in *E.P. Thompson: Critical Perspectives*, edited by Harvey J. Kaye and Keith McClelland, Cambridge: Polity.

Thompson, Edward Palmer 1978, *The Poverty of Theory and Other Essays*, London: Merlin.
Thompson, Edward Palmer 2014 [1957], 'Socialist Humanism: An Epistle to the Philistines', in *E.P. Thompson and the Making of the New Left: Essays and Polemics*, edited by Cal Winslow, New York: Monthly Review.
Trotsky, Leon 1957 [1924], *Literature and Revolution*, New York: Russell & Russell.
Trotsky, Leon 1972 [1936], *The Revolution Betrayed: What is the Soviet Union and Where is it Going?*, translated by Max Eastman, New York: Pathfinder.
Trotsky, Leon 1988, *Schriften 1: Sowjetgesellschaft und stalinistische Diktatur, Band 1.2 (1936–1940)*, Hamburg: Rasch und Röhring.
Vack, Klaus 2011 [1977], 'Eine Institution geworden', in *Begegnungen mit Leo Kofler*, edited by Uwe Jakomeit, Christoph Jünke and Andreas Zolper, Cologne: PapyRossa.
Wallerstein, Immanuel 1989, '1968, Revolution in the World-System: Theses and Queries', *Theory and Society*, 18, 4: 431–49.
Wallerstein, Immanuel 2002, 'Revolts against the System', *New Left Review* II 18: 29–39.
Williams, Raymond 1983, 'Culture', in *Marx: The First Hundred Years*, edited by David McClellan, London: Fontana.
Wolf, Frieder Otto 2008, *Humanismus für das 21. Jahrhundert*, Berlin: Humanistischer Verband Deutschlands.
Woods, Ellen Meiksins and Foster, John Bellamy (eds.) 1997, *In Defense of History: Marxism and the Postmodern Agenda*, New York: Monthly Review.

Works Cited in Kofler's Essays in This Volume

Briefs, Goetz 1952, *Zwischen Kapitalismus und Syndikalismus*, Munich: Lehnen.
Friedmann, Georges 1953 [1950], *Zukunft der Arbeit: Perspektiven der industriellen Gesellschaft*, translated by Burkart Lutz, Cologne: Bund.
Horkheimer, Max and Theodor W. Adorno 2002 [1947], *Dialectic of Enlightment: Philosophical Fragments*, translated by Edmund Jephcott, Stanford: Stanford University Press.
Kofler, Leo 1960, *Staat, Gesellschaft und Elite zwischen Humanismus und Nihilismus*, Ulm/Donau: Schotola. New edition in two volumes under the title *Vergeistigung der Herrschaft* [1986–7], Frankfurt am Main: Materialis.
Kofler, Leo 1964, *Der proletarische Bürger: Marxistischer oder ethischer Sozialismus?*, Vienna: Europa.
Kofler, Leo 1970, *Stalinismus und Bürokratie: Zwei Aufsätze*, Neuwied: Luchterhand.
Kofler, Leo 1981, *Geistiger Verfall und progressive Elite: sozialphilosophische Untersuchungen*, Bochum: Germinal.
Lukács, Georg 1951, *Existenzialismus oder Marxismus*, Berlin: Aufbau.

Lukács, Georg 1972 [1923], *History and Class Consciousness: Studies in Marxist Dialectics*, translated by Rodney Livingstone, Cambridge: The MIT Press.

Mannheim, Karl 1943, *Diagnosis of Our Time: Wartime Essays of a Sociologist*, London: Kegan Paul.

Marcuse, Herbert 1964, 'Der eindimensionale Mensch' (excerpt), in *Ideologie: Ideologiekritik und Wissenssoziologie*, edited by Kurt Lenk, Neuwied: Luchterhand.

Marcuse, Herbert 1968, *Kultur und Gesellschaft II*, Frankfurt am Main: Suhrkamp.

Marcuse, Herbert 1974 [1955], *Eros and Civilization: A Philosophical Inquiry into Freud*, Boston: Beacon.

Marcuse, Herbert 2002 [1964], *One-Dimensional Man: Studies in the Ideology of Advanced Industrial Society*, London: Routledge.

Marx, Karl 1975 [1843], *Contribution to Critique of Hegel's Philosophy of Law*, in *Marx and Engels Collected Works*, Volume 3, London: Lawrence & Wishart.

Marx, Karl and Frederick Engels 1975 [1845], *The Holy Family*, in *Marx and Engels Collected Works*, Volume 4, London: Lawrence & Wishart.

Marx, Karl and Frederick Engels 1976 [1848], *Manifesto of the Communist Party*, in *Marx and Engels Collected Works*, Volume 6, London: Lawrence & Wishart.

Marx, Karl 1977 [1849], *Wage Labour and Capital*, in *Marx and Engels Collected Works*, Volume 9, London: Lawrence & Wishart.

Marx, Karl 1986 [1857–8], *Economic Manuscripts of 1857–58*, in *Marx and Engels Collected Works*, Volume 28, London: Lawrence & Wishart.

Marx, Karl 1989 [1875], *Critique of the Gotha Programme*, in *Marx and Engels Collected Works*, Volume 24, London: Lawrence & Wishart.

Marx, Karl 1996 [1867], *Capital, Volume I*, in *Marx & Engels Collected Works*, Volume 35, London: Lawrence & Wishart.

Marx, Karl 1998 [1894], *Capital, Volume III*, in *Marx & Engels Collected Works*, Volume 37, London: Lawrence & Wishart.

Tomberg, Friedrich 1963, 'Utopie und Negation: Zum ontologischen Hintergrund der Kunsttheorie Th. W. Adornos', in *Das Argument* 26: 36–48.

Index

'1848' 165
20th Party Congress 63, 81

Abendroth, Wolfgang 11, 43, 127
Absolute Spirit 206–7
Ackermann, Manfred 3
actually existing socialism 46, 54, 66, 70, 118, 120
Adenauer, Konrad 10
Adler, Max 6, 7, 19, 21, 31, 53
Adorno, Theodor W. 43, 109–10, 124, 127, 134, 136, 213, 216, 219
    and fascism 125–6
    and Lukács debates 109–11, 117–21, 123, 128–9
aesthetics 60, 120–1, 123, 138, 186, 237
Agartz, Viktor 11, 127
aggression drive 93
'Agreement of the People' 154
alienation 85, 108–9, 111, 116, 129–30, 133, 149, 171–2, 177, 182, 186–7, 193, 195, 199, 203, 208–9, 224–5, 236
Alth, Michaela von 215
Althusser, Louis 13, 83, 93–4, 98
America *See* United States of America
Andere Zeitung 63, 113
Anderson, Perry 47, 137–8, 139
animals 193–4
anthropology 92, 201
    bourgeois 227, 234
    humanist 91
    See also Marxist anthropology
anti-globalisation movement 47
anti-humanism 79, 86, 94, 100, 152, 181
Apollonian and Dionysian 221, 223
art 185–6, 220
asceticism 91, 183, 224, 232
Der asketische Eros 130
Asiatic despotism 46
Austromarxism 6, 9, 35, 51, 53, 70
avant-garde 109–12, 113, 116, 119–20, 129

Bachofen, Johann Jakob 238
Bad Boll 182
Bad Godesberg Programme *See* Godesberg Programme

Balzac, Honoré de 159
Bauer, Otto 5, 37, 53
beauty 236–7
Beckett, Samuel 112
Beijing 46
Belgian Revolution 156
Bello, Walden 49
Betto, Frei 50
biological determinism 93, 194, 227–8, 233
Bismarck, Otto von 158, 160
Bloch, Ernst 134
Die Bochumer Studenten-Zeitung 1
Bourdieu, Pierre 48
bourgeois ideology 157
bourgeoisie 76, 133, 155, 157, 159, 161–8, 173, 175, 179, 203, 206
    liberal 156, 158, 169, 172, 179
Bové, José 49
Brecht, Bertolt 40, 113–115, 186–188
Briefs, Goetz 170, 173–5
Brieler, Ulrich 27
Bristol 156
Britain *See* England
Brückner, Peter 43, 66
bureaucratisation 35, 37, 48, 53–4, 56
    Stalinist 55–62, 69, 72, 74, 82, 84, 152
Bürger, Peter 109, 119n

Calvin, John 154
campism 66
Camus, Albert 236
capital 199
Capital 151, 196, 233
capitalism 27n, 47, 151–2, 159, 170–1, 173, 203
capitalist class society *See* class society
Cardorff, Peter 45
Carlyle, Thomas 159
Carnegie, Dale 176
chartism 156
Churchill, William 159
citoyen 161–8, 173, 175
class relations 169, 197
class society 89, 91, 96, 150, 162, 183, 185, 197, 203, 205–6, 221
    bourgeois 149, 168, 179, 192–3, 203
    capitalist 85, 175–6, 186, 193

class struggle   105, 133, 135, 175, 178
Cold War   11
Colletti, Lucio   73
Cologne   9, 128, 135
commodity   193, 203, 209, 224, 230
Communist liberalisation policy   11
Communist Manifesto   154
Communist Party (KPD)   11
consciousness   7, 15, 19, 21–4, 67, 69, 71, 73, 89, 90, 103, 134, 177, 192, 194, 196, 199, 206–8, 223, 228, 230, 233, 238
   bourgeois   154
   bureaucratic   60
   proletarian   76
   social   208–9
conservatism   158
   See also social conservatism
contingent dialectic   136
critical theory   126, 136
Cromwell, Oliver   154
cultural revolution   64–5
culture   90, 151, 185, 219
Czechoslovakia   71

Dadaism   121
Dahrendorf, Ralf   233
degenerated workers' states   77
dehumanisation   172
Demirović, Alex   127, 139
democracy   162, 164–5, 168, 170–1, 174, 178
   and elections   69
   and liberalism   166, 175–6
   bourgeois   154, 156, 169, 175
democratic socialism   56
demonstrations   173, 175
de-Stalinisation   58, 61–3, 70, 77, 80–1
Deutscher, Isaac   3, 58
dialectical thought   76
dialectics   *See* subject-object dialectic
direct action   48
Disraeli, Benjamin   157–8, 160
division of labour   89, 150–1, 179, 183, 204
Dominicans   174
Dubček, Alexander   62, 65

Eagleton, Terry   78, 90, 93, 96, 104, 123
East Germany (German Democratic Republic, GDR)   47, 69, 153

economism   152
education   1, 76–7, 139
egoism   210–1
Eibl-Eibesfeldt, Irenäus   93
Eichler, Willi   10
Enclosures movement   156
enfranchisement   155
   elective   159–61
Engels, Friedrich   89, 196, 228, 238
England   156, 158
English Revolution   154
Enlightenment   99, 179
Eros and Civilization   184
the erotic   1, 15, 90, 195, 233
Evangelical Academy   182
existentialism   162–3, 189–190
expressionism   111
externalisation   91–2, 195, 201, 234
extra-parliamentary opposition (APO)   46, 110

family   194
fascism   27n, 135–6, 170, 183, 187
feudalism   150, 155–60, 203
Feuerbach, Ludwig   199
Fleischer, Helmut   101
Florence   170
France   156
Die Frankfurter Rundschau   125
freedom   8, 24, 31–2, 69, 104, 133, 152, 162, 165, 167–8, 184–5, 189–90, 192, 205, 214, 219, 234
   bourgeois   149, 157, 170, 190
   class character of   29
   economic and political   85–7
   individual   169, 179, 193
   negative and positive   151, 153
   of action   83, 86
   of competition   86
   social   151–2, 154
   socialist   151, 206
French Revolution   154, 160, 164, 210
Freud, Sigmund   184–5, 233
Freudian psychology   219–20, 222
FRG   *See* West Germany
Friedmann, Georges   175–6
Fromm, Erich   83
Funken   113

GDR *See* East Germany
Gehlen, Arnold   93, 94n, 234
Geneva   154
Geras, Norman   96, 99
German idealism   126
German Ideology   89, 208
Geschichte und Dialektik   54
Gladstone, William Ewart   156, 158, 159
God   163
Godesberg Programme   11, 36, 63, 109
Goethe, Johann Wolfgang von   160, 177
Gorbachev, Mikhail   14, 46, 67
Grundrisse   234

habeas corpus   156
Habermas, Jürgen   129, 131–2, 135–6
Halle   8–9, 128
Hardt, Michael   49
Hatschek, Julius   156
Hayek, Friedrich   153
Hegel, Georg Wilhelm Friedrich   7, 19, 70, 123, 130, 192, 206–7, 211–2
Heller, Agnes   235
Hess, Moses   104
historical materialism   59–60, 194, 197, 200–2, 205, 209, 230
    and anthropology   227–9
history   26–7, 181–2, 186, 192, 195, 200, 202, 205–6, 219, 228–9, 232
Hobbes, Thomas   153
Hobsbawm, Eric   107
Horkheimer, Max   127
human development   168
human essence   99–100, 104, 167, 187, 200
humanism   1, 8, 15, 47, 50, 64, 67, 94, 101, 137, 181
    bourgeois   27–8, 84–5, 95, 99, 101, 157
    radical   7, 16, 60, 85
    socialist   78, 80–5, 95–8, 101, 105
    See also anti-humanism
humanitarian intervention   79
human nature   90, 105
    See also human essence
Hungary   63

idealism   90, 138, 212, 214, 229
individualism   15, 28, 31–2, 84–5, 126, 135, 152, 163
    See also freedom

Inquisition   174
Institute for Social Research   138
Introduction to Modernity   121
irony   186–9

Jacobin   154
Jameson, Fredric   116, 119
Jaspers, Karl   236
Judaism   2, 3
    See also non-Jewish Jew
July Revolution   156

Kafka, Franz   112
Kant, Immanuel   154
Kautsky, Karl   7, 101
Khrushchev, Nikita   63, 81
Klein, Naomi   48
Krahl, Hans-Jürgen   125, 127, 135, 136–7, 139
Kürbiskern   130

labour   90, 104, 184, 193–4, 196–7, 199, 201, 230, 234
    See also division of labour
Labriola, Antonio   17, 22
laissez-faire   167
Landauer, Gustav   13
Lassalle, Ferdinand   3, 159–60
Lebowitz, Michael A.   98
Lefebvre, Henri   37, 70, 95, 107–9, 115, 121–2, 124
Lenin, Vladimir   57, 64
Lessing, Gotthold Ephraim   160
Levellers   154
liberalism   29, 153, 158–9, 165–7, 169–171, 173, 177, 179
    See also democracy
Liburne, John   154
Linguet, Simon-Nicholas Henri   179
Die Linke antwortet Jürgen Habermas   135
linguistics   55
Locke, John   154–5
Lorenz, Konrad   93
Löwy, Michael   50
Lukács, Georg   7, 13, 53, 55, 70, 81, 109–10, 117–8, 124, 128, 131, 207–8

management   172
Manchester   156
Mandel, Ernest   72, 73, 75

Mann, Thomas   237
Mannheim, Karl   178
Maoism   64
Mao Zedong   64
Marcuse, Herbert   13, 43, 131, 133–4, 138, 184–5, 217–26
markets   71, 94
Marx, Karl   7–9, 89, 151, 157, 184–5, 192–4, 196, 197–200, 202–4, 206–8, 222, 231–2, 236, 238
Marxism   56, 123, 208
Marxist anthropology   23, 78, 87–8, 96, 99, 227–39
Marxist ethics   103
Marxist sociology   19
Marxo-nihilism   43, 47, 128, 134, 222–3
Marx: The First Hundred Years   22
Maschke, Günter   94n
materialism   194, 199
McLennan, John Ferguson   238
means of production   149, 197
Mehring, Franz   101
Merleau-Ponty, Maurice   81
Middle Ages   159, 164, 206
Milton, John   155
Minima Moralia   219
modernism   108, 119–20
monarchy   159
monopoly capitalism   126, 166, 178
moralism   101
More, Thomas   101
Moser, Tilmann   51
mystification   199

naivete   188
National Assembly   154
National Liberal Party   160
naturalism   111
nature   151, 196–7, 199, 231
Negri, Antonio   49
Negt, Oskar   17, 128
neoliberalism   73, 94, 166–8, 178
New Left   11, 12, 41, 43, 45–6, 48, 66, 81, 109, 135, 139
nihilism   46, 114, 119, 123, 129, 163, 181, 220
   See also Marxo-nihilism
nonconformist conformism   119, 136
non-Jewish Jew   3–5
nuclear armament   182

objectivity   195–7
Oelssner, Fred   9
'On the Jewish Question'   161
opportunism   44
Origin of the Family   238
Othmar, Spann   166

Party of Democratic Socialism (PDS)   14, 47
pauperism   204
Perestroika   68, 71
personality   151
Perspektiven des revolutionären Humanismus   13, 42, 135
petty bourgeois   33, 43, 76, 156, 236
phantasy   185
Pirker, Theo   127
Pitt the Younger   156
planned economy   57–9, 68, 70
play   91, 151, 184, 220–1, 233–6
Poland   63
Pope   174
Popular Front   81
popular sovereignty   154–5
positivism   59, 130
post-war capitalism   132
Prague Spring   65, 71
primitive accumulation   54, 56, 67–8
primitive communism   197, 202
private property   *See* property
productive activity   195
productive forces   25, 197, 203
productivity   184–5
progressive elite   11, 39–47, 49–50, 113–6, 120, 123, 130, 132–3, 135, 136–7, 181–91
proletariat   86, 156, 165–6, 203, 215, 217, 233–4
   as revolutionary class   109
   international   50, 73
Der proletarische Bürger   76, 129
property   28, 30, 84–5, 155, 164, 168, 172, 179, 197
Prussia   156
psychoanalysis   126, 138, 176, 185
public   167

Raith, Werner   101
rationality   185, 200
Reagan, Ronald   66

INDEX   251

realism   119, 189
reason   185
reform Communism   7, 12, 50, 61–2, 70–2
reification   59, 68, 89, 95, 126, 131, 133, 136–7,
    149, 152, 199, 213, 216, 231
relations of production   197, 202, 209
Renaissance   163
revolutionary elite   82
revolutionary subject   43, 127
Robespierre, Maximilien   155
romanticism   188
Röpke, Wilhelm   153, 167
Rousseau, Jean-Jacques   179
Ruhr University   1, 13, 14
Russian civil war   57
Russian Revolution   152

Sartre, Jean-Paul   190
Schiller, Friedrich   150–1, 236
sectarianism   44
self-denial   185
self-determination   14, 69, 179
self-realisation   195–6, 233–5
senses   232
Seppmann, Werner   33
Serge, Victor   80
Six Acts   156
slavery   154, 185, 198, 202, 205–6
Smith, Adam   166
social being   193–4, 201
social conservatism   158–60
social democracy   36, 160
Social Democratic Party (SPD)   10–11, 14, 35,
    38
Social Democratic Workers' Party of Austria
    (SDAP)   5–6, 14
socialism   124, 137, 150, 161–2, 171, 175, 178,
    181, 204
    ethical   10, 36
socialist democratisation   71
Socialist German Student League (SDS)   12,
    125–8, 135
socialist realism   113, 120–2
Socialist Unity Party (SED)   9, 14, 54, 64
sociality   193–5, 197
social movements   50
social ownership   175
social relations   25, 74, 197, 231
    of production   99, 199

social state capitalism   11, 30–33, 36, 85
Sodomism   189
Soviet Union   46, 53, 56, 62, 67–8, 73–4, 152–
    3
Species-being   86, 95, 233
*Staat, Gesellschaft und Elite zwischen Human-
    ismus und Nihilismus*   132, 220
Stalin, Joseph   7, 55, 83
Stalinism   10, 37, 50–2, 55, 57–8, 60, 62, 63–
    4, 67, 73, 75, 77, 82, 97, 137, 151, 166, 168,
    216
Stalinismus und Bürokratie   52
Steinbach, Ernst   182–3
Stendhal   122
strikes   173, 175
Subcomandante Marcos   49
subject-object dialectic   7, 19, 59, 92, 192–3,
    207–9
subjectivity   111, 181, 195–7
surrealism   121

telos   24–5
Thatcher, Margaret   66
Theories of Surplus Value   208
theory and practice   20, 126, 136–8, 196
Third World   73
Thompson, E.P.   81–4
Threepenny Opera   188
Tito, Josip Broz   61
trade unionism   162, 167–71, 173–4, 181, 214–
    5
transitional society   56, 67
Trevelyan, G.M.   156
Trotsky, Leon   24, 72, 74
Trotskyism   71
'Two Treatise'   154

Ulbricht, Walter   64
United States of America   172
USSR   *See* Soviet Union
utopianism   114, 134, 184–7, 189

Vack, Klaus   17
Vienna   2, 3, 5, 19
voluntarism   60
vulgar materialism   7, 59, 76–7

Wallerstein, Immanuel   49
Weber, Alfred   173

West Germany (Federal Republic, FRG)   47, 139
Wider den missverstandenen Realismus   117, 128
Williams, Raymond   22–3
Die Wissenschaft der Gesellschaft   8, 53, 54, 123
Wolf, Frieder Otto   100
Workers' movement   12, 34–5, 38, 51, 85, 97, 133, 136, 181, 182, 186, 187, 189
working class   160, 164, 173, 175, 178
world spirit   211–3

Yugoslavia   153

Zapatistas   49
Zur Geschichte der bürgerlichen Gesellschaft   7, 54
Zur Theorie der modernen Literatur   111, 113, 115, 123, 128

www.ingramcontent.com/pod-product-compliance
Lightning Source LLC
Chambersburg PA
CBHW070917030426

42336CB00014BA/2445